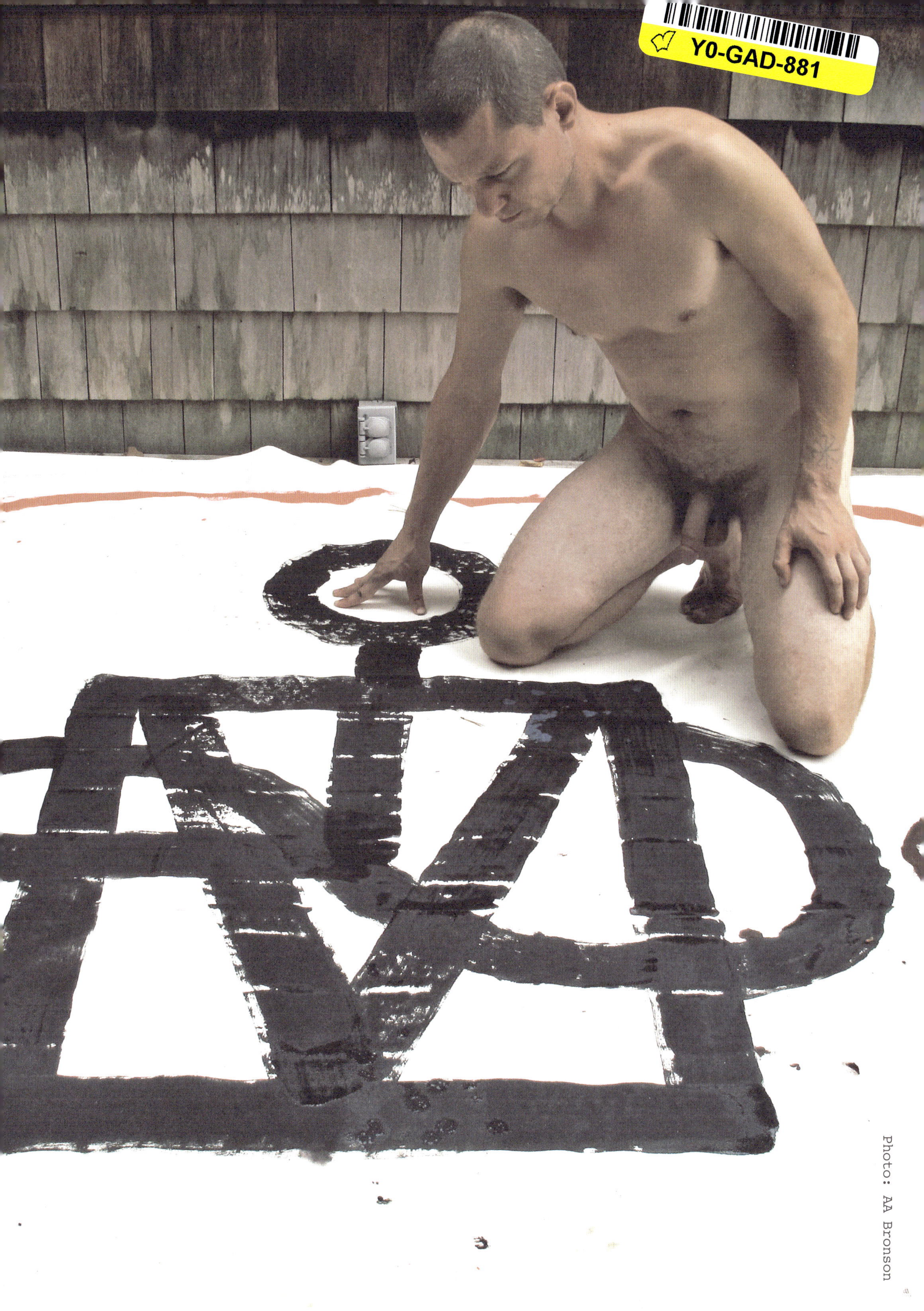

Photo: AA Bronson

LA Art Book Fair 2016
Fundraising Edition
By Sterling Ruby

Printed Matter, Inc.

FEATURING

Aneta Bartos

Shane Book

Ana Božičević

Paul Burgess & Louise Colbourne

Elijah Burgher

Nicola Canavan & Dawn Felicia Knox

Julia Cohen

Todd Colby

Sara Cwynar

Jen Davis

Andy Fitch & Danielle Pafunda

Benjamin Fredrickson

Robert Heinecken

Matthias Herrmann

Philippe Jusforgues

Maria Lassnig

Sugar Magnolia & King Snake

Sergey Melnitchenko

Niina Pollari

Marcelle Sauvageot

Dina Seiden

Jeremy Sigler

There is the satisfaction of being able to look at the image without flinching. There is the pleasure of flinching.

– Susan Sontag

This is the age of easy-exhibitionism. Where exposing yourself to a potentially massive audience is as simple as pushing a button, and the possibility of going viral can result in next-day notoriety. But the millions of eyeballs that focus on you today will quickly blink and move on. Your dangerous, personal work, destined to be overwritten with the next image-search results page.

With this issue, we want to present you with intimate work that has the depth and resonance to stay with you. Powerful words and images meant to move well beyond the initial gaze, to lodge somewhere in your being, permanently. With your willing participation, the following pages become exhibitionistic. And you: the voyeur.

I am hopeful that the experience of reading this third issue of *Secret Behavior* will make your eyes happy, and your mind satisfied. In the meantime, we will be carefully gathering more human pictures and stories to further excite and enrich.

-James Gallagher

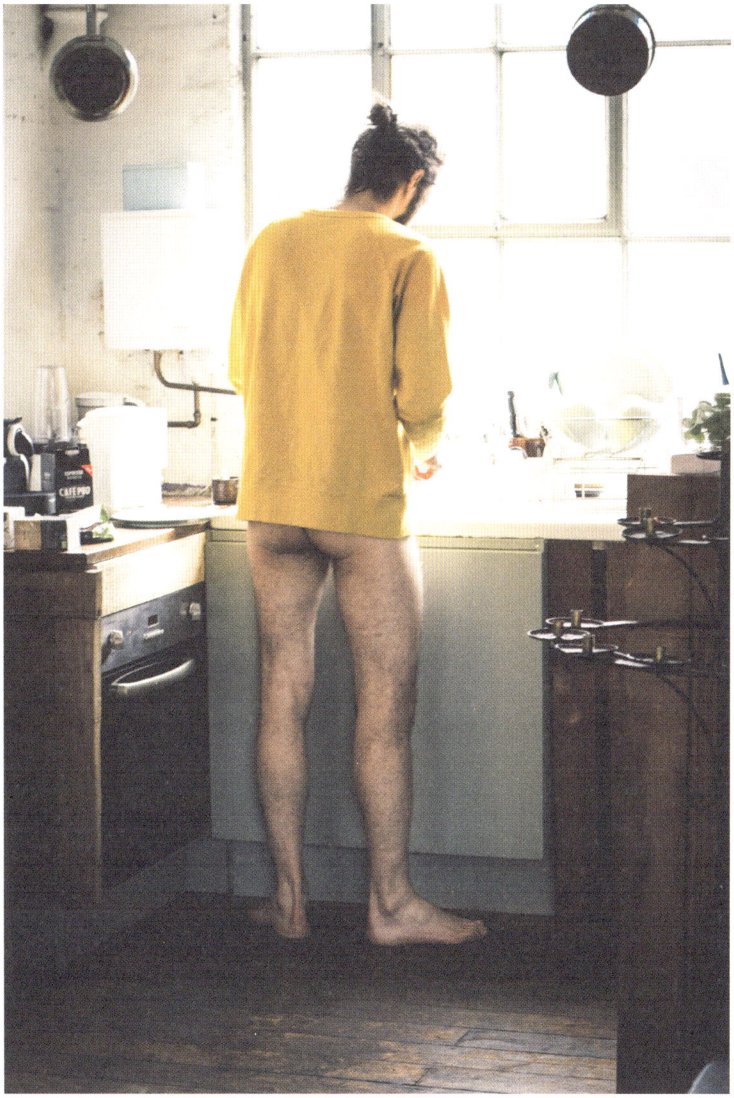

slide-2-unlock / King in Kitchen / 2015

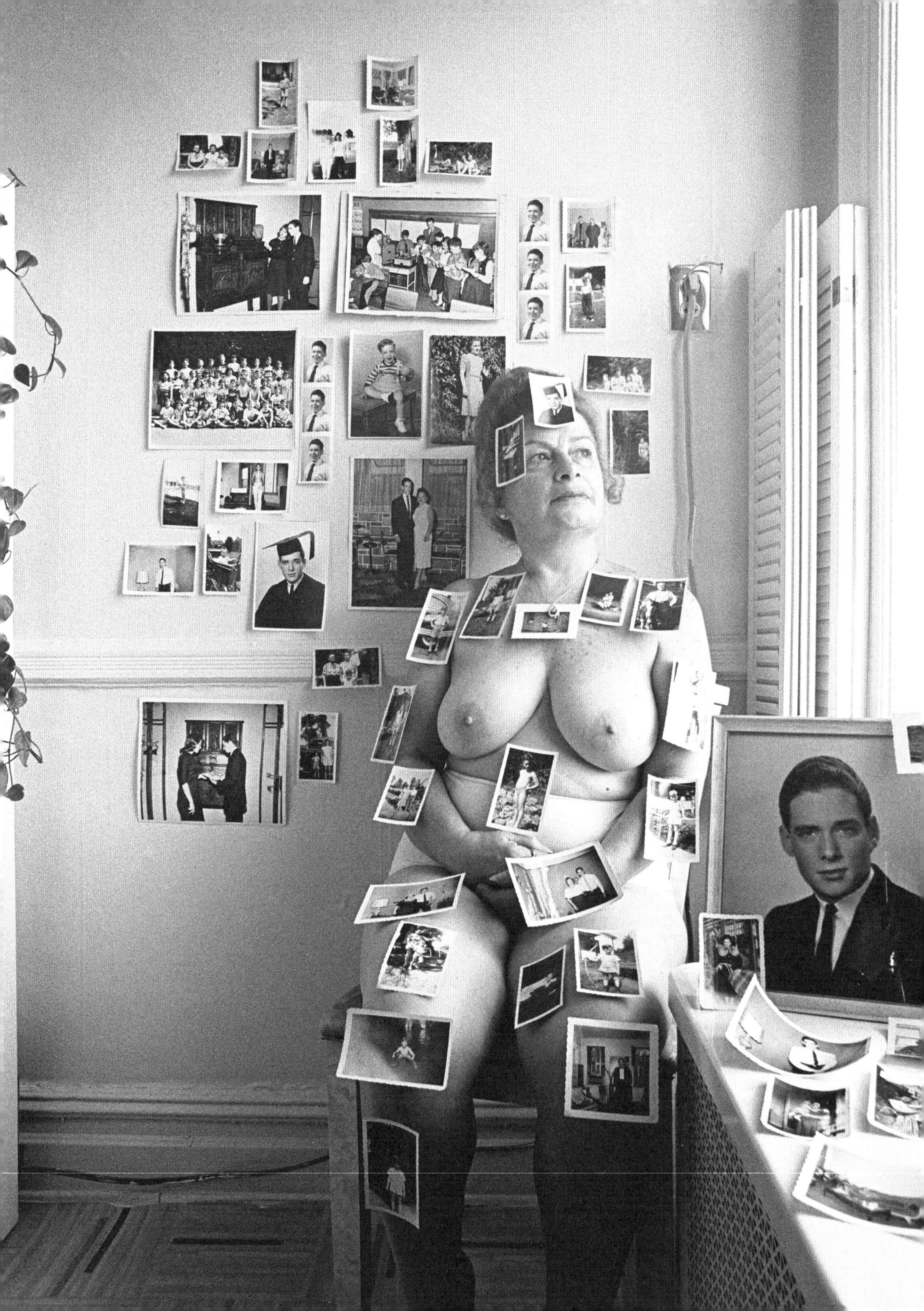

CONTENTS

Front cover: Aneta Bartos / Mirror: Dad Series / 2015. Opposite page: Les Krims / Mom's Snaps / 1970 / (Sally Krims, June 13, 1910 - September 25, 2005 / Printed by Les Krims, in a Basement in Buffalo, New York - A Failed Border Town where the Stank of Goverment Cheese Meets the E.coli Scented Lake Erie Breeze).

E
Y
E

DISPLAYED

In this civilized universe, (public) nakedness points towards a more elemental stage of our development: a baser, more animalistic humanity. Naked bodies are sites of imagined sin, representing—as they do—the wilds of the past.

Maybe it all goes back to the big Edenic transgression, where a woman—naked and pleased—brought shame into the body; allowed the outside world to enter for the first time. The body was no longer a vessel of sensual pleasures, turned instead into a locus of judgment and suffering, a thing that would wither and eventually end. With the awareness of death and time came the idea of the naked body as an affront to creation and, eventually, of the 'nude' body as deliberate display.

If we accept that 'naked' means 'exposed' and 'nude' means 'unclothed and on view,' then perhaps we can thank the last couple centuries of tasteful, artistic nudity for a more-recent, creative embrace of nakedness. With the disrobed figure giving itself over, the revelations bouncing around inside the artwork, the artist's corpus splayed across the gallery walls: the artist, the curator, and the nude/naked model—sometimes all the same person—do what they can to bare it all, and bodies—pained and difficult as they are—keep being revealed.

-Mike Newton

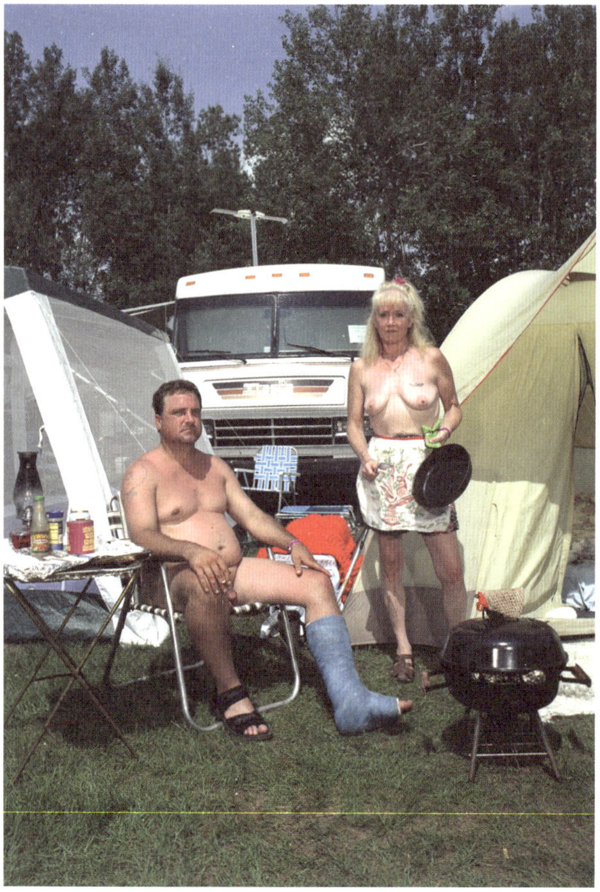

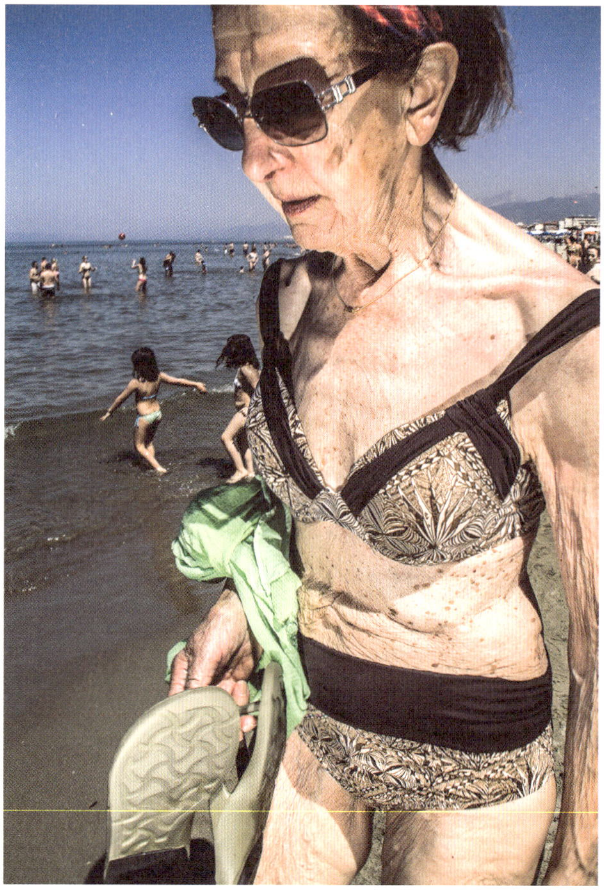

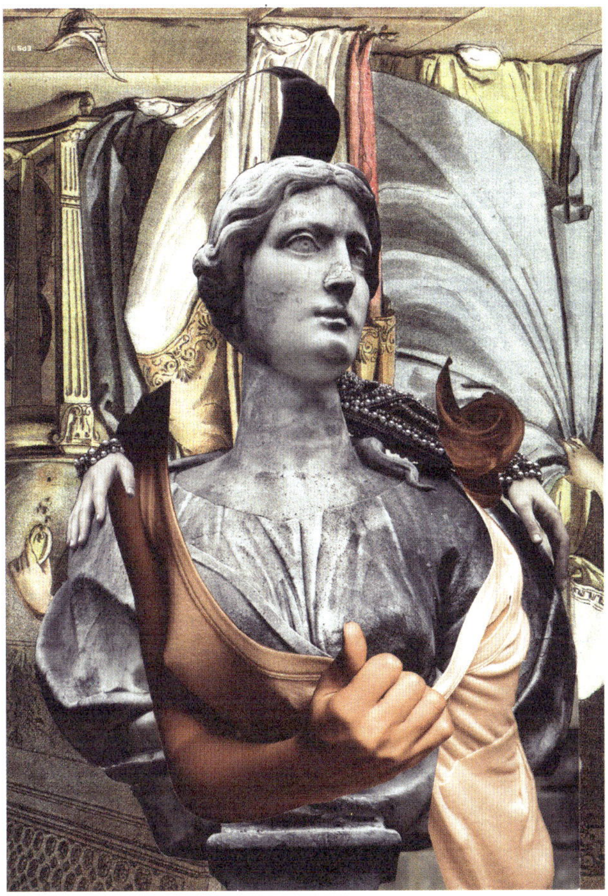

Clockwise from top: Cless / Untitled / 2014. Franz Falckenhaus / Footprint / 2015. Lula Hyers / Me and Stella Stuck in Texas / 2015. Salvatore Matarazzo / From Project Street Photography Versilia / Viareggio, Italy / 2014. Naomi Harris / Broken Leg and Barbecue / Swingstock / Duxbury, MN / 2004.

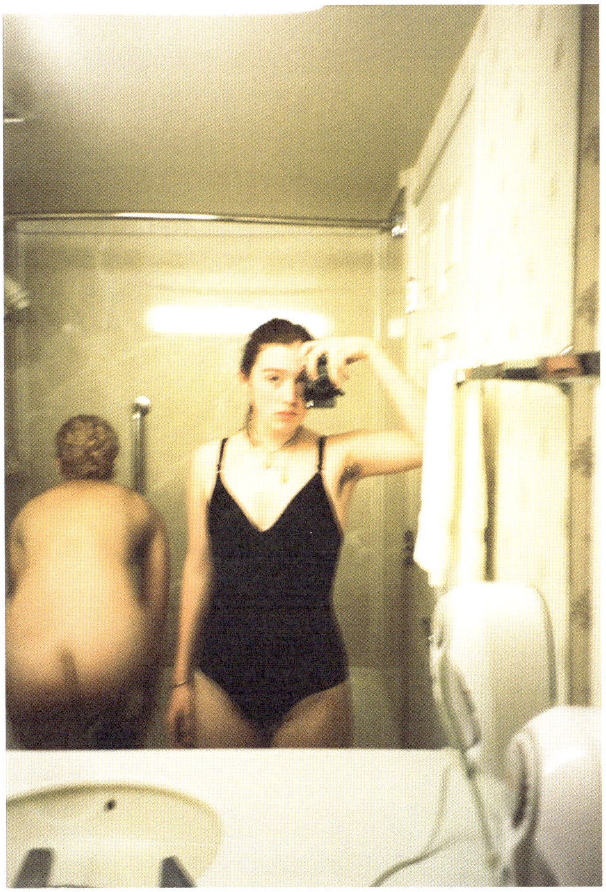

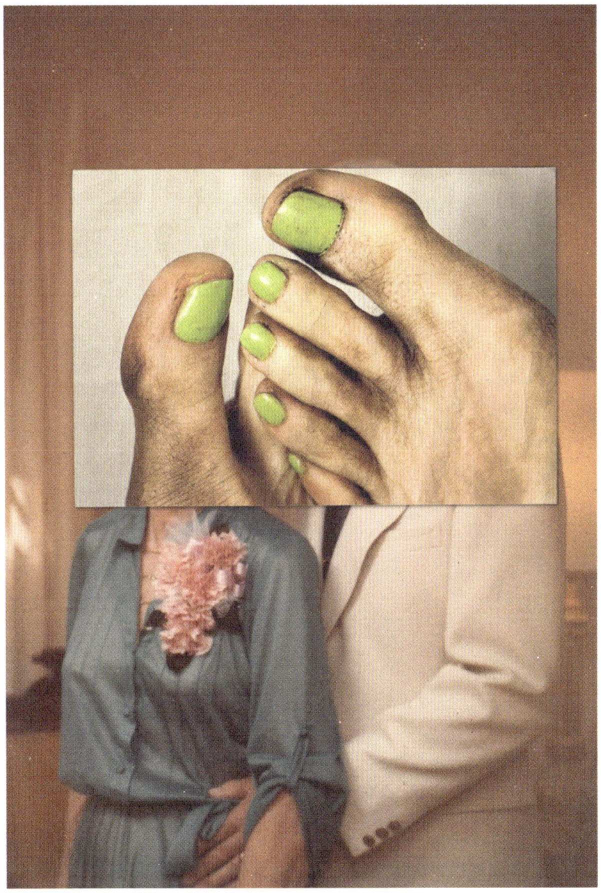

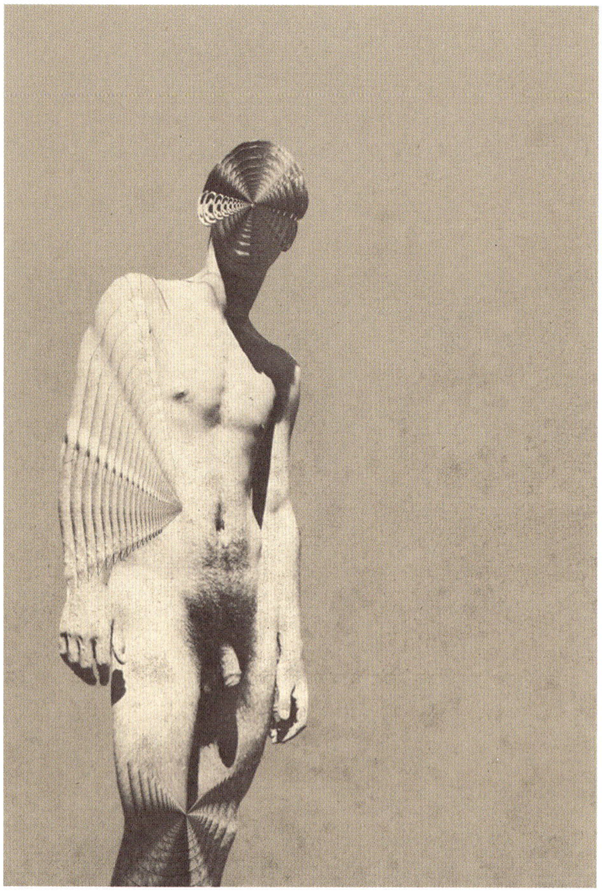
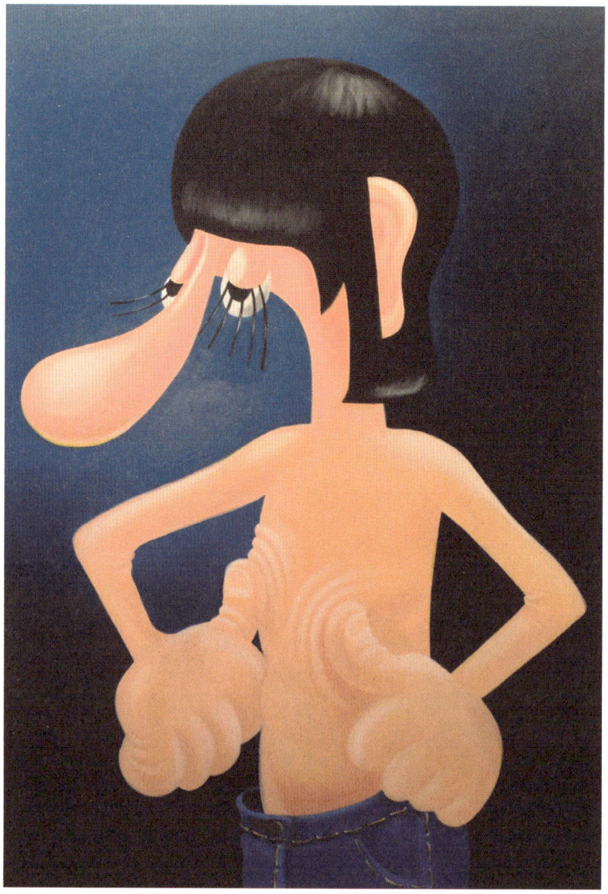
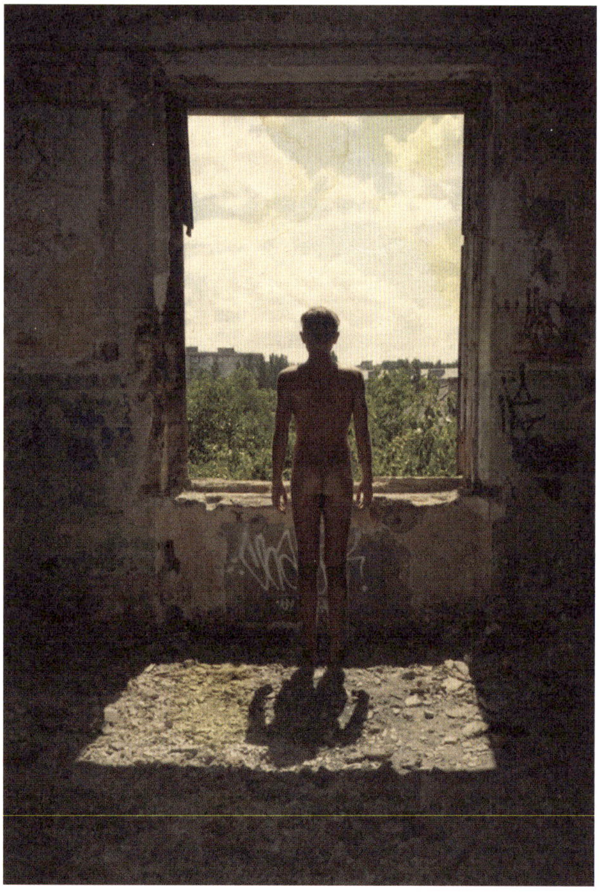
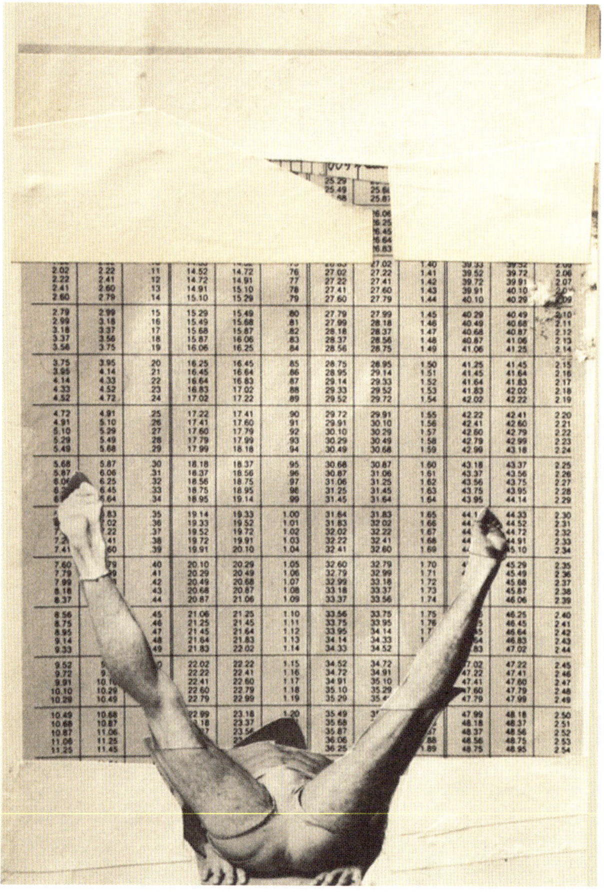

Clockwise from top left: Tomasz Malka / Boy Cut #3 / 2011. Louise Bonnet / Christophe / 2015 / Courtesy of the collection of Christophe Suter. Christian Patterson / Pin-up Girls, From the series "Redheaded Peckerwood" / 2009 / From the collection of the artist / Courtesy of ROSEGALLERY. Anna Ostoya / Exposures / 2011 / Courtesy of the artist and Bortolami, New York. Borys Makary / They Were: Part III / 2013. James Gallagher / Calculations / 2011. Sergey Melnitchenko / From "Fashion Magazine" / 2012-2013.

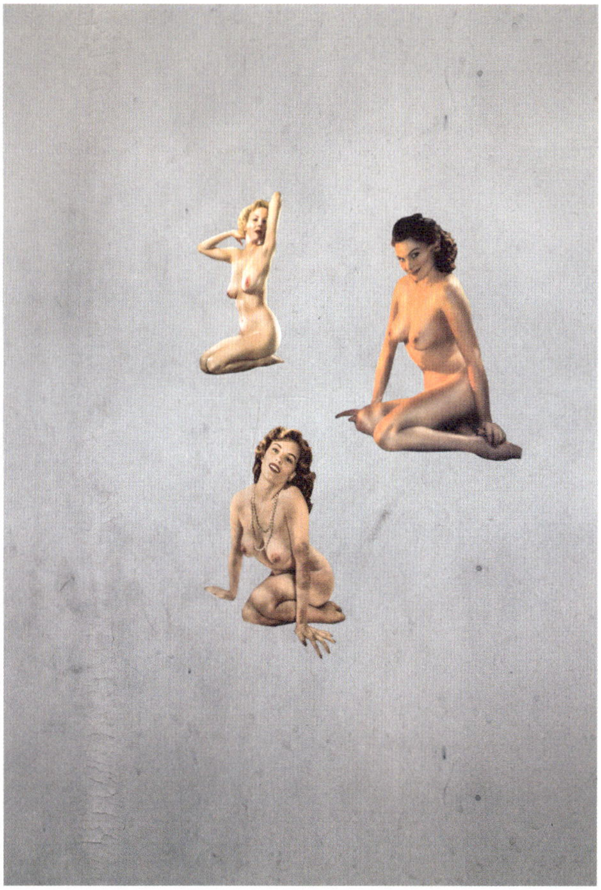

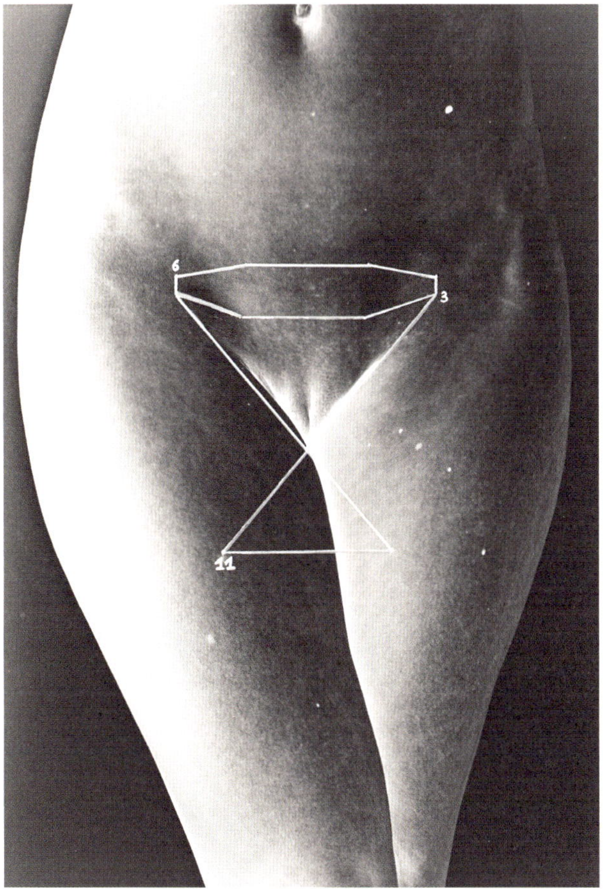

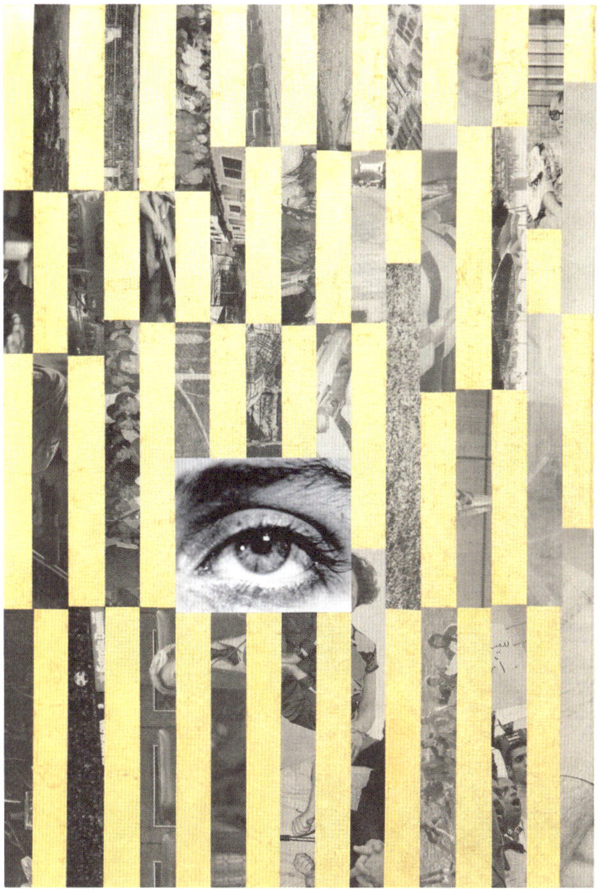

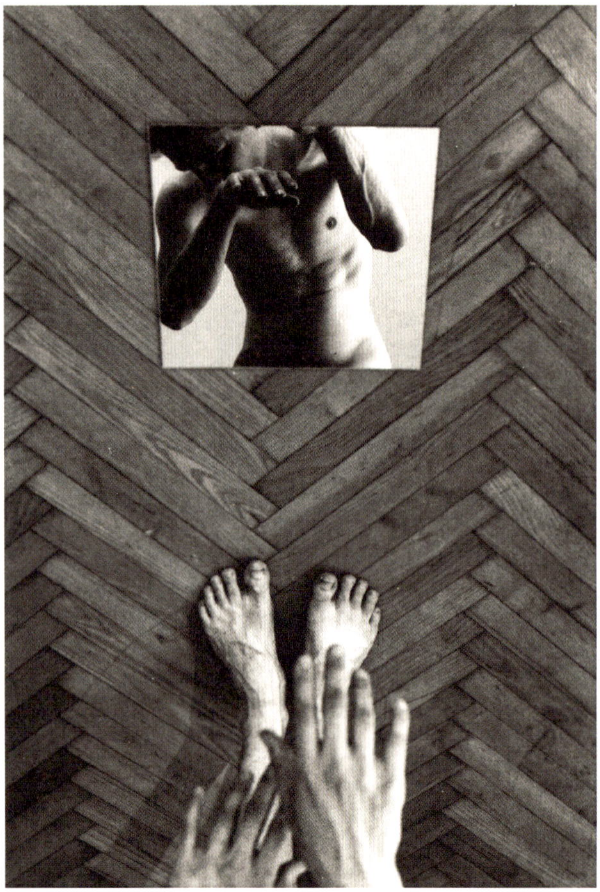

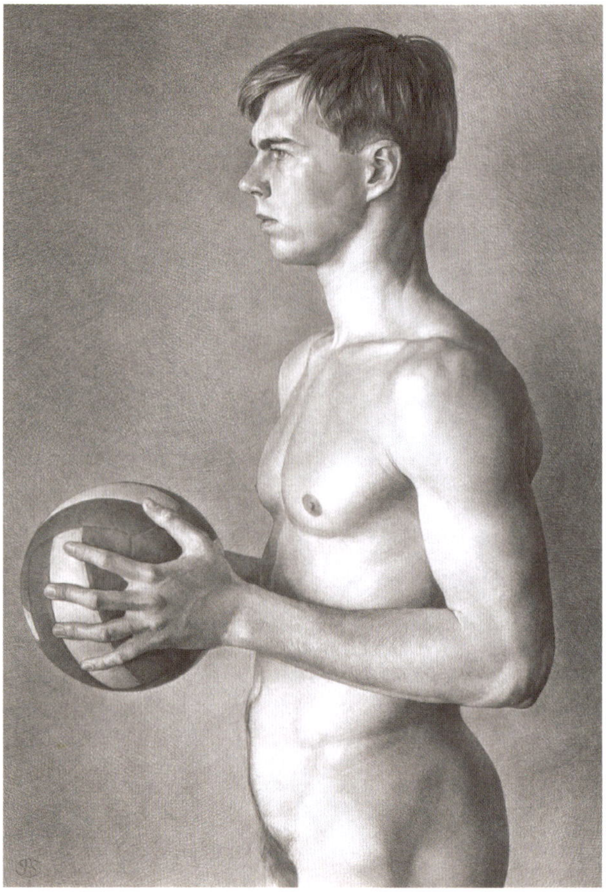

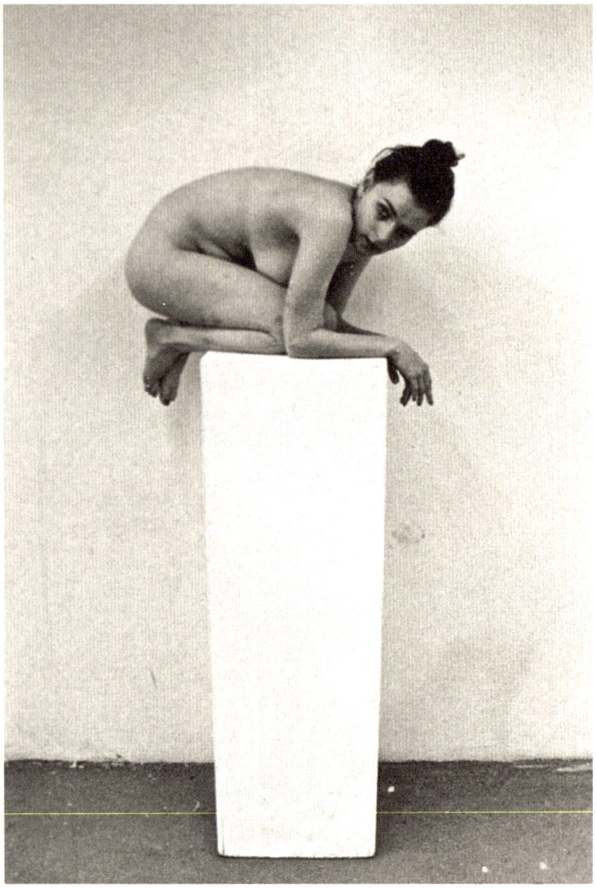

Clockwise from top left: Esthaem / Untitled / 2014. Sergey Svetlakov / Youth with Ball / Pencil on paper / 2002. Ryan James Caruthers / Self Portrait / 2014. Alexis Vasilikos / Portals #17 / 2013. Peter Berlin / Self Portrait on the Piers II, NYC / Circa 1970s / Vintage gelatin silver print / Courtesy of ClampArt, NYC. George Hajian / Folding Tests (a) / 2015. Liv Fontaine / Plinth Piece / 2012.

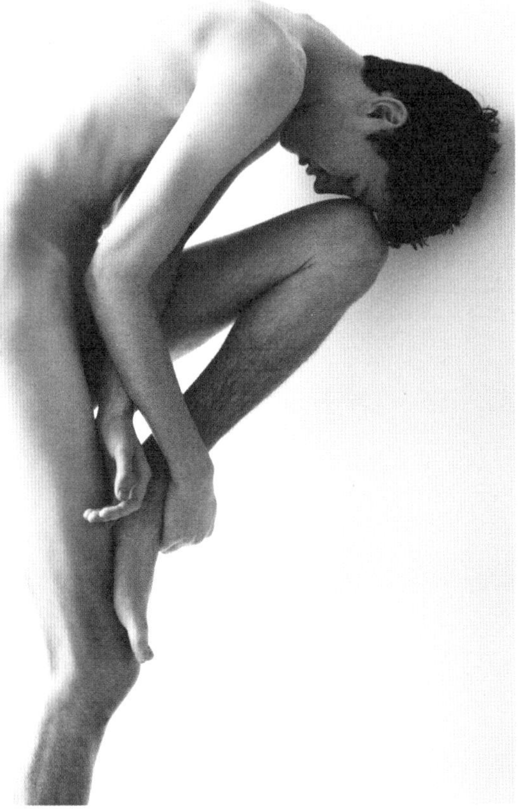

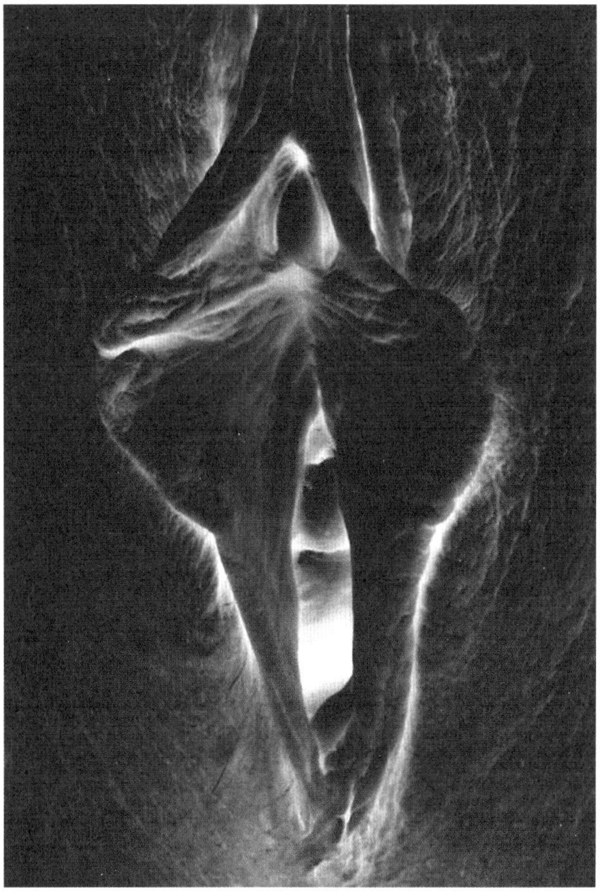

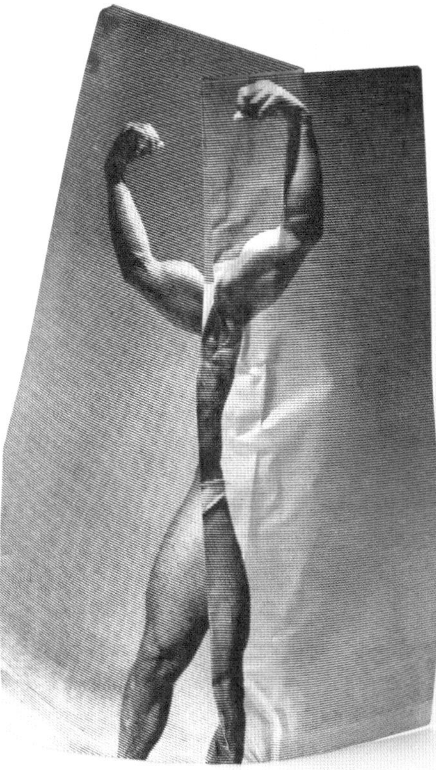

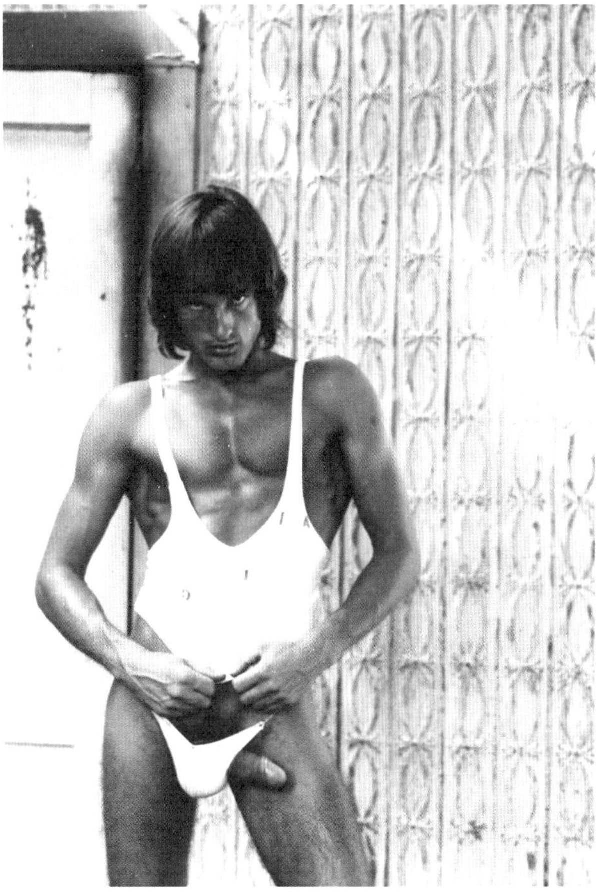

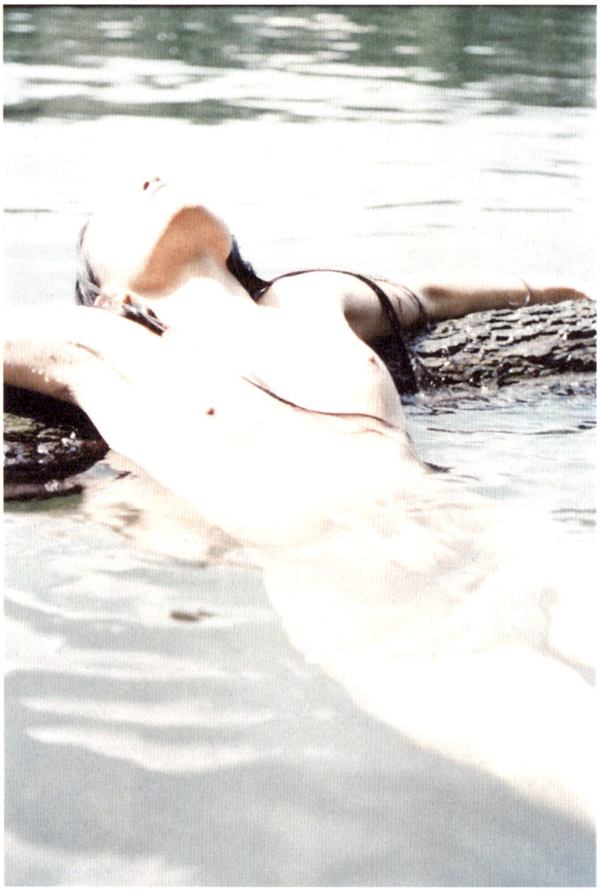

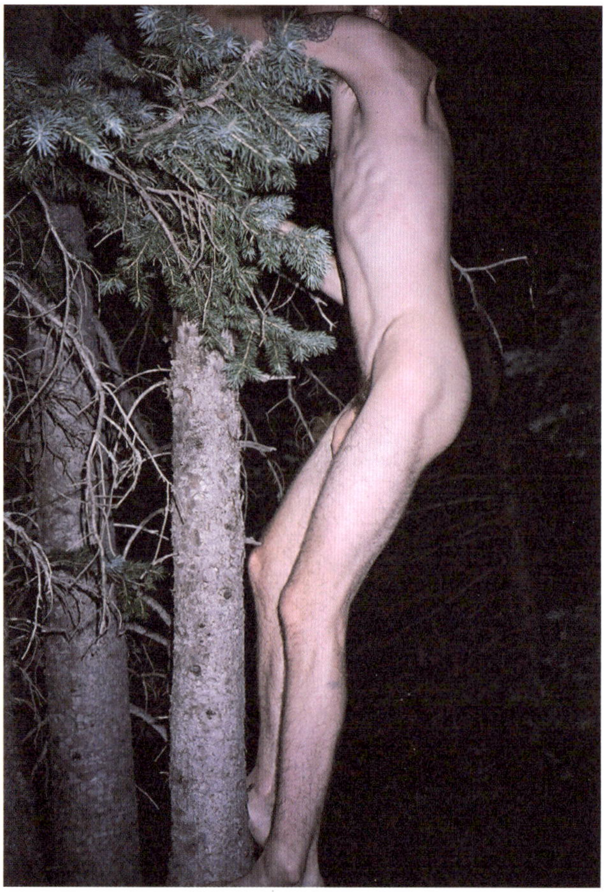

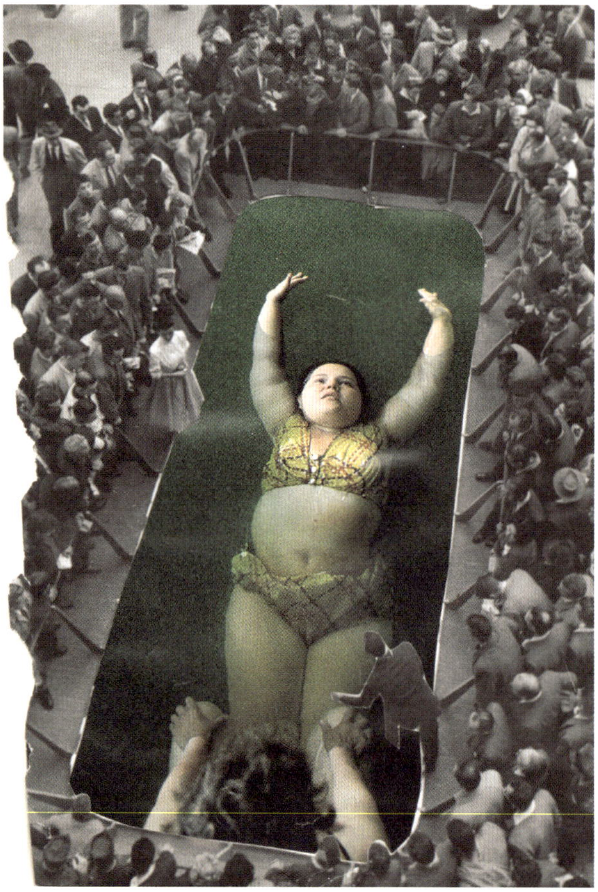

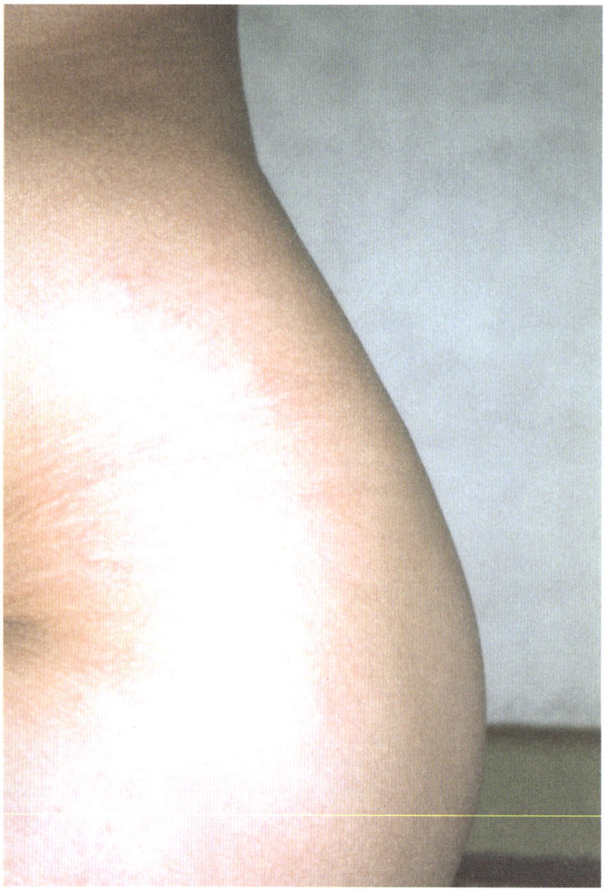

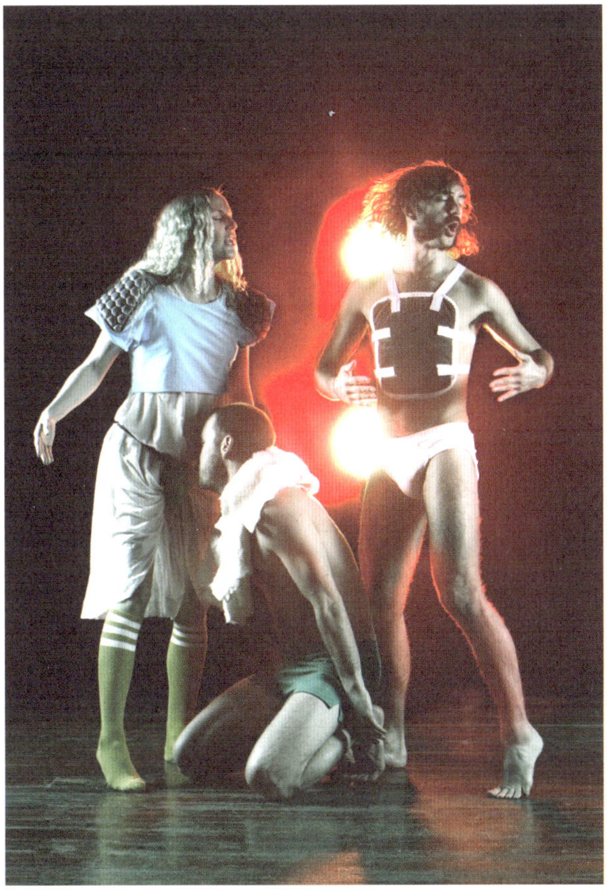

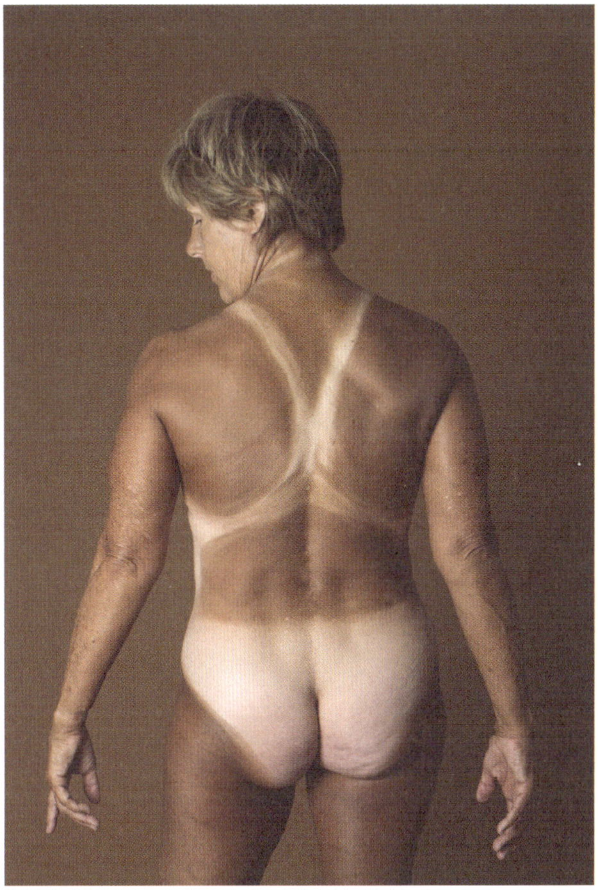

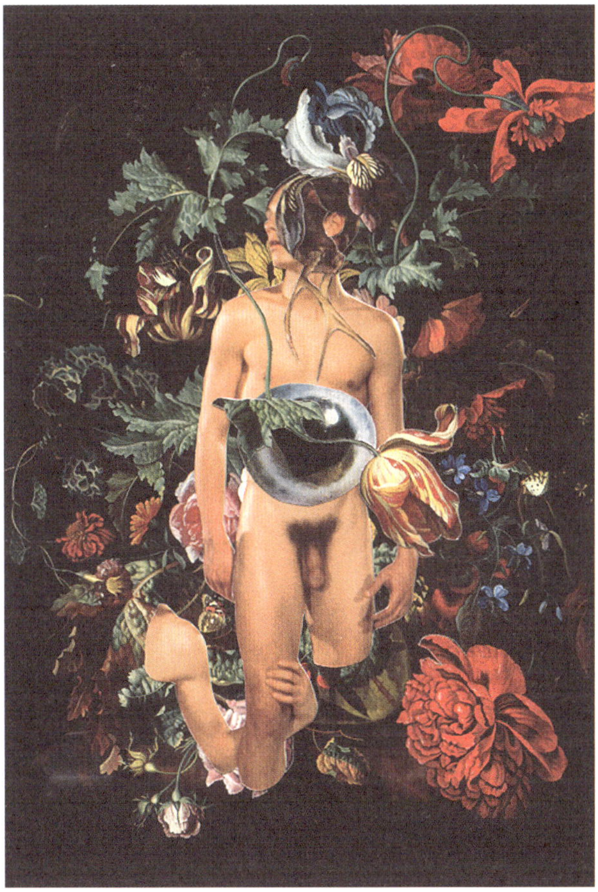

Clockwise from top left: Luna Leung / Water Lily / Berlin / 2014. Jamie Knowlton / Reaching for Home / 2015. Luke George / NOW NOW NOW / Photo: Jeff Busby / 2013. Catherine Opie / Diana Nyad / 2011 / Courtesy Regen Projects, Los Angeles © Catherine Opie. Ashkan Honarvar / Creed Adam #1 / 2013 / Courtesy of Steven Kasher Gallery, New York. Daria Hristova / Untitled / 2015. Ben Giles / Untitled / 2011.

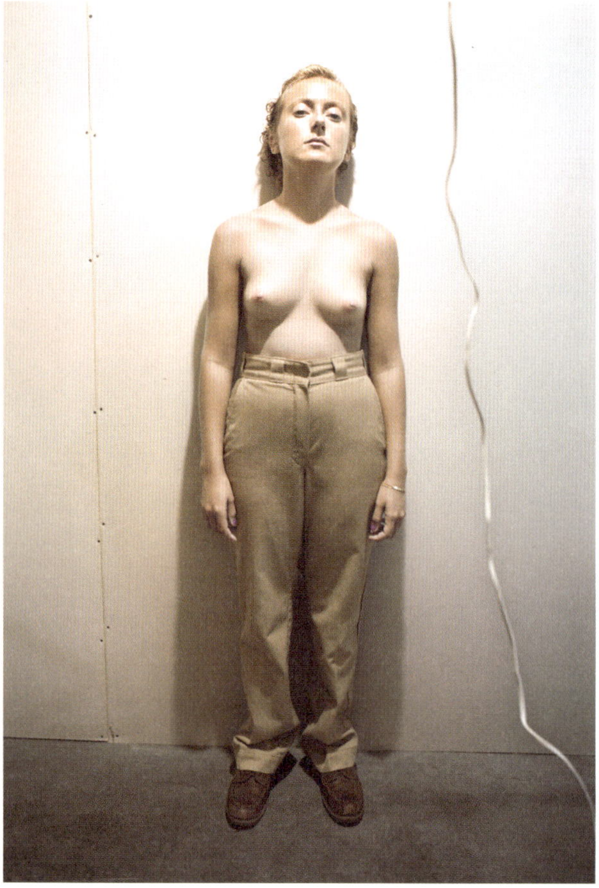

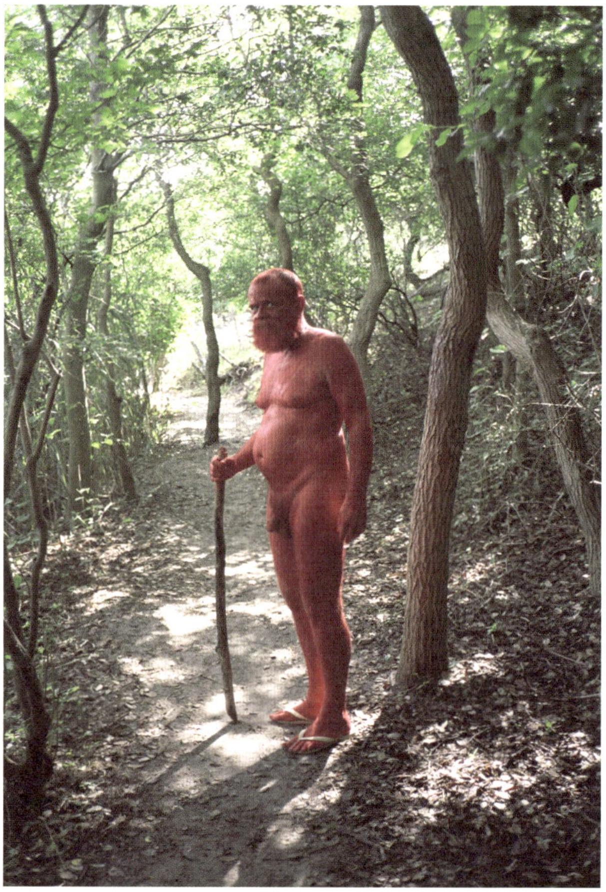

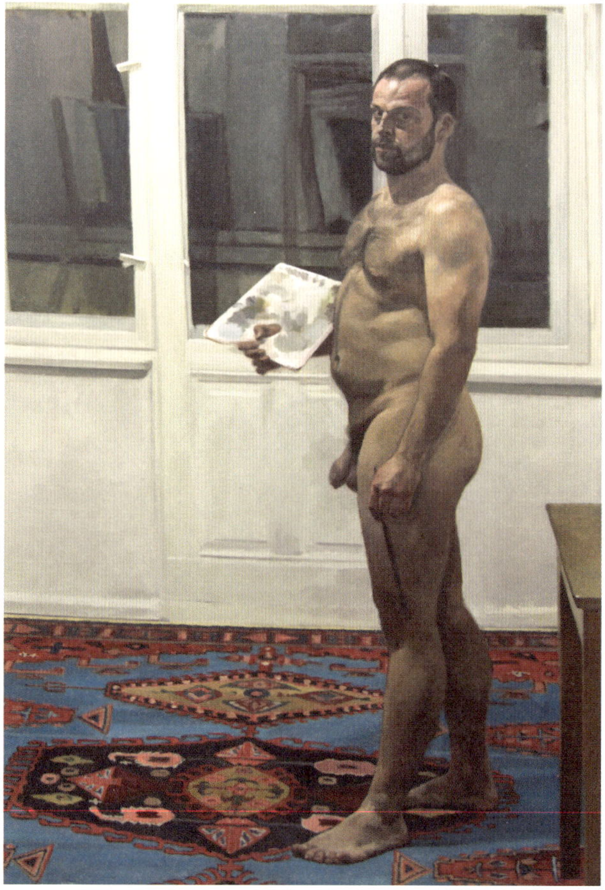

Clockwise from top left: Jo Ann Callis / Untitled, From Early Color Portfolio / Circa 1976 / From the collection of the artist / Illustrated in: *Jo Ann Callis, Other Rooms*. Aperture, 2014 / Courtesy of ROSEGALLERY. AA Bronson and Ryan Brewer / Red / Duratrans Transparency in Lightbox / 2011 / Courtesy Maureen Paley, London. Unknown / 1966 / Courtesy of Jason Brinkerhoff and Ampersand Editions. Jack Early / Studio Image of Strawberry Yoko, Boysenberry Yoko, and Grape Yoko, 2012 / Plywood, Ink, Metal / Courtesy of Fergus McCaffrey, New York / Photo: Carol McCranie / 2015. John Kayser / Circa 1960s / Courtesy of Myles Haselhorst and Jason Brinkerhoff. April Valencia / Feelings I Replaced / 2014. Dimitar Hristov / Selfobserving / 2014.

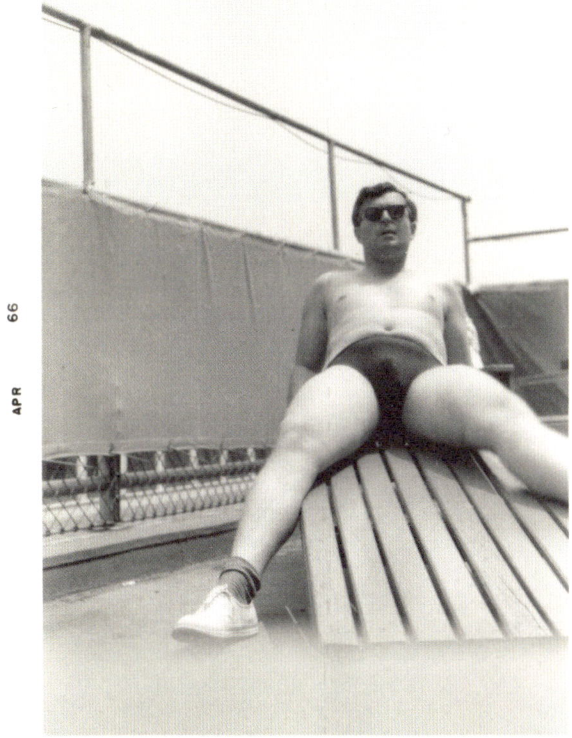
APR 66
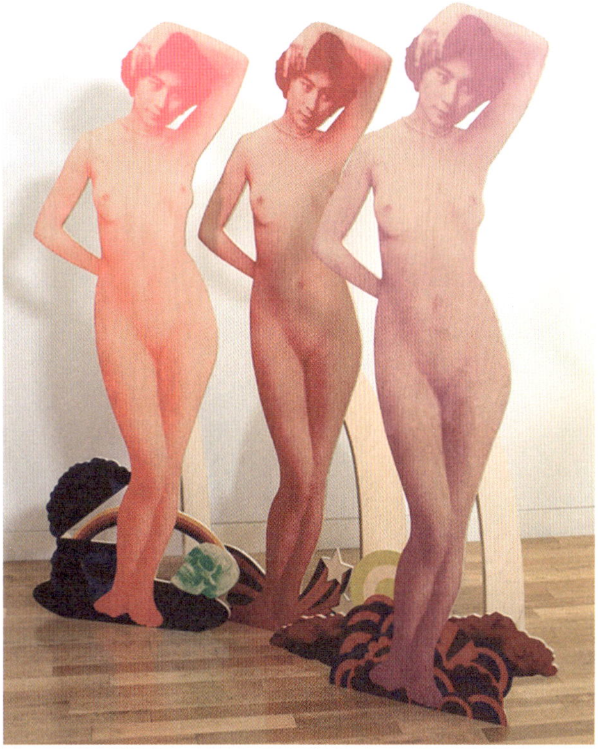
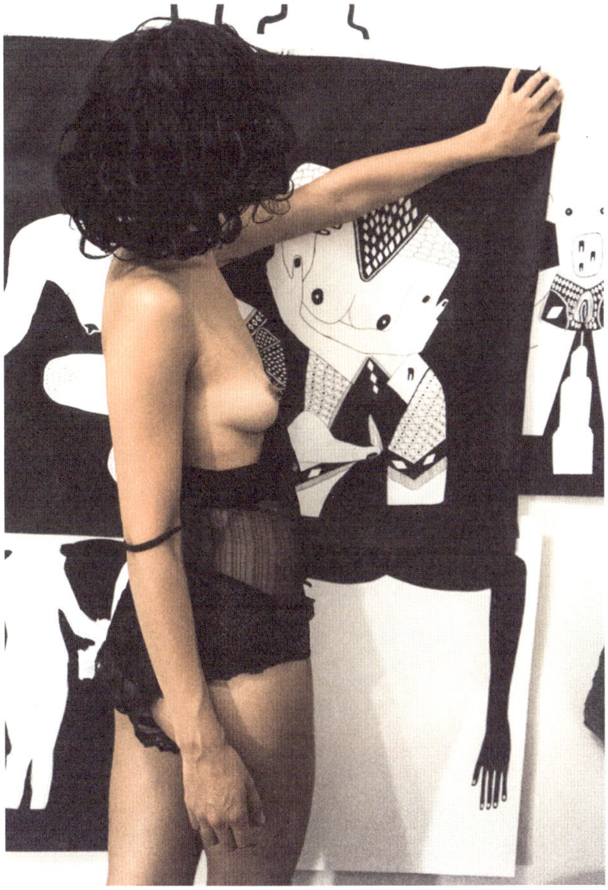
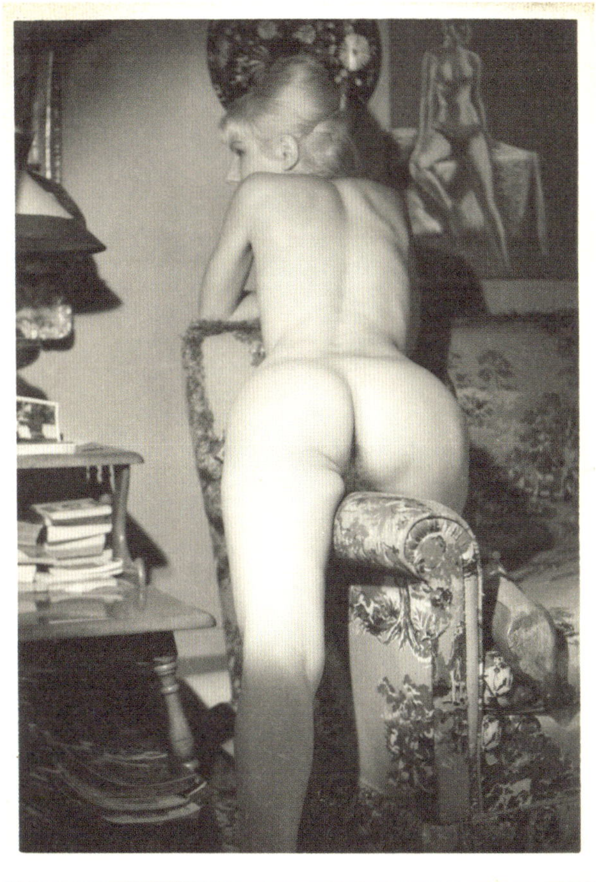

E
XP
OS
UR
E

BODY ISSUES

Jen Davis in the cold light of day

Opposite Page: Untitled No 29 / 2008. Pages 24-25: Steve and I / 2006. Page 27: Untitled No 24 / 2007. Page 28: Untitled No 4 / 2004. Page 30 (Top): Untitled No 53 / 2012. Page 30 (Bottom): Untitled No 59 / 2014. Page 31 (Top): Untitled No 39 / 2010. Page 31 (Bottom): Untitled No 26 / 2007. All images courtesy of Jen Davis and Lee Marks Fine Art, IN and ClampArt, NY.

There's an element of fantasy in Jen Davis's photographs, with their carefully composed scenes, and bits of milky flesh in clear, pale daylight. It's a fantasy constructed around a very particular reality: that of Davis's own vulnerable body.

Davis started taking pictures of herself after years of thinking—a lot—about her body. The first of her mature images (made when she was only 23) shows Davis at the beach, her body in marked contrast to those of her lithe, skinny friends. Davis is, unavoidably, pretty big, and her self-portraits draw off an awareness that this is, sometimes, a difficult thing to be. Her mood in these photos is not one of particular pride or shame, but there is often a sense of burden: that Davis is now setting down for some hard but necessary work, doing what must be done. Part of that burden must have been in the making of the images themselves—it doesn't look easy to share so much with the world (Davis has said that if she knew how many people would eventually see these photos, she might never have made them at all).

Davis's body is clearly on display; it's not a front-facing, sexualized display, but rather the daily display before lovers and mirrors (though some of Davis's lovers are imaginary, just props). Davis is enacting a self formed from within and without: the simple truths of a naked body created, in part, by its surrounding world.

Now in her 30s, Davis has been steadily losing weight. She's much smaller, but she continues to document herself and her body; it's not like her body is about to stop being problematic, after all. Without even trying, the female body is endlessly politicized. The bigger a body gets, the more it seems to become a sort of projection screen for cultural anxiety and fear, or a convergence point for all manner of assumed recklessness and turpitude. In the selfie era, fat women are scolded for their pride and instructed to hate themselves more. In the public imagination, it becomes even easier to divorce the body from the human.

How little it takes, to make a young woman into a symbol, to make a body bear more than its own weight. How complicated it all gets, once the light hits.

-Mike Newton

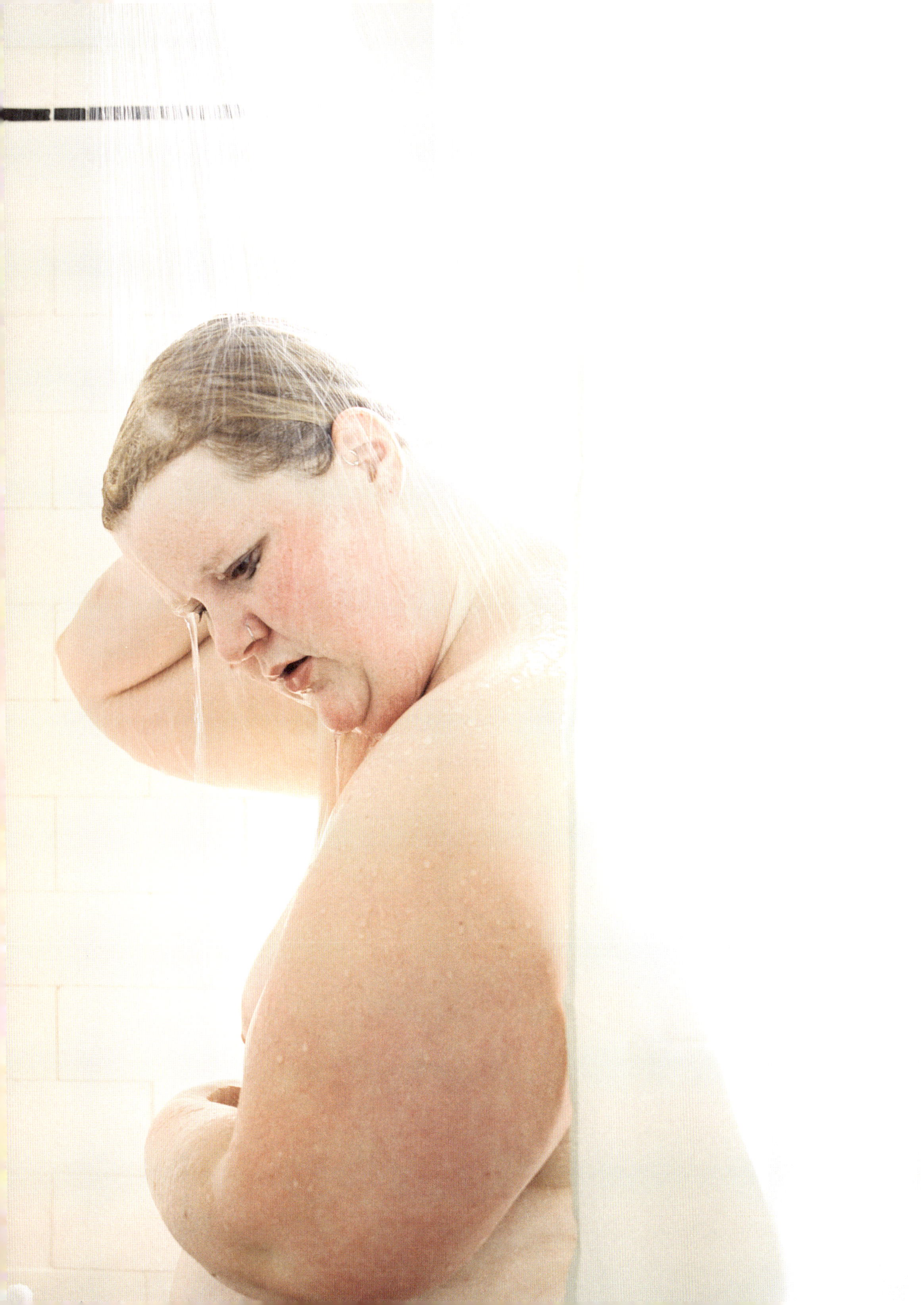

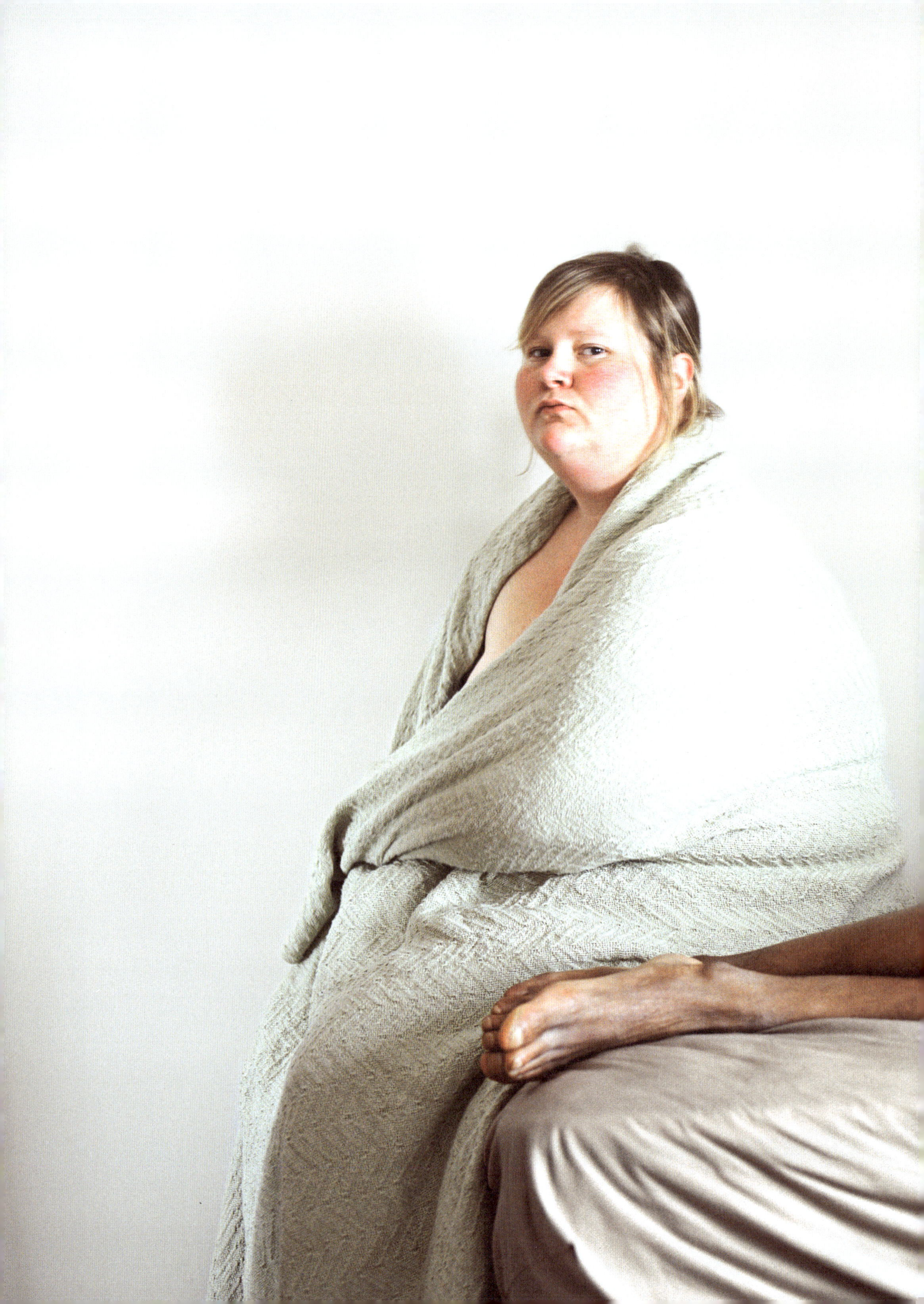

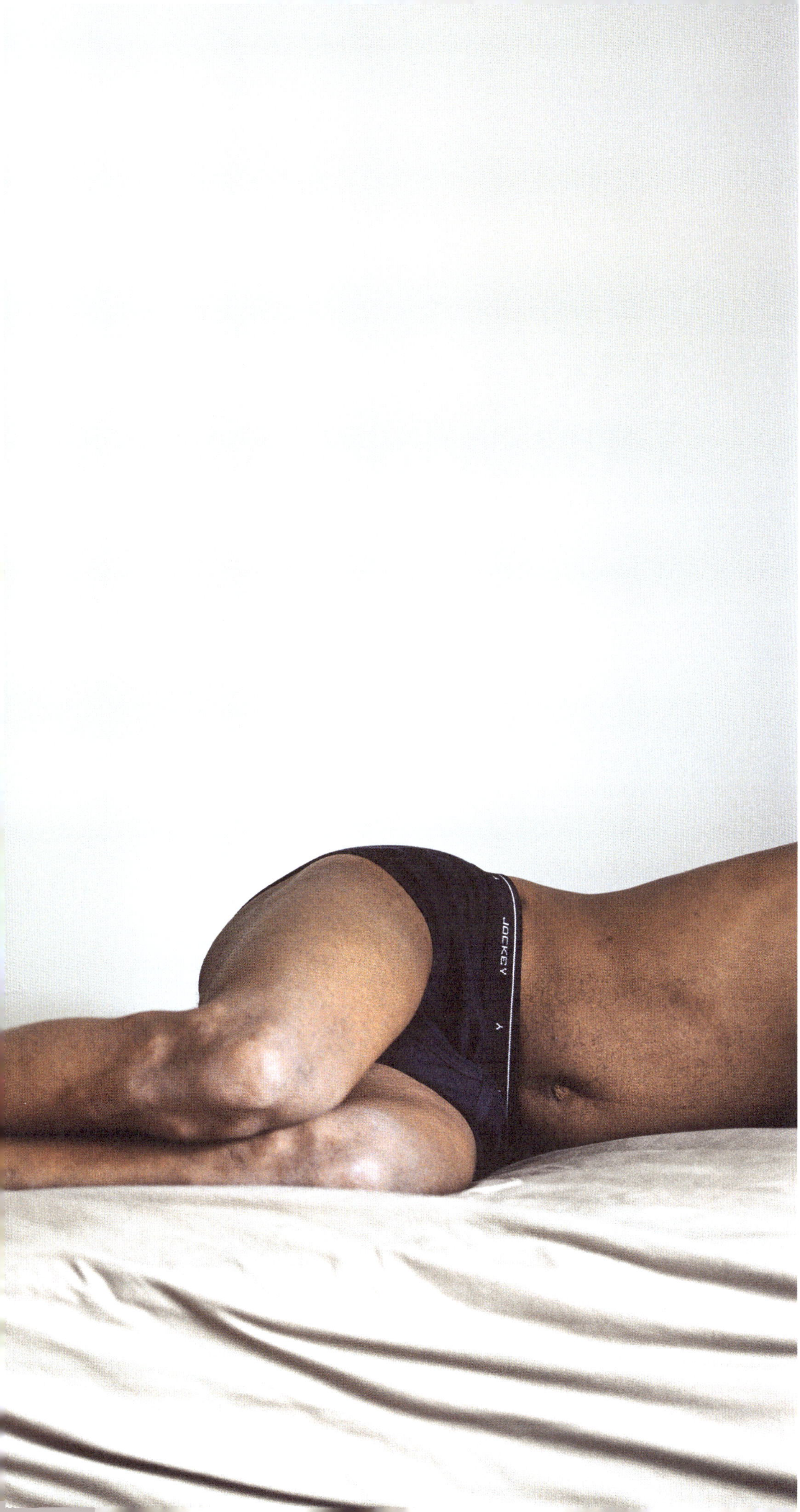
JOCKEY

TWO POEMS

by Ana Božičević

EINE KLEINE

This with you
It's like masturbating at
five years old in a pool of gold
sunlight

Blissful bee
Vertigo train
Snow hinge

The warmth that comes when
outside there's only death.

DARK AND DEEP

Two women today told me
I was most beautiful and yet
I schlafe allein

I kiss one and wear the other's
Underpants

No one knows and
No one cares not
Even them, with whom I play

Deep dark forest games in the winter
snow

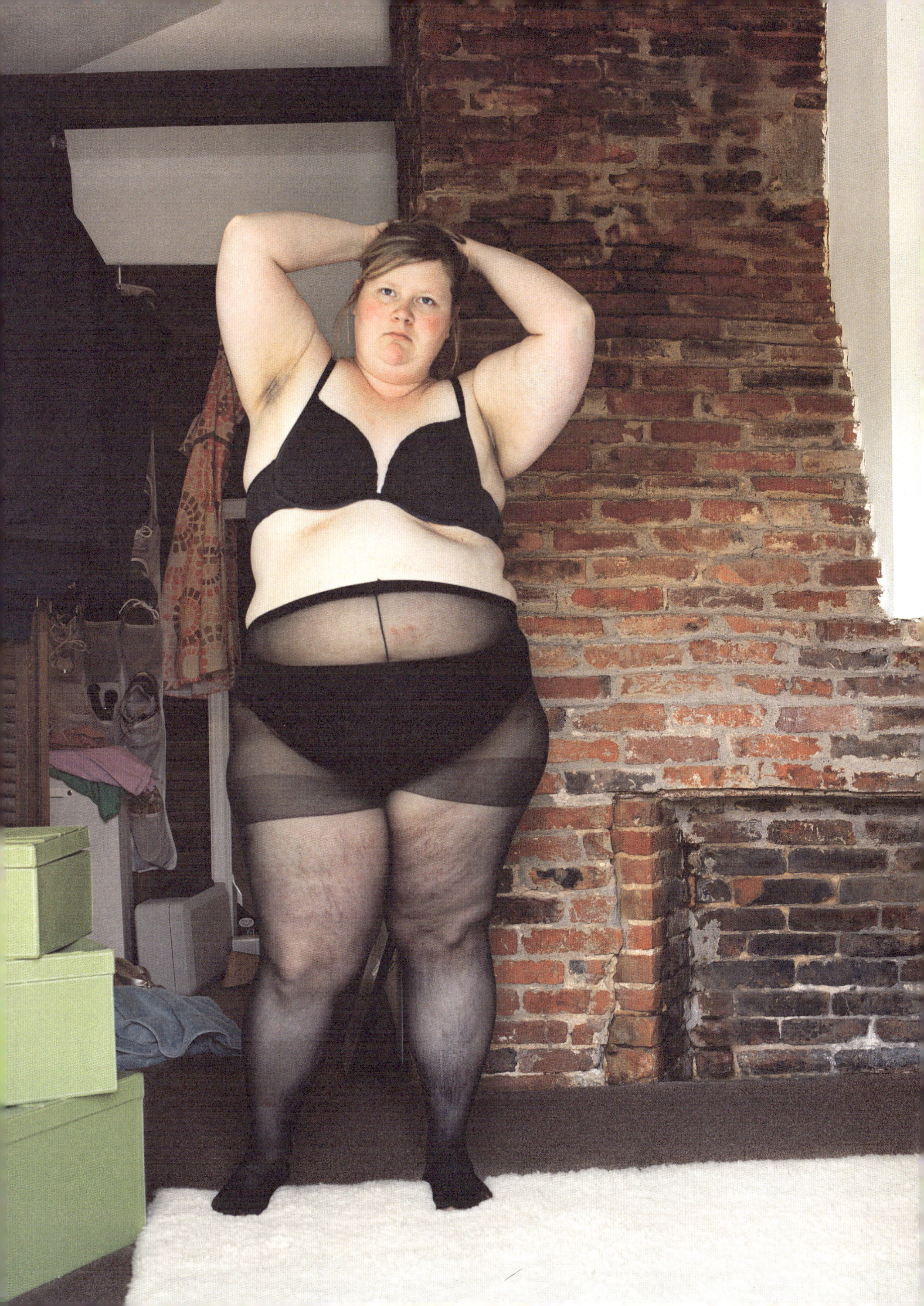

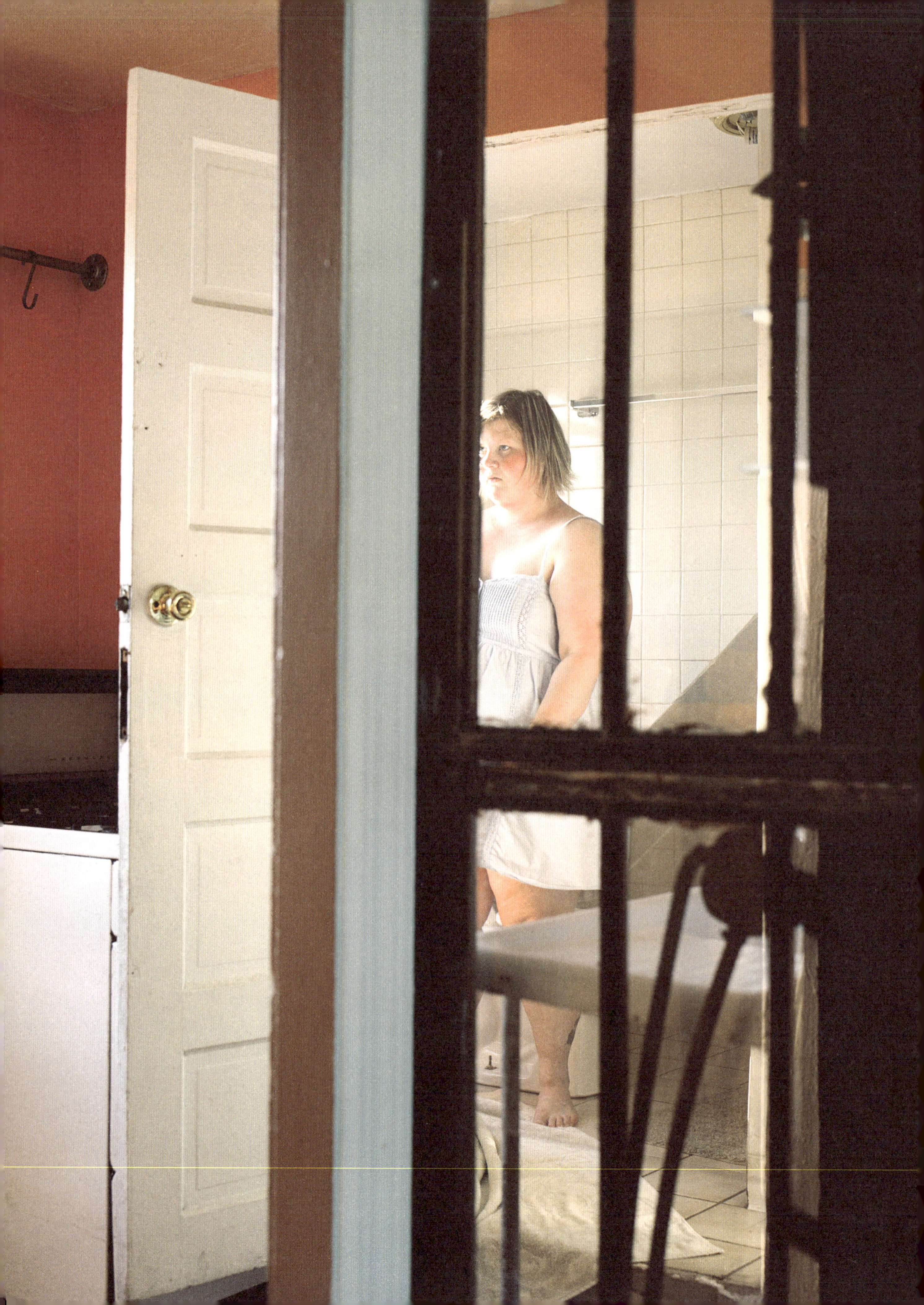

BEING TOUCHED, MONDAY 5/19

by Niina Pollari

My skin feels like a Wooly Willy toy filled with metal shavings and any person could drag a magnetic wand over it to pull them up into living features. Produce ridges or eyebrows all over me. Make it fur. In the room with a curtain this prose itches me into agreement. A field of stars spreads across my skull like diffused particles from the propulsion of a sneeze. For a long time it's possible to not be touched at all by anything except clothes and shoes. But this turns you into an expansive starving field. It's monstrous then because then you are unable to use the verb "want." I am full of shavings of all kinds. Every single metal hair. If you touch them all out of me I am going to dissolve.

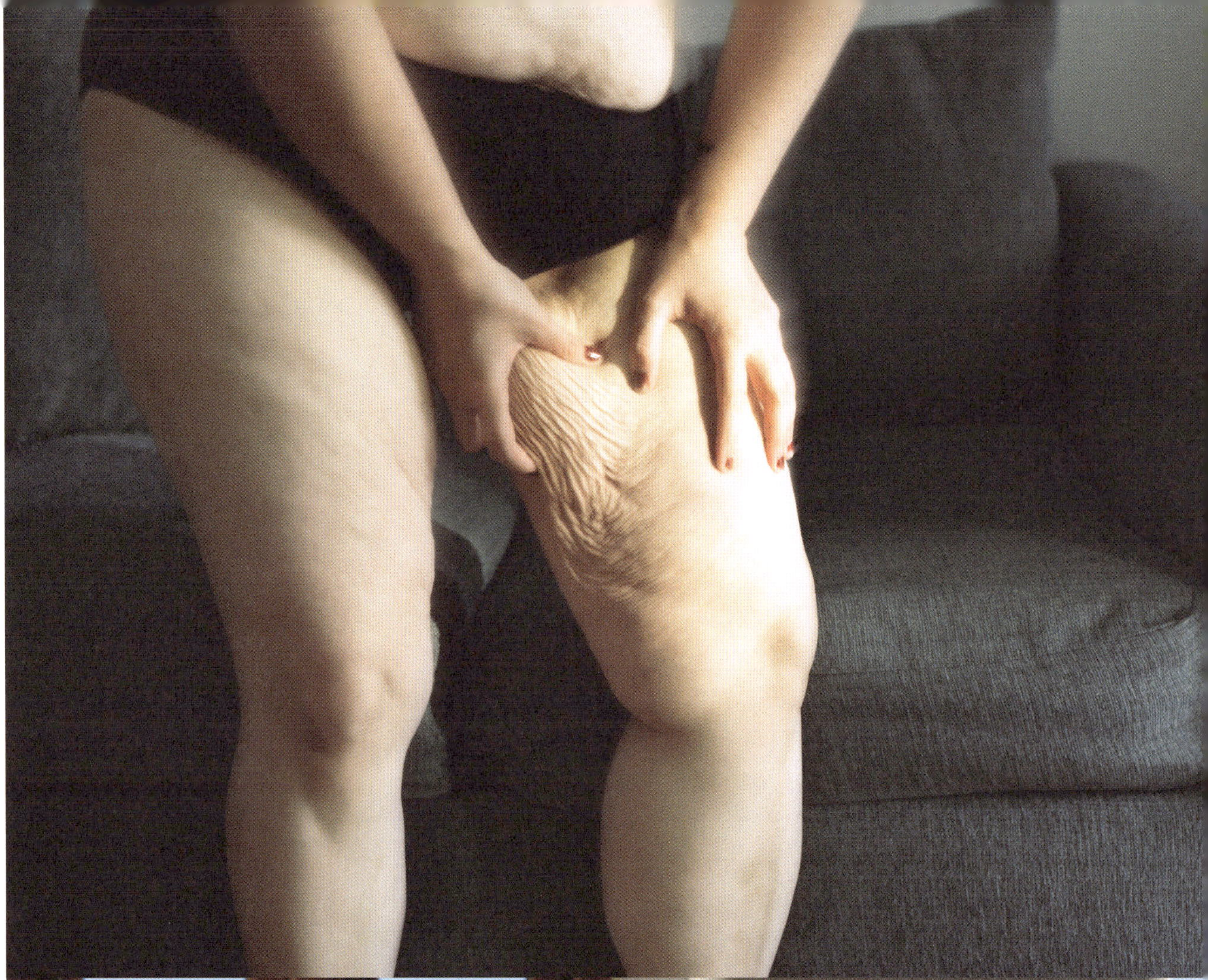

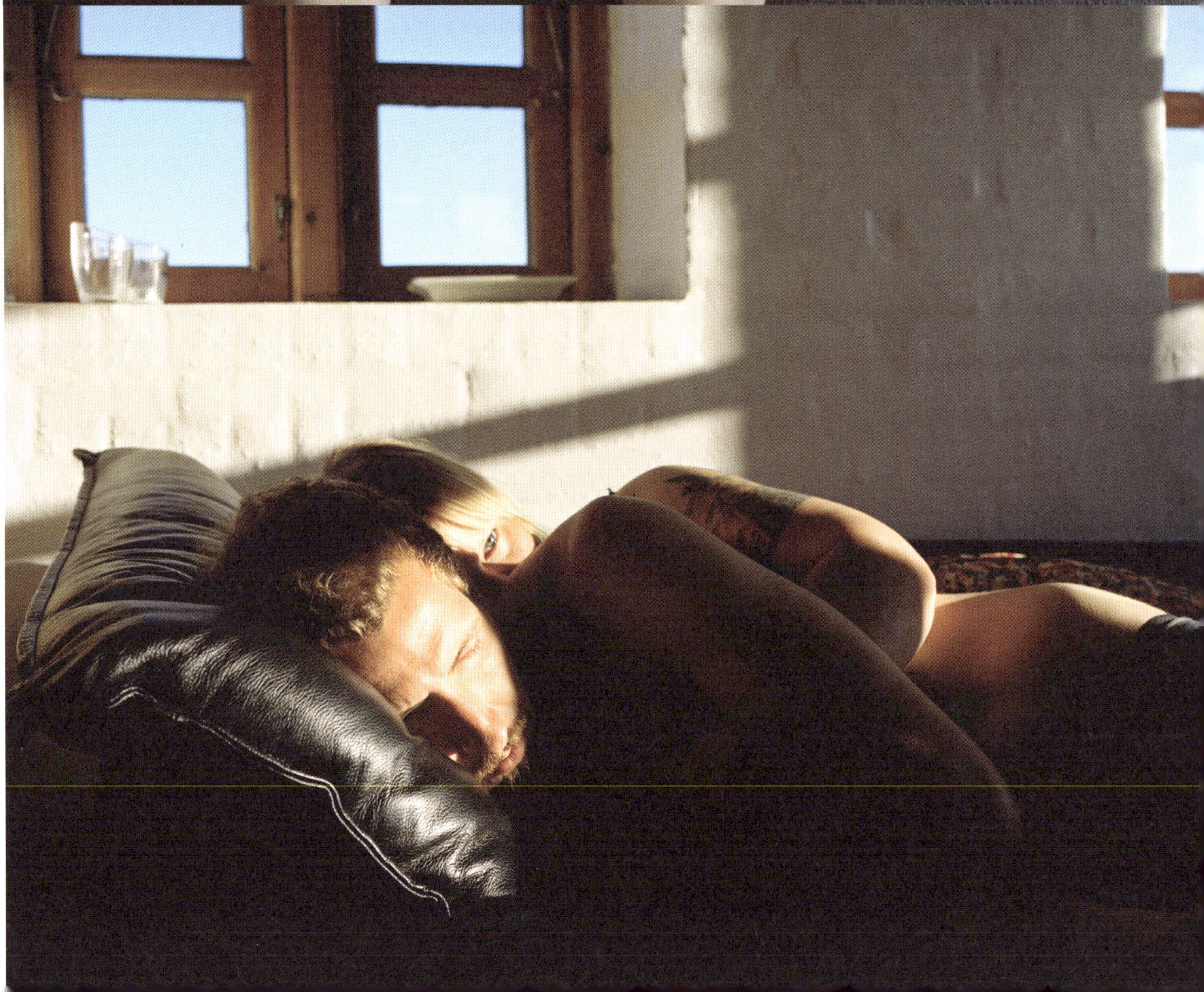

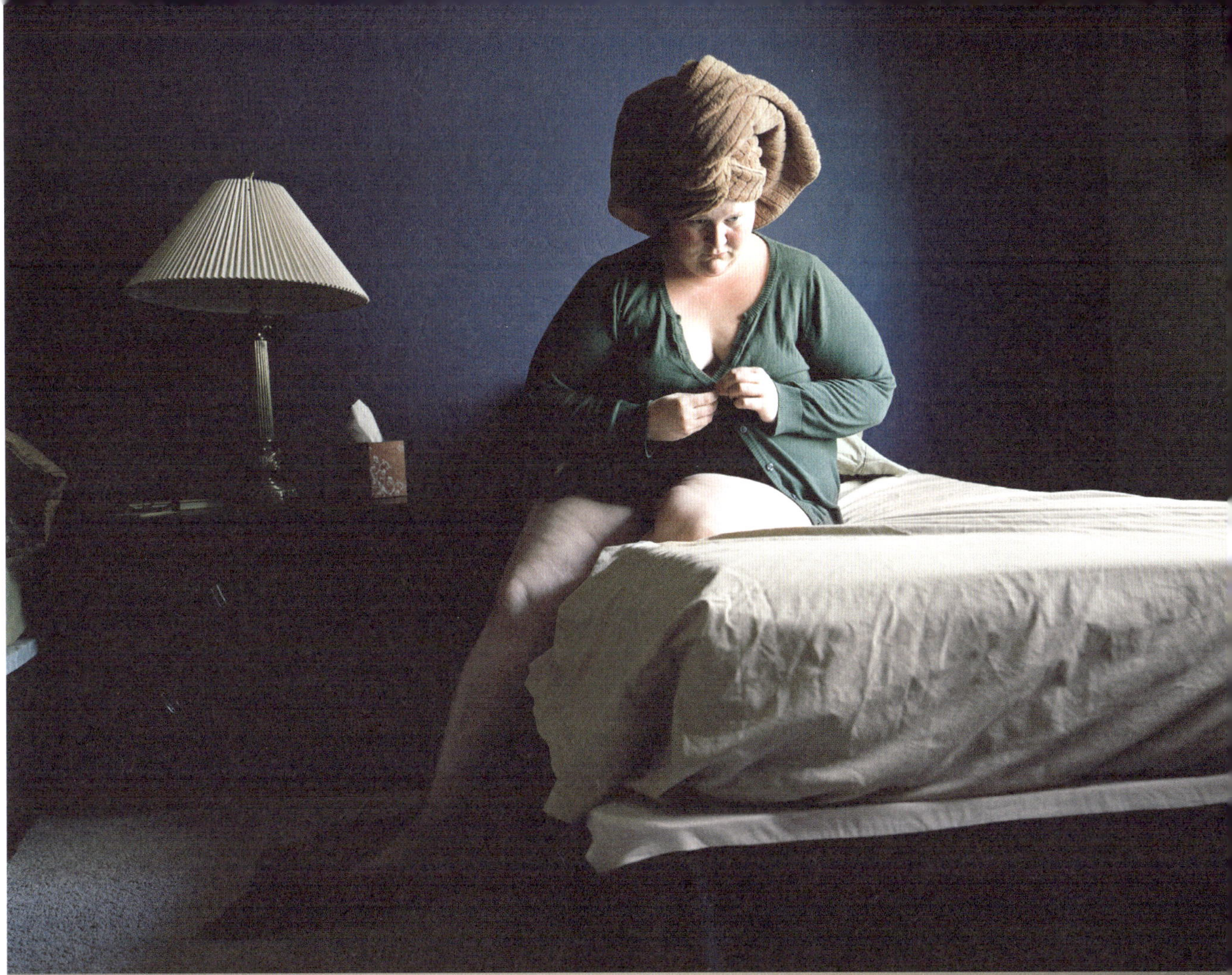

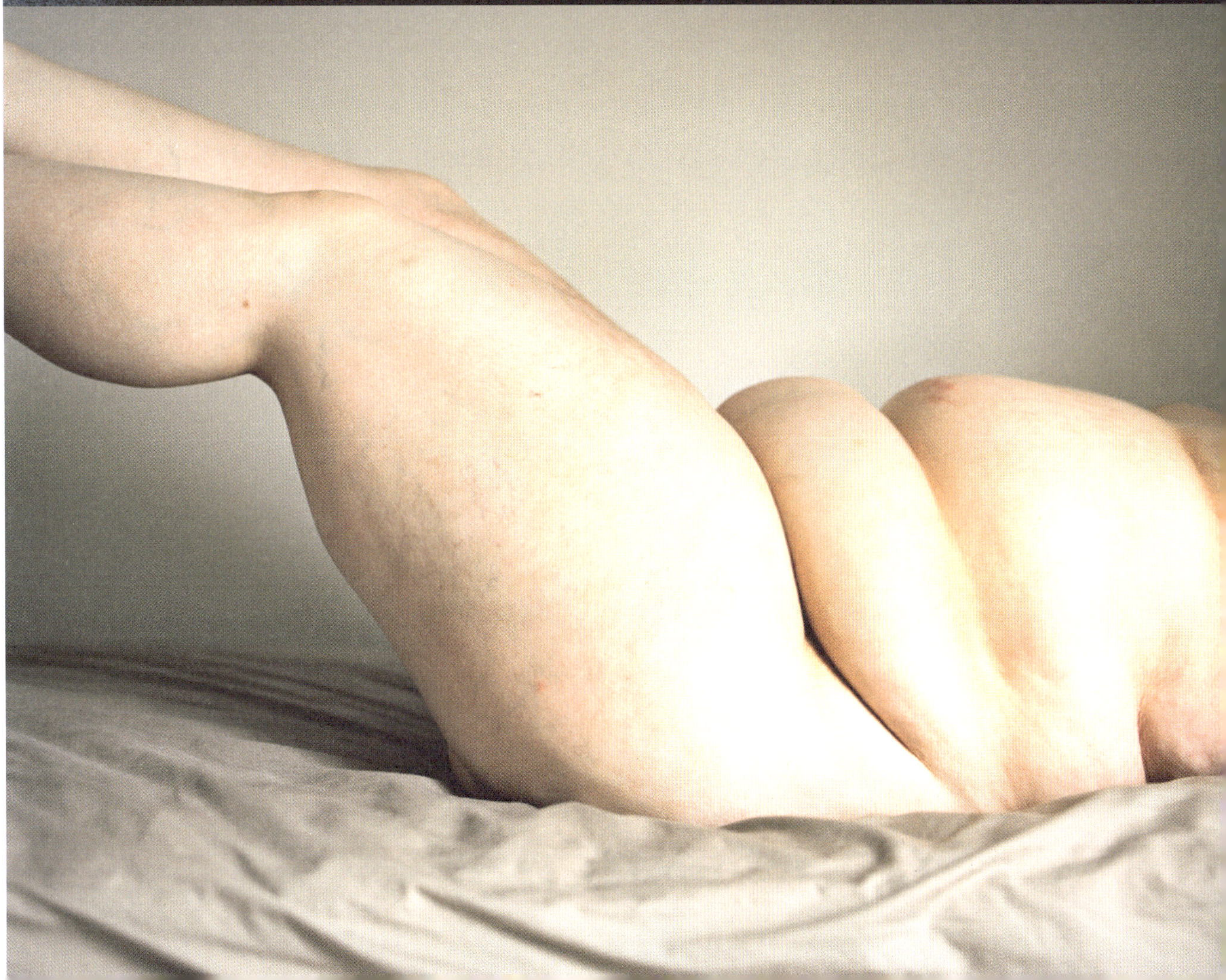

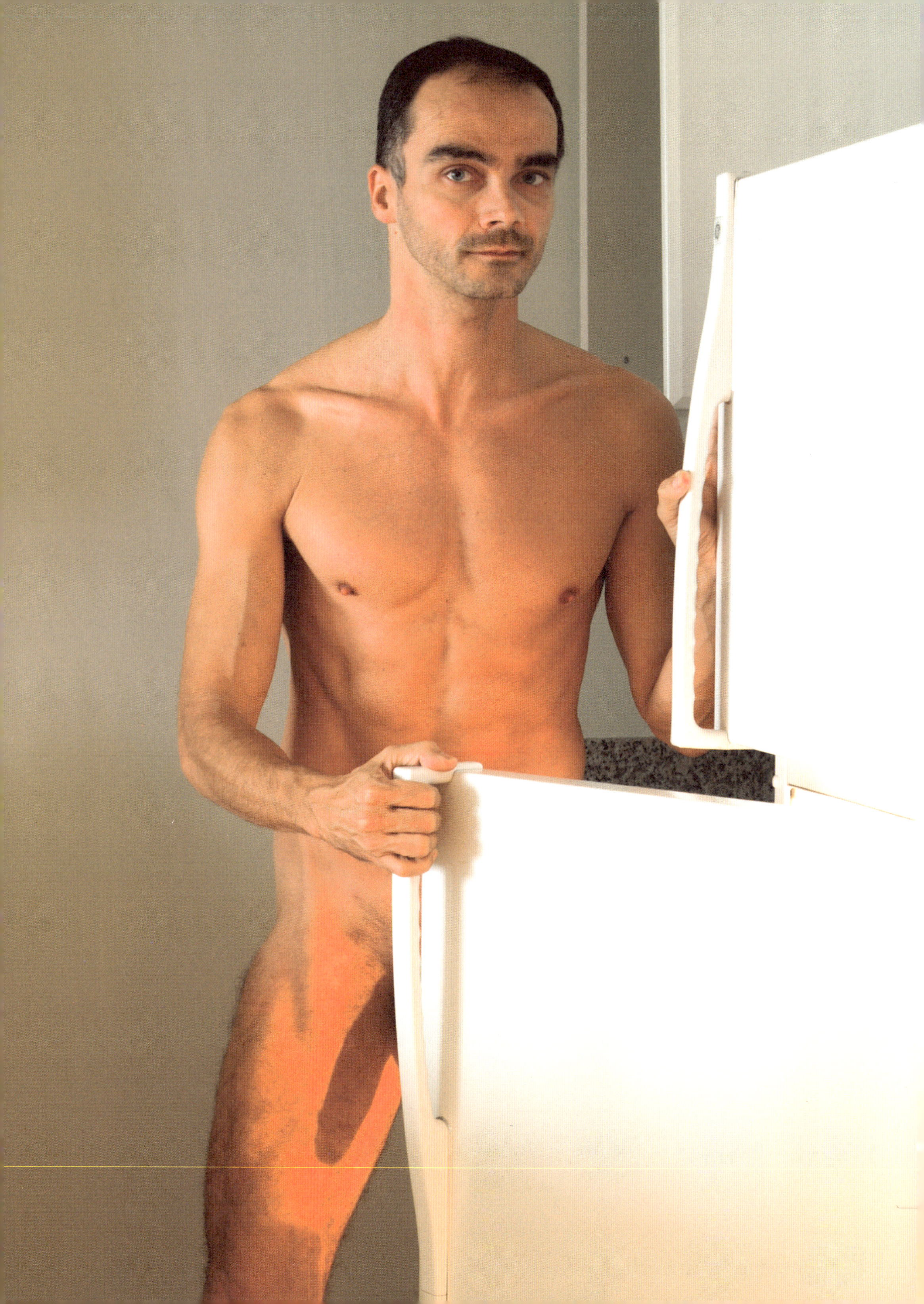

MALE FACTOR

Matthias Herrmann in flux and danger

Opposite Page: Phillips Club, NYC / 2012. Page 34: Untitled (Blue) / 1999. Page 35: Fremont Hotel, Tokyo (Hatsuta) / 2001. Page 36: from the series Toscana Dance / 2009. Page 39: au Naturel / Shirtology, Paris / 2003. Page 40: from the series Toscana 2 / 2007. Page 41: Untitled (Blue Dick) / 1995/2015. All images courtesy of Matthias Herrmann and Galerie Steinek, Vienna.

It's difficult to discuss the work of Matthias Herrmann without also discussing his cock. Herrmann's performative self-portraits don't always include his penis but when they do, they really do. Sometimes it's the only part of him in the photo.

Still, as part of the world of sexualized male nude photography, Herrmann's work is unusual for its politeness. It doesn't get into the totemic dick-worship common to porn, or the casual extremities of S/M photography. Herrmann's photos don't emerge as directly or desperately confrontational, but with his smirking face and bulging crotch he lightly teases a confrontation out of the viewer; a gentle confrontation.

Herrmann often stages his photos in places that aren't exactly public, but aren't really private either, like hotel rooms, or the woods near his house. Outside of private space, of course, the naked body is criminalized: not the child's innocent body, but the adult body, the changed body—that can get you arrested. Herrmann's body is doubly criminalized by an imagined sexual/cultural malignancy: the still-common idea that homosexuality—male homosexuality especially—is a threat to normal, down-home decency; regressive notions that still define public policy in so many countries. His body is further complicated by HIV—something that he's incorporated into his art. In a 2003 interview, Herrmann said that he feels "Like I have an endangered body. [...] I'm what they call a fast progressor: the HIV progresses faster into AIDS than usually. So yes, I think of my body as being in decay." Herrmann's is a body in flux.

Herrmann performs a masculinity not in crisis, but still in conflict. He looks for ideological zones and modes of presentation like a bird looks for a place to build its nest, seeking places to put his naked body. He's a nice European guy and also a serial malefactor, a gentleman-thief. Like everyone else, he has a criminal body: like everyone, he has a lawlessness beneath his clothes just waiting to spill over. In his photos, he can appear almost withholding, or half-hearted, like he doesn't really want to be there. As if he's a child dragged on-stage by his parents—maybe he doesn't particularly want to perform and yet, he has to. We all do.

-Mike Newton

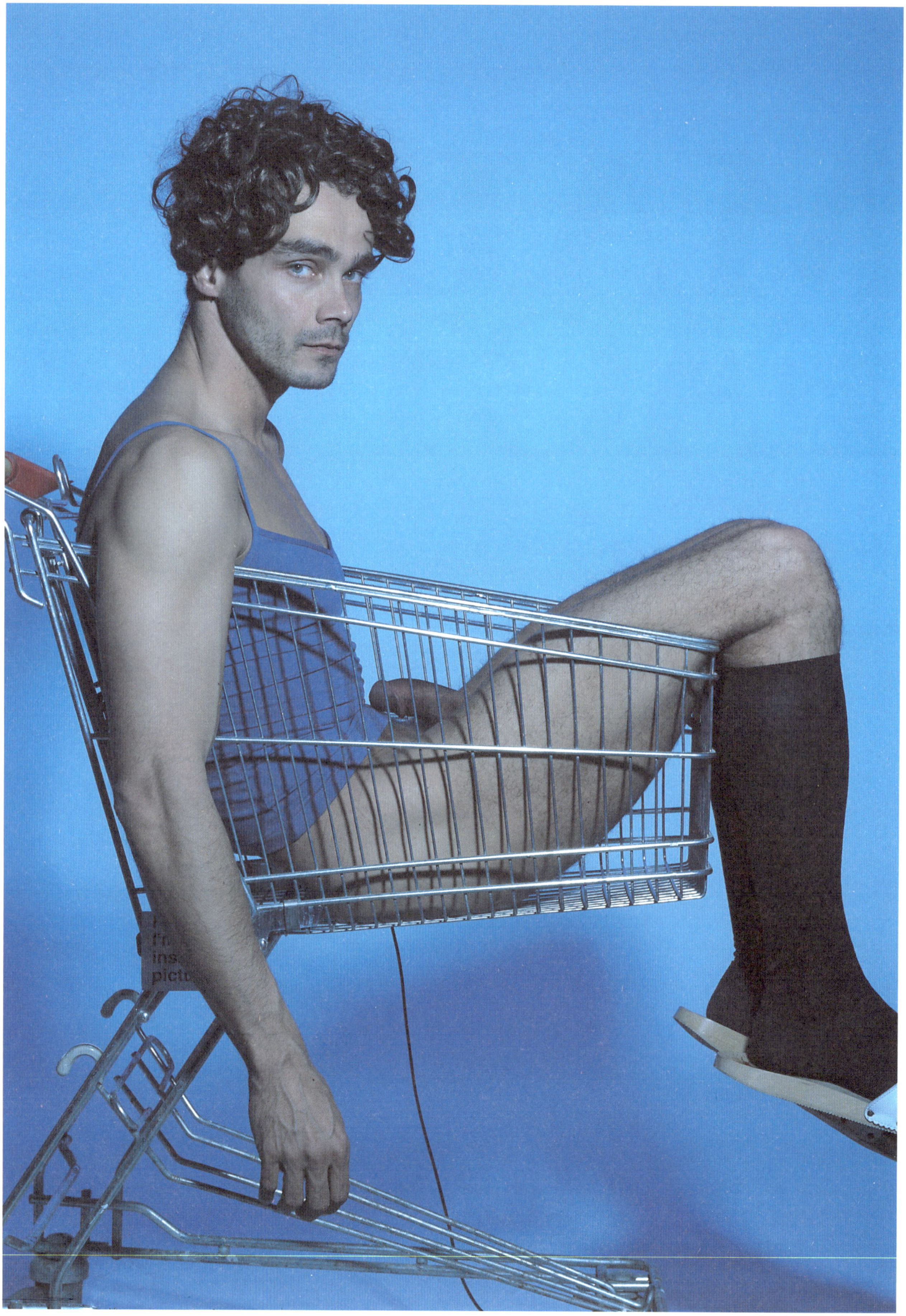

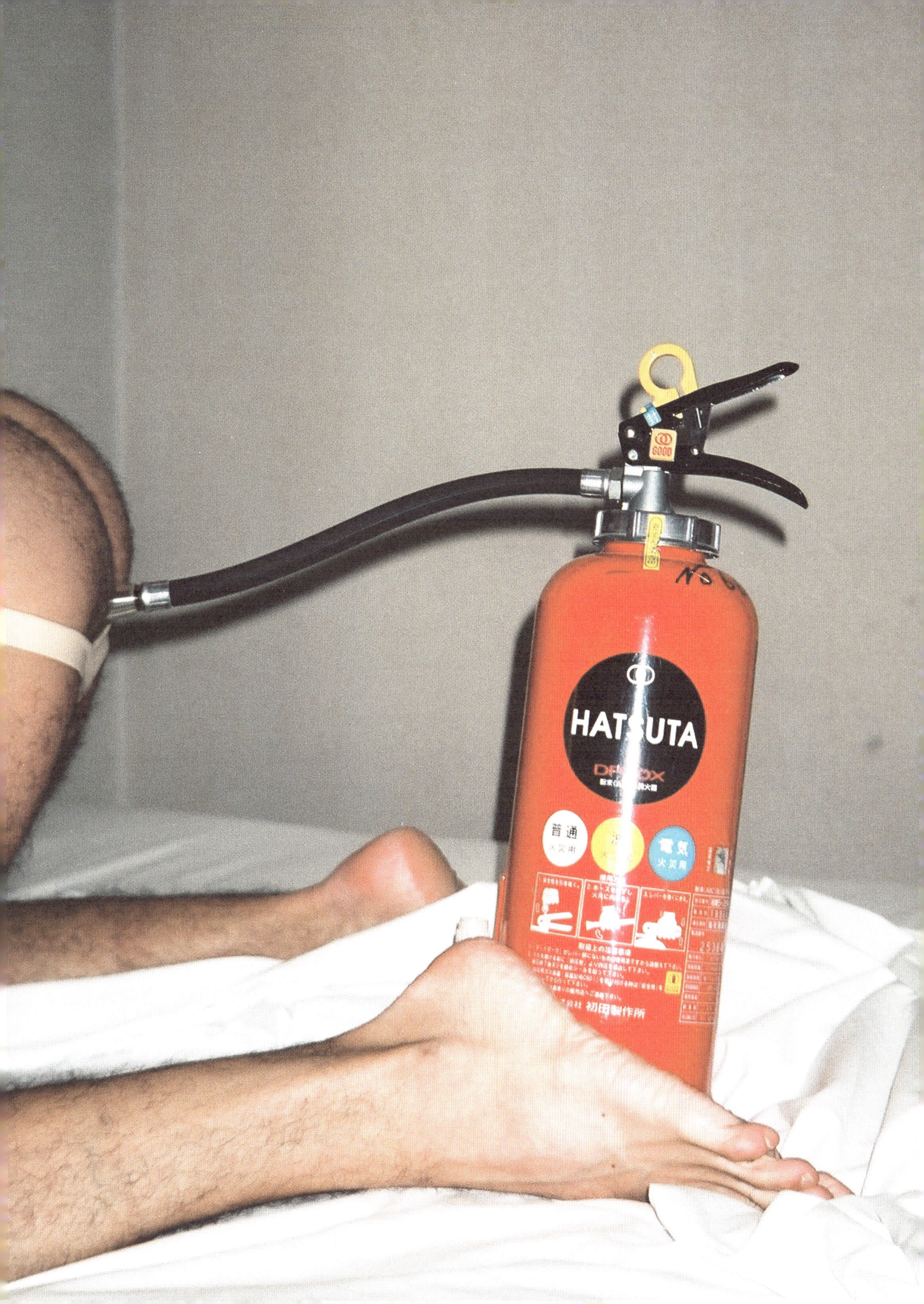
HATSUTA
普通
電気

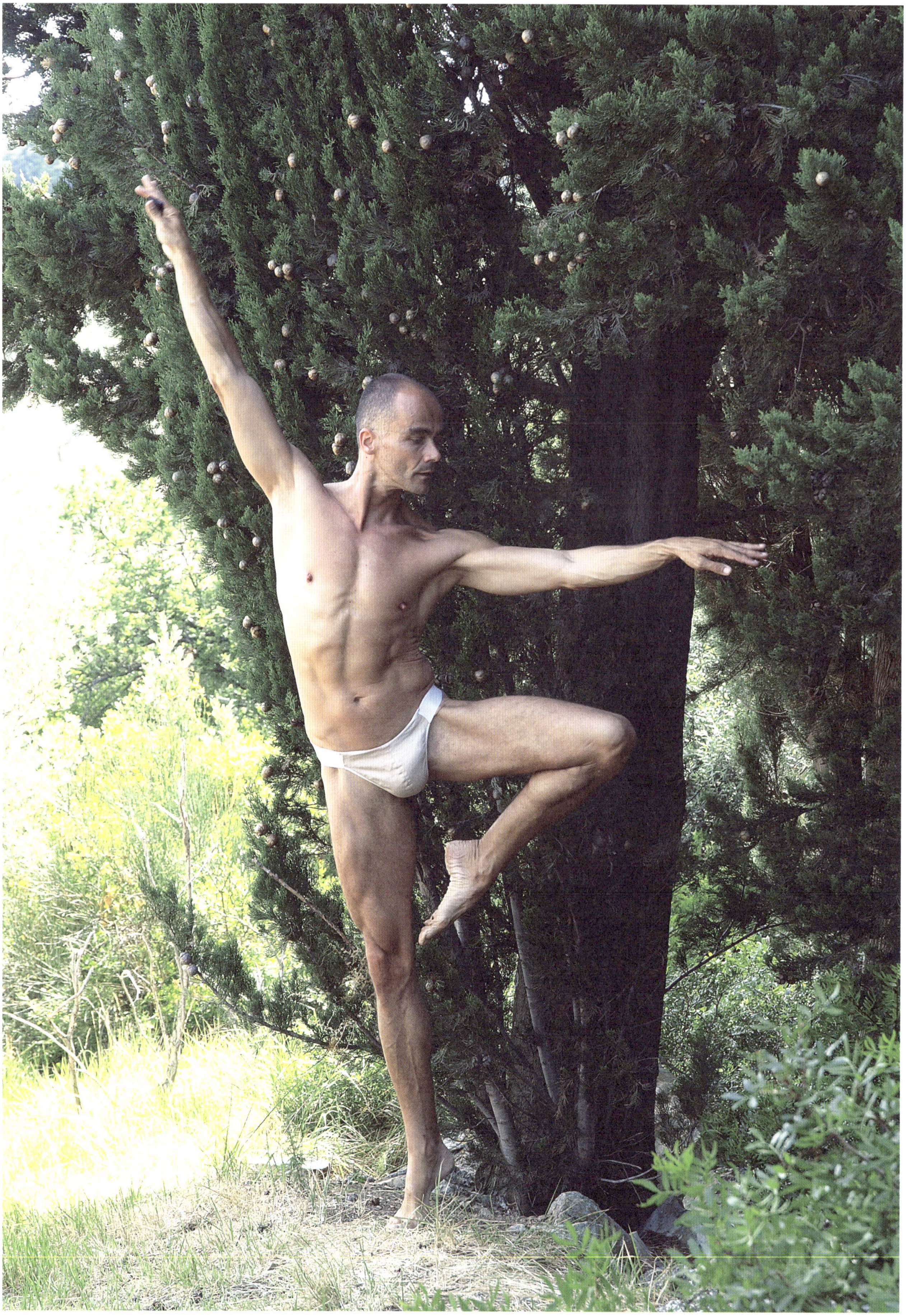

HOW TO LOOK LIKE EVERY THING IS OKAY IN PHOTO GRAPHS

by Todd Colby

Is your house making
you feel large? Do your curtains
reveal a shimmering dust when
you pat them gently in the sunlight?
Is your kitchen a "no fuck zone?"
Does your bathroom smell of bleach
or the fragrant after-sprinkle of talc?
When you enter your house
are you greeted with the whoosh
of dander, or a plush degenerative
offal gush? Is your desk littered
with broken hair and pencil shavings?
Do you fix your hair in a
proper room? Do you enjoy gazing
out the window absentmindedly,
only to discover someone is looking
back at you from the adjoining building?
When you ate your breakfast this morning
did you think of me?

AT PRETTY MUCH EVERY PARTY SOMEONE ASKS ME TO TELL THE STORY OF MY A.P.C.'S

by Jeremy Sigler

I wear my A.P.C jeans every day for about two years. They are my only pants. They never get washed. Washing them is forbidden. I'm not sure where this rule is officially stated, but I certainly live by it. And after about two years, when they've been tamed, broken in—by the time my boxers are visible through the void in my frayed crotch—I know it is time to bring them in.

I enter through the door of the boutique, and an attractive shopkeeper looks me up and down and nods approvingly. Off she goes to a shelf at the back of the store, quickly returning with a brand new folded pair, in just my size. She hands the stiff, navy square to me, and I force my legs into them, turn up the cuffs, and squat five times, feeling the seizure of my crotch as I struggle to button them up.

Meanwhile, my soft gems are laid across the oak counter, and examined, as if by a palm reader. Every crease and crinkle is deeply studied and admired. She pops off the top of a Sharpie and hands me the pen. By now I know the drill. I sign my initials discreetly on the inside of the waist band.

At this point my jeans are swept off to the back of the boutique and hung on a special rack—a rack that gets wheeled out for A.P.C. V.I.P.'s (Here's where I used to throw in the detail, "for V.I.P.'s like Madonna," although I have since changed it to "buyers on the Asian market"). Even with a tethered hole where my testicles once fought a war for room (and won, thank you!), the jeans can fetch up to 3 grand.

I know what you're thinking. And the answer is N-O. Why wouldn't I go ahead and sell them on e-bay? Good question. I guess I must enjoy the glamour of walking into A.P.C. and initializing my work. I enjoy this rare moment of acknowledgement.

So there I was, at Eva's apartment, dragging out my story, throwing back one of the last Red Stripes in the fridge, when I noticed it was past 2 and my audience had dwindled down to me and, like, 3 other alcoholics. This was when I had a sensational idea. "Eva," I announced, "I've decided to give you a very special birthday present!" I'd already begun to unbuckle my belt and rip apart my button fly. "I want you to have my A.P.C.'s."

Eva smiled but didn't seem so thrilled.

"But Eva," I continued, letting my pants drop to my ankles, and stepping out of them in just my boxers, "I want them to be hung right here on this wall. OK?"

And before she had time to say no, I found some pushpins, climbed up on a chair and hung them above the fireplace mantle. Horizontally! Then I stepped back to observe my work. There they were. A stranger to me now. With my old leather belt still in the loops. And with my leather wallet still protruding from my back pocket. And with my credit cards, and drivers license, and metro card. And with maybe 50 bucks.

About an hour later, I arrived by foot in front of my stoop. I was in only my boxers and sneakers. I went to dig for my keys, which is when I realize I had no pocket, nor pants, nor keys. They were all hanging sideways on Eva's wall.

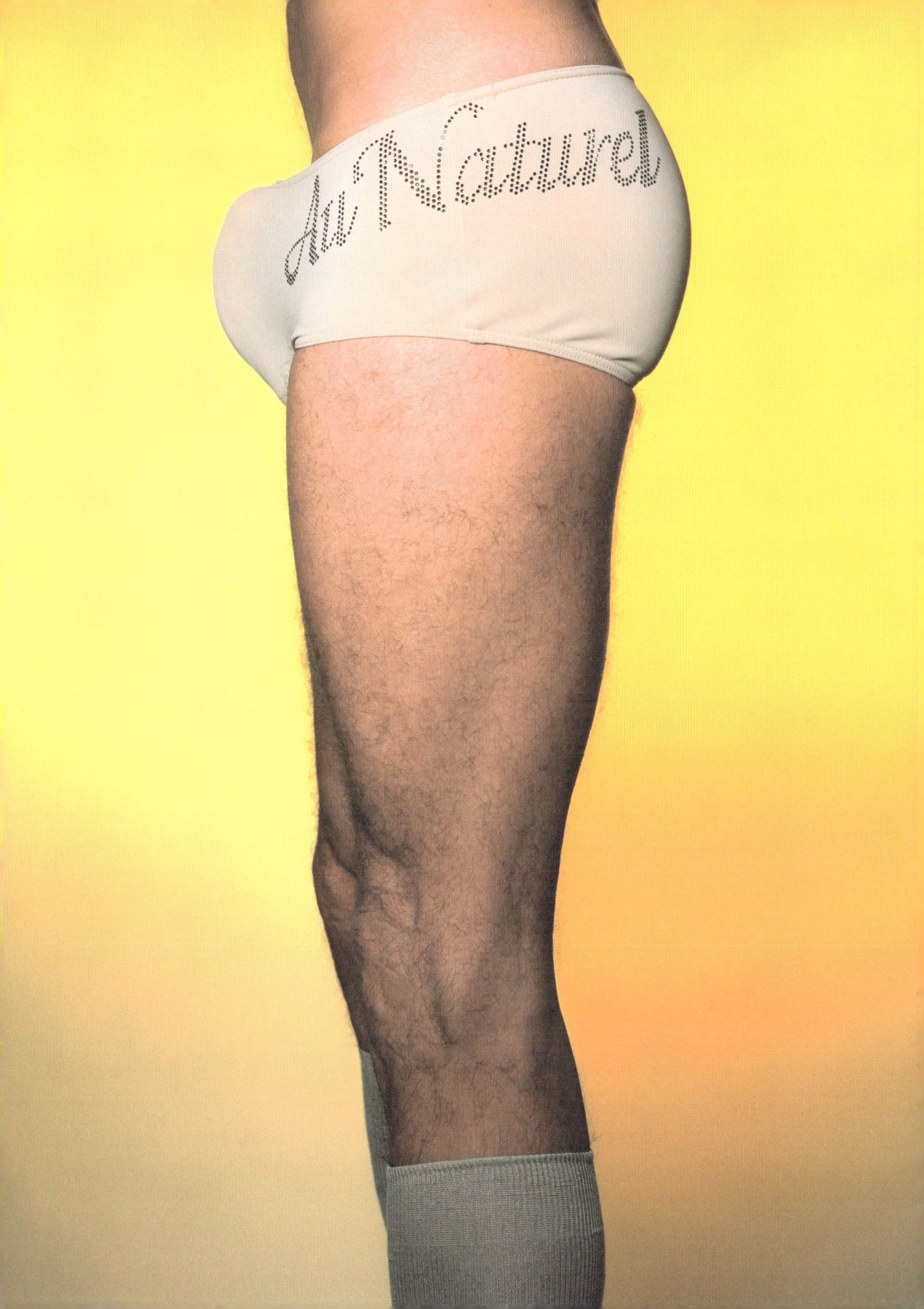
Au Naturel

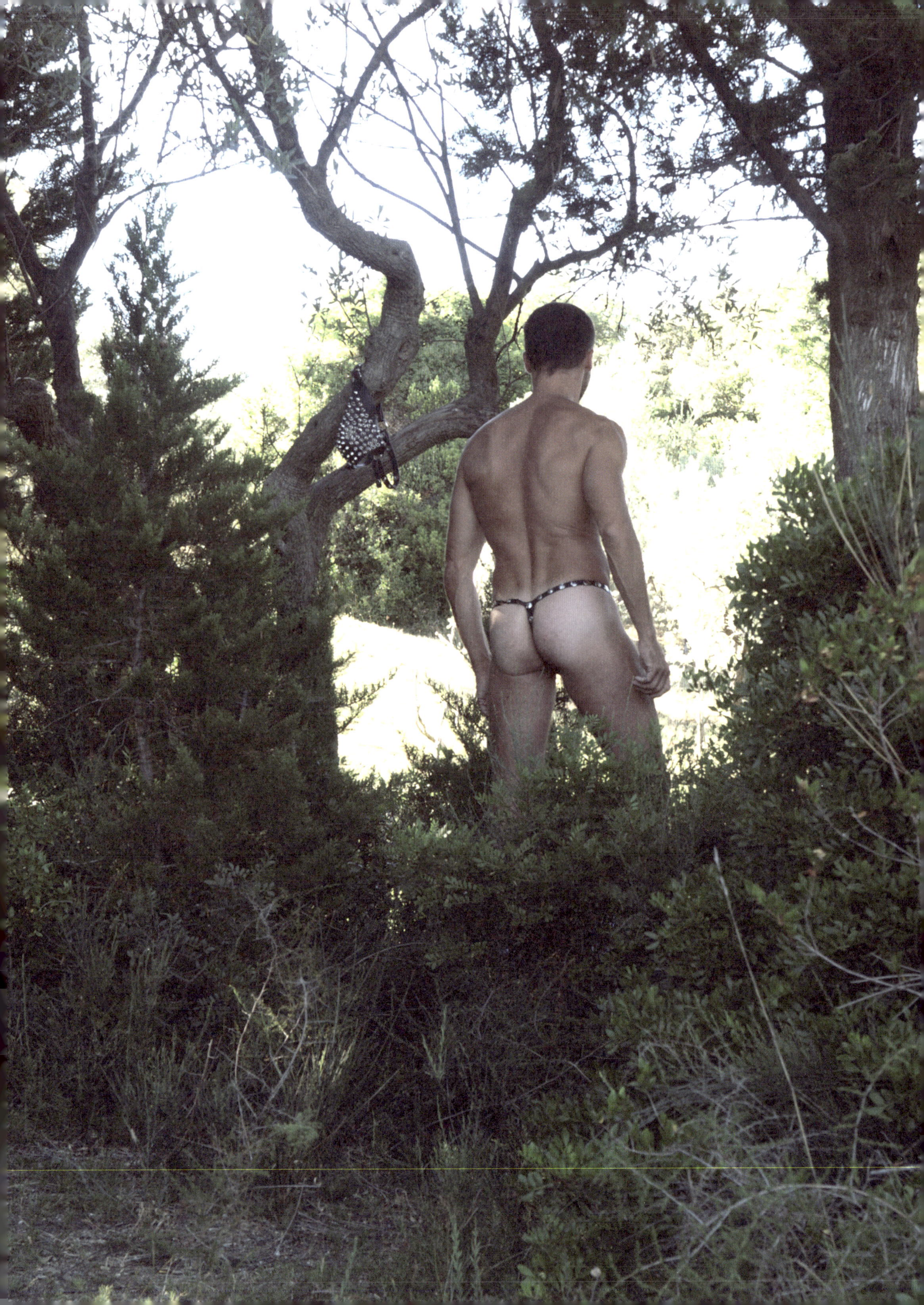

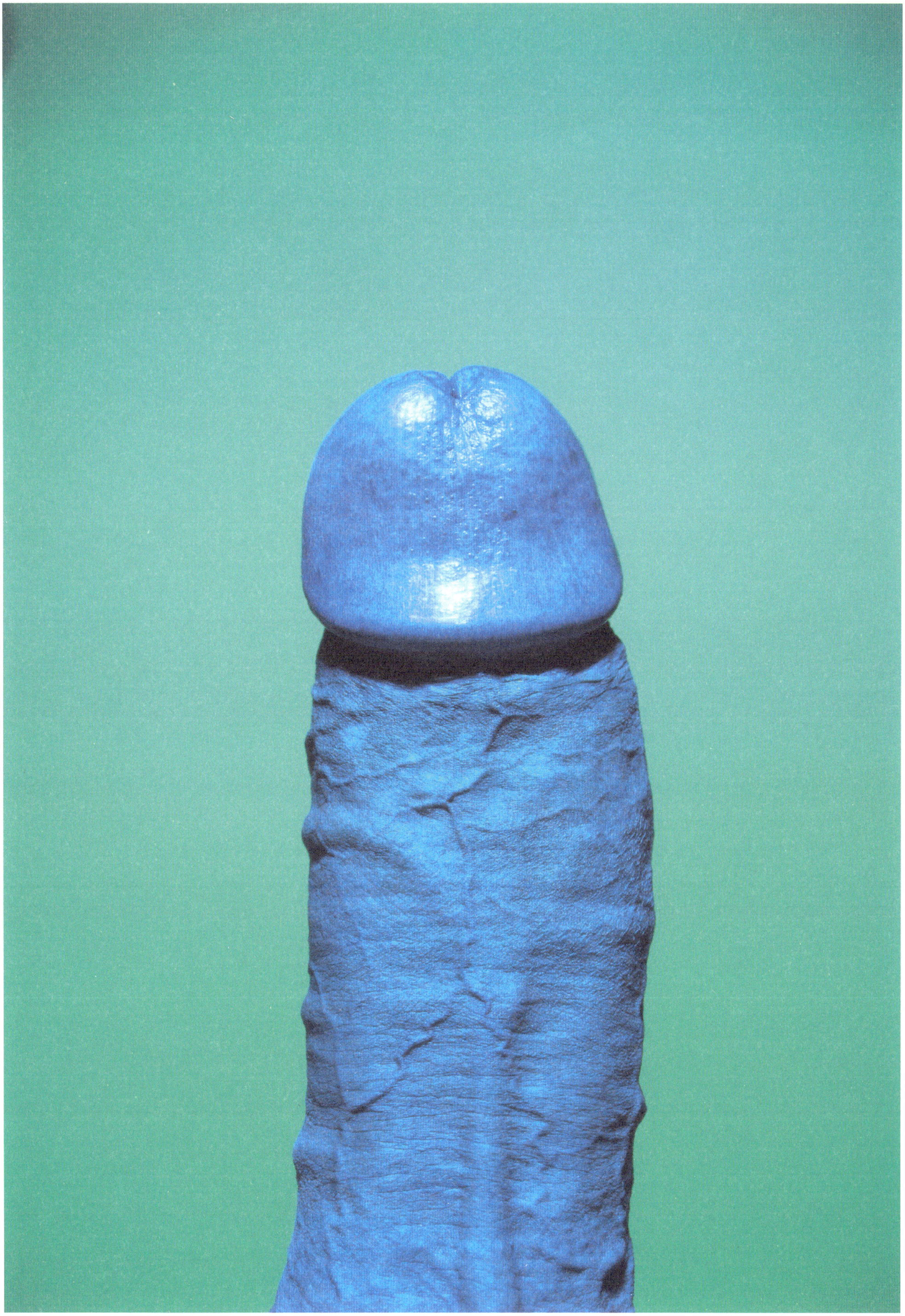

E
XP
RE
SS
IO
N

DREAMS

by Andy Fitch & Danielle Pafunda

DREAM 1

"In this field the interest of analysis seems to [us] to be quite wrongly directed. Instead of an enquiry into how a cure by analysis comes about (a matter which [we] think has been sufficiently elucidated) the question should be asked of what are the obstacles that stand in the way of such a cure."—Freud

In New York, a person could walk for hours without bumping into anyone we know. It's more than that. Walk for hours without being seen. Now to walk is a visible crime. To walk while white, safer, to walk while feminine less safe. To walk in the day she trades anonymity, to walk at night she trades the illusion of safety. To walk in the alleys, to walk in the streets, to walk on the prairie, to walk without haste. After awhile, walking affords few recognizable pleasures. People want us to experience its new pleasures, but do we want to? Bright-sided. Brained. Sometimes we walk together and then it is pleasurable, but also without leisure. Oh, we are very funny, and we are able to make a plan or two, and we shed the problem in clear terms. We are unable to walk for hours. The weather, the time, the dog, the children, the limits of the town, the encounters, the houses we avoid as cracks in the sidewalk and every voice carries on the wind, but where she carries we dunno. We just heard it in a dream.

The wonders of Canada. **Big, beautiful Niagra Falls, what stays in Vegas, forever west, the sunshine state, left my heart in el Segundo.** We reach the Toronto Meditation Center built into the dewy hillside around 6 PM **[the grammar of just being built]**, just as night comes on **[a beast, a change of lighting, a sudden retching of the horizon]**. All of my senses stir with anticipation. **[Let a lesser analyst at it!]** All seats, individual, at first resemble mediation pillows, but bench-sized—built both of fabric and fresh, cool leaves. We face a stage people now set up. So this meditation center also seems a church or stadium. Everything makes me feel fresh. I try to get Kristin to appreciate this moment's beauty, but as I myself pay more attention I realize we've sat in somebody's seats. **[Spoiled, spoiler alert, spoiling, molting, the mildewed smell of wet leaves in a bag, they were crisp when we collected them, I feel embarrassed by my poor planning, caught in the net of the very nostalgia I've been writing about—in the very parenting I've been writing about—except not writing so much as planning—I was just trying to give them a nice memory, to counteract what must be the accumulation of dull or encumbered memories. Saddened, I chuck them before the children can see the extent of the damage.]** Someone owns each seat in this place. The owners of our seats have in fact come down the aisle almost right behind us (I glimpse them through our row's coiled laurel branches), so we keep moving almost before sitting down. Later, after thinking/laughing in an elevator ride by myself, I reach the hallway to our hotel suite. **[Where you can be sure who's paid for which spot. Where it smells of industrial soap bad and industrial soap fancy, but not really much else, we hope. If we find a hair in the carpet, let's not talk about it, this time.]** Not only can you see down eight stories, with the hall just a rickety cable bridge, but soon the cables become more like flapping yellow wooden arms. They have sharp elbows. I have to swing from one hall to the next, but the cables swing too. They clutch at loose rock walls while I clutch at them. **[*Inception* (2010)**

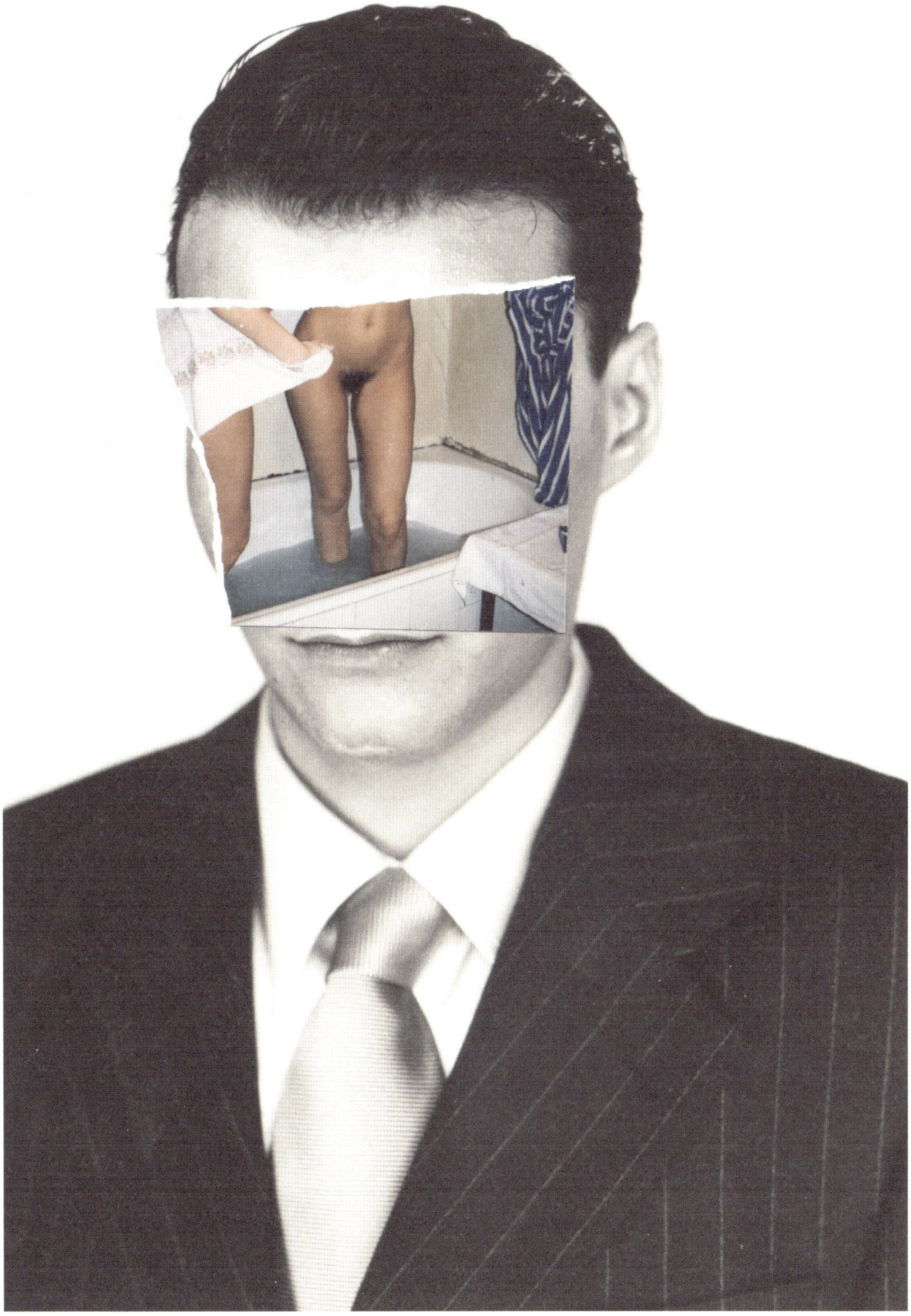

Philippe Jusforgues / Untitled / 2014

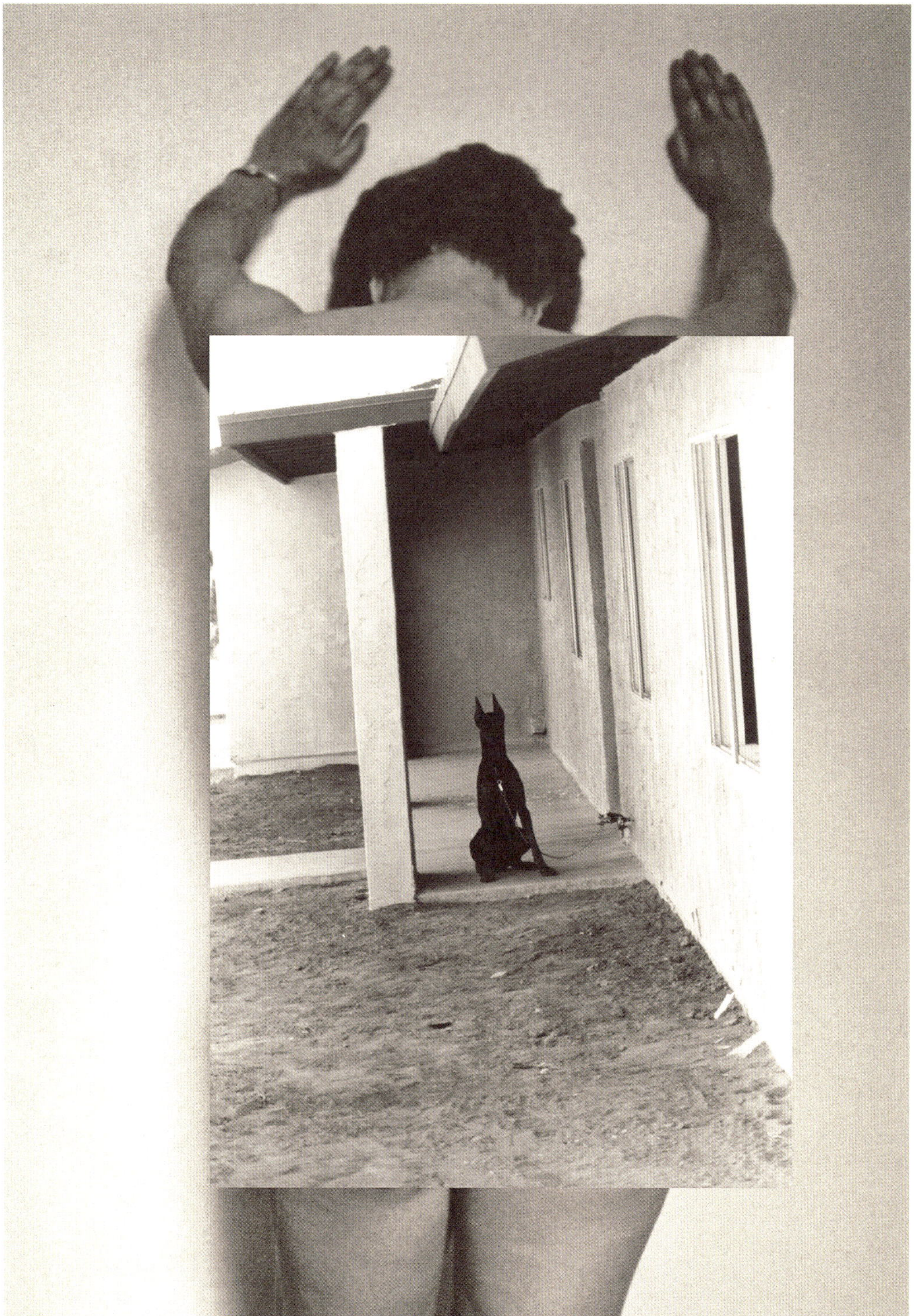

Philippe Jusforgues / Untitled / 2014

(that's a guess, but we're right, like our recent history resides in us, called to the surface reluctantly if fairly reliably, and those weren't Leonardo DiCaprio's dreams, either.)] Sometimes the cables swing "with" me, sometimes "against" me. I stay both scared and casual, and laugh somewhat nervously. I surprise myself by supporting all of my weight with just a dangling pink belt for a while. I probably should swing more cautiously, more attentively, but don't. I'll need to fling myself through a porthole basically. Kristin stands, or hovers, inside the suite already, complaining about these dangerous accommodations, but she surprises me by not complaining **[issuing our own complaints for us, we want to complain, we want to say everything is quite off kilter and unsatisfactory, what can you pay for that's beautiful? What can't you pay for that's doleful, dangerous, or disappointing? Where is the thrill we felt before we saw dirt so clearly as germs, grime so clearly as grime, when our own grassy knees protected our noses from the dull stupidity of the chemical era's baroque collapse? We take a trip to an island made entirely of plastic. When we cry, we add plastic because plastic now originates within and without us]** more. I can't believe Kristin already has made it through the **[plastic]** porthole, and with her heavy **[plastic]** suitcase. ***remainder unnecessary—speaker preoccupied with dog's evacuation, per uszh.**

DREAM 2

Only one of us knows that this dream is coming for a walk with us. Only one of us, lagging a moment behind the other, will casually let it slip from the notebook; the path we'll return upon, a to-and-fro. But that one of us will wait until after dark, slip back out as the other sleeps, and fetch the page. What is the dream, now, when it's been orphaned on the path. When it's been for animal, mineral, or vegetable. If there were time, we might bury this dream over the winter and dig it up again in the spring. We might lodge it beneath the rock that, when lifted, revealed a colony of ants and eggs. We might do this with another dream, on another day, when nothing feels particularly pressing. Meanwhile, we might hope for a bit of rain, excitement, some theft or a bird's nest. Or we may find it, looking like this:

On Mackinac, or at least an island, Pat (Kristin's dad) tells me that with so much family arriving tonight, I probably should sleep elsewhere. He has rented me space in a communal boarding house. The place seems still, bright, breezy in the day, but I have to pick one bed in a room of four or five. Later, as I approach Kristin's parents' place at night, I feel desperate for returning so soon, so I swing around back to the water. In the dark light I spot a smiling seal, often skipping across the surface. I've never seen a seal out here before. It comes close and I get to scratch its belly. With me now in the water, another mammal, maybe a beaver, swims over. When I step back onto the dock, under stars, I find a girl I once met in Berlin, a Harvard student studying opera production. We lie next to each other talking, touching sides of our bodies. Kristin runs by, not noticing us, to tell two female cousins, further out on the dock: "Susan called—she's fine." Everybody rejoices. Kristin turns around, heading back in, and finds me. Her relief and happiness linger, but I can't imagine what she thinks of me: already returned, lying beside this girl. As Kristin and I talk, my mind moves back to the boarding house. During the afternoon I'd read in an historical book that on one night 12,700 people crammed into its few bedrooms. It amazes me how families scrimp on vacation. At least I have a full bed to myself, but I panic because I can't picture where it is, in which room. I'll walk in past midnight and wake everyone up. Then I realize I don't have my computer playing white noise, so everybody will wake me, all night and morning, arriving and exiting. I'm still at Kristin's parents' condo the next afternoon. I'm already a couple minutes late to a tennis lesson scheduled for Kristin and I, but

If there were time, we might bury this dream over the winter and dig it up again in the spring.

I incomprehensibly dawdle and miss 40 more minutes. I get the sense I'll skip the whole lesson. I step out once, quickly return. Lawson, a five-year-old family friend, lets me back in. In the basement, wiping my butt, I run out of toilet paper and start using laundry. It becomes especially shameful to unravel dirty socks to use. I realize Ryan, Kristin's cousin, probably can see me from the kitchen, through an internal window. I have to put the socks back in the laundry, but now the little kids want to play in the laundry pile. I find Kristin back upstairs. She says there's no use taking the lesson now, as the sky darkens.

or maybe some part of a reservoir system? Water runs over the edge of a concrete bar. In the water, something I identify as a baby marmot, but Shanna will later tell us is a northern river otter plunks over the bar, swims up under it, mechanically cocks its head at us, dribbles back down. We're glad of its presence and I take a picture to post to Facebook later. I'll tell Facebook I was out walking with Andy, but right now I tell Andy about my predicament and he asks clarifying questions. He wears a sweater. I have a premise. I'm hung up on a bar of the heteronormative matrix. Plunk. Then we have a dream.

how does that make you feel? don't answer that.], a face in a round frame (a cameo) shouts, "I'm on my way." Mom **[that's your mom]**, watching with me at her friend Louise's condo, sighs, turns from the screen and says, "I should express my own sundry vaudeville distaste for this topic." **[We/women/feminine are loathe to participate in a system wherein our men colleagues' and counterparts' abuse of masculine privilege costs us time and dignity. A feminine economy rejects this in the baroque language and desultory floorshow that is its only recourse at present.]** I decide finally to open Pilgrim's Progress, still not knowing what it's about. The book

No one doubts that love is possible in a patriarchy, even when love is compulsory.

DREAM 25

"In the following pages I shall prove that there exists a psychological technique by which dreams may be interpreted, and that upon the application of this method every dream will show itself to be a senseful psychological structure which may be introduced into an assignable place in the psychic activity of the wa[l]king state."—Freud The Interpretation of Dreams 1913

Andy & I cross the park. It's relatively treeless. A thin cover of grass shivers there. We've been walking awhile, and I've lost feeling in my fingers, which is just the Reynaud's kicking in. Needles run their tips. There's a pond here,

Nobody in my design class completes the editing assignment as expected. Each person's book looks different. Dan, the new student, even thought he had to buy a book to bring in. I tell Dan **[this boy this boy this boy]**, "We'll just talk after class." Dan **[this boy, son, sword, hoof, boy]** wears red flannel. In a Shining-like scene, Shelly Duvall **[me, oh]** gasps, "He's back" as she notices the toilet seat flipped up **[We might note that nothing, nothing comes out of the navel. It is not an orifice. Any longer.]**. A body seems to slump behind the opaque shower curtain. **[Yes, that's true. It's also in The Shining. The body is a hag. That's me, too.]** As she opens it **[I open it; you continue to dream about me;**

becomes one of those magazines focusing on a place—Vail or Breckenridge. At the backyard patio table my sister Kati and I sit drinking tea, as snow falls, on us, all around, but we feel warm. In our shared steaming teakettle float orange flowers. **[Shhh, shhh. Let's stay, here. Trouble's coming. Shhhh.]** At the mountain-side **[aiyyyyyyiiiiiii]** restaurant Diva I keep wanting more jelly for my lamb chops, no matter how much I spread. The waiter **[we ordered it, after all]** brings a can of peaches and a can opener **[I dreamed the baby was made of gelatin, not yet set, it was not a baby made of gelatin, it was gelatin shaped as a baby, and through it ran multicolored wires, many of which were tacked**

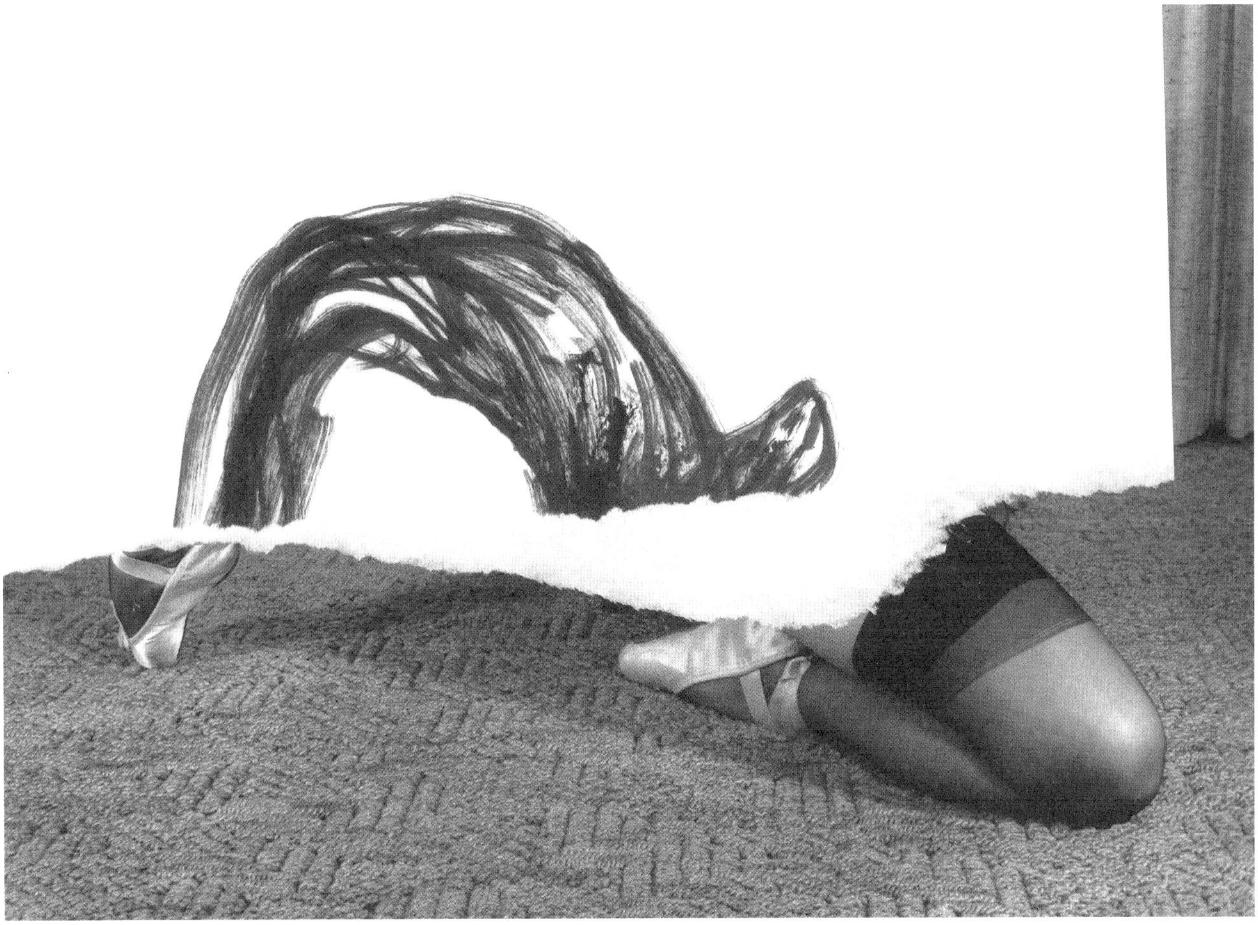

Philippe Jusforgues / Untitled / 2014

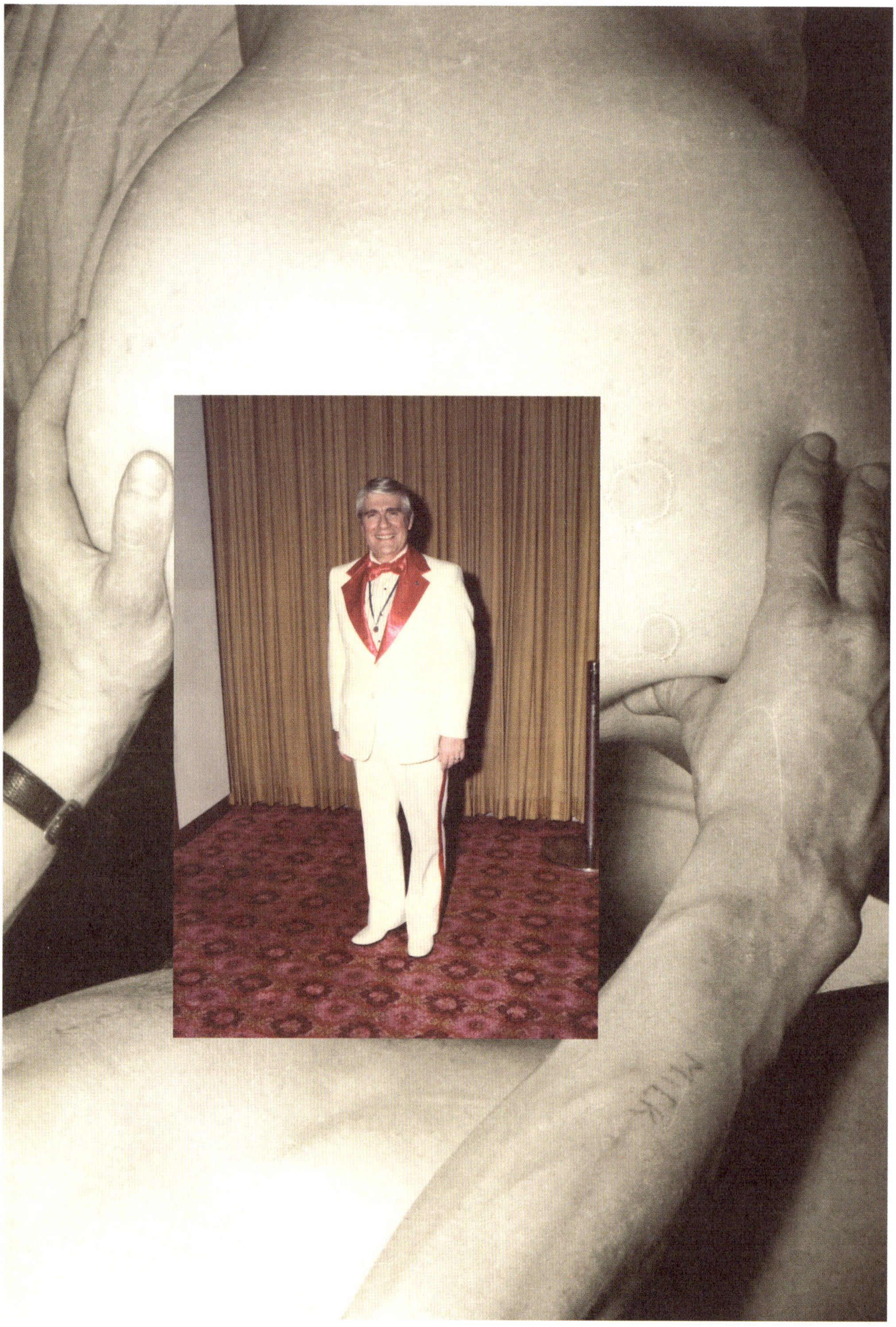

Philippe Jusforgues / Untitled / 2014

to the board on which the baby glistened, but around it no liquid seeped. I turned to this man, not the waiter, this other man, he was not prepared to father]. I slice my finger on this can's rim. A burnt-toast smell intensifies. A paper boat with drops of blood floats toward the ocean. **[That's what happened, of course. A cultural event occurs in the body and presents its evidence through the body's chemical transmissions, which can now be captured as rabbits themselves, but when the cultural event ceases to occur, one watches her paper boat, white paper, red droplets, if it's quick enough the blood is very red, if it's quick enough the blood makes for a wave and the boat makes for the horizon. Women describe themselves as "living tombs," women describe themselves as lucky, women describe themselves as persons undergoing an experience. Huchkkkh, huchkkkh, unghhhh.]** A tennis volley goes on forever, at the net with no bounces. I can't see my opponent—just myself frowning. A big yellow truck rolls over the rubble of our house, searching out Fanky with its shovel (I feel secure that Fank's fine). **[In Carol Emshwiller's germinal text Carmen Dog, the women become animals and animals become women. The beloved family golden retriever, slipper-mouthing, child-cuddling footrest badgirlgoodgirl tit-ular Carmen becomes heroine. Bark bark bark, she says, in human wordwords. Bark the patriarchy, bark operatic bark, the first time a woman is allowed to speak it is in labor and the second time it is on the stage from beneath her Viking trim.]** Tim Johnson, the senator who had a stroke, stands by, on the scene with a microphone. Orange crepe paper, at first fluttering and decorative, soon gets smeared stuck on everything, unwanted **[flowers, tea pot, crashing the party]**. Kristin finally consents to ordering pulpo **[see above]** for an appetizer, amid ongoing job negotiations. With her first bite she says, "Chewy, just as predicted." We have to return to the business room in 10 minutes. **[Crypt/cryptic]** The widescreen TV's comedy show offers one celebrity after another stepping into a crappy car. Our new living-room's tall plants' dark leaves lean over me, comforting. Video/experiential scenes of real life happening in our house (Kristin and I lacing hightops) get framed, blended, as if one single, static picture. **[No one doubts that love is possible in a patriarchy, even when love is compulsory. Hissssss. Hisssssssssss. Hisss.]** From inside this frame, I sense that somebody, outside, just picked it up. **[Hisssssss.]** "History plants" **[Gingkos in spring, clobbering the city with the littoral stench]** get given away on the last day of the semester. A blonde woman pulls them from the stone fireplace in her classroom. The last question I ask my huddled journal-production team (as the alarm rings): "So did do this?"

Philippe Jusforgues' Poetic Surgery

There is a lawless quality to the collages of French artist Philippe Jusforgues. It the lawlessness of our inner and outer lives, our perceptual and physical realities, overlapping, entangling, taking each other's places. As a collagist, Jusforgues is unconcerned with the seamlessness many other artists look for in their work. He uses broad strokes, jagged edges, and striking juxtapositions to create a sense of visual, spatial, and psychological discord. Often applying only a single cut-out over a single base image, Jusforgues works with a minimalist approach for maximalist effect. His placement is highly strategic, one image concealing or exposing another. Context creates meaning, or erases it, just as meaning can either re-contextualize or de-contextualize an otherwise unremarkable image.

Jusforgues, who moved from Paris to Monaco in 2010, had discovered collage six years earlier while looking at family photo albums. The discovery initiated a radical change in his artistic practice:

"One moving day I found a suitcase full of family pictures. Most of them were copies and I could use them without destroying the familial inheritance...

"I started to change faces and all the images were overwhelming... My characters became real and the range of emotions became larger.

"I became addict with the rapidity of execution and possibility of surprise. The realism of the photography and the lightness of the drawing mixed together... I consider my images like drawings with flesh and blood. A poetic surgery..."

The idea of "poetic surgery" echoes the "dissecting table" in Lautréamont's famous phrase—"as beautiful as the chance meeting on a dissecting table of a sewing-machine and an umbrella" —which served as a touchstone for the Surrealists' first experiments in appropriation and displacement. Jusforgues' own "operations" may or may not heal that which they put under the knife, but what they sew back together is startlingly vivid and alive.

-Keith Newton

EXPRESSION #2

MACK DADDY MANIFESTO

by Shane Book

"Ultimately, when stubborn historical facts had dispersed
all intoxicating effects of self-deception, this form of
Socialism ended in a miserable fit of the blues."
—Marx & Engels

A spectre is haunting Europe
but I feel the sun cocooning
in a triple-breasted track suit

when I think of you. Thus we
obtain our concept of the unconscious
from the theory of repression, a sweet finish

after the bitter pills of floggings and bullets,
my Tender-roni, my Maytag Blue –
for real, you like them dresses? I'll bag the whole rack – let
the ruling classes tremble

"But you Communists would introduce
community of women!" screams
the chorus.

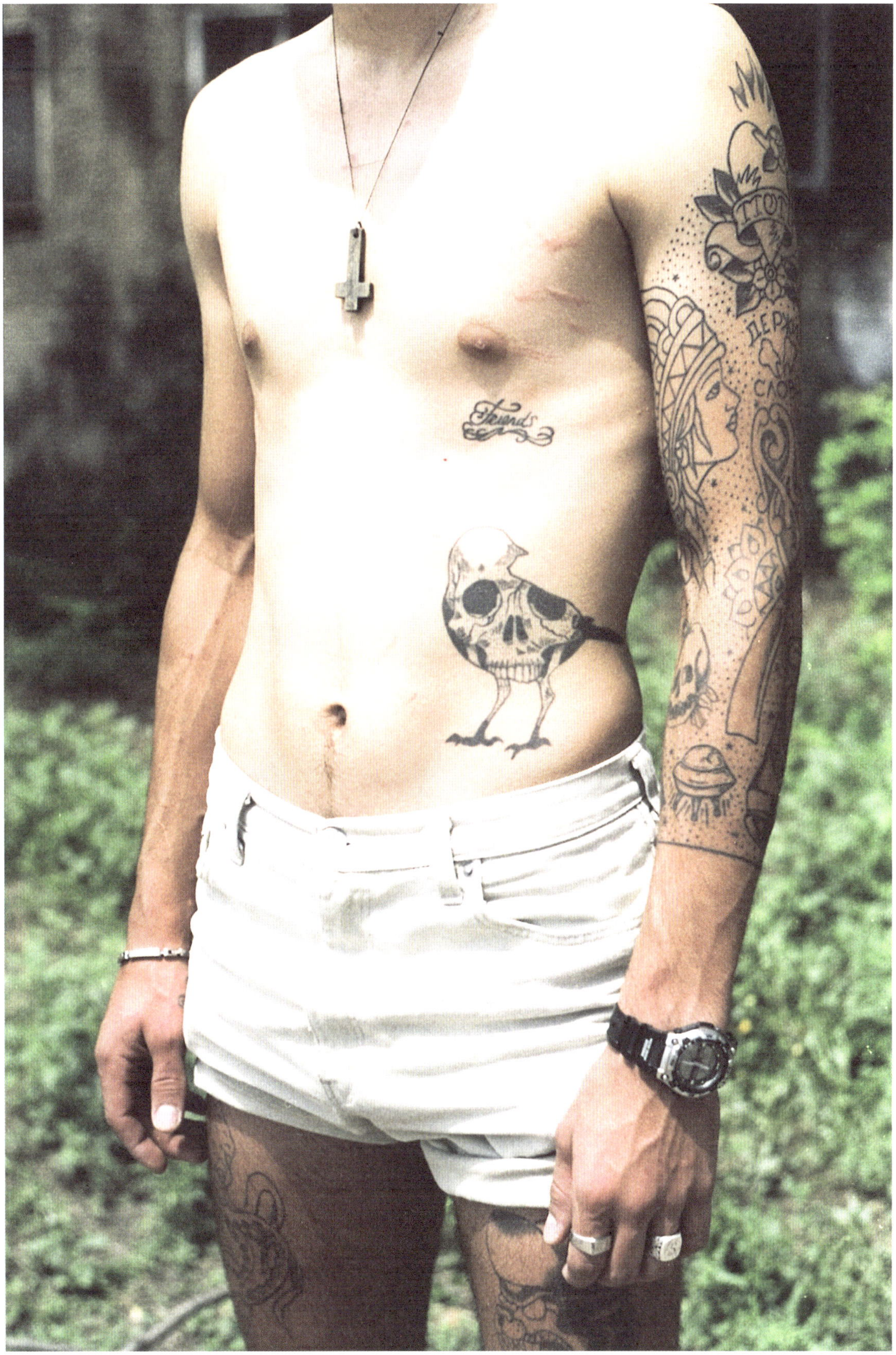

Sergey Melnitchenko / Semyon: Boys & Tattoos / 2013

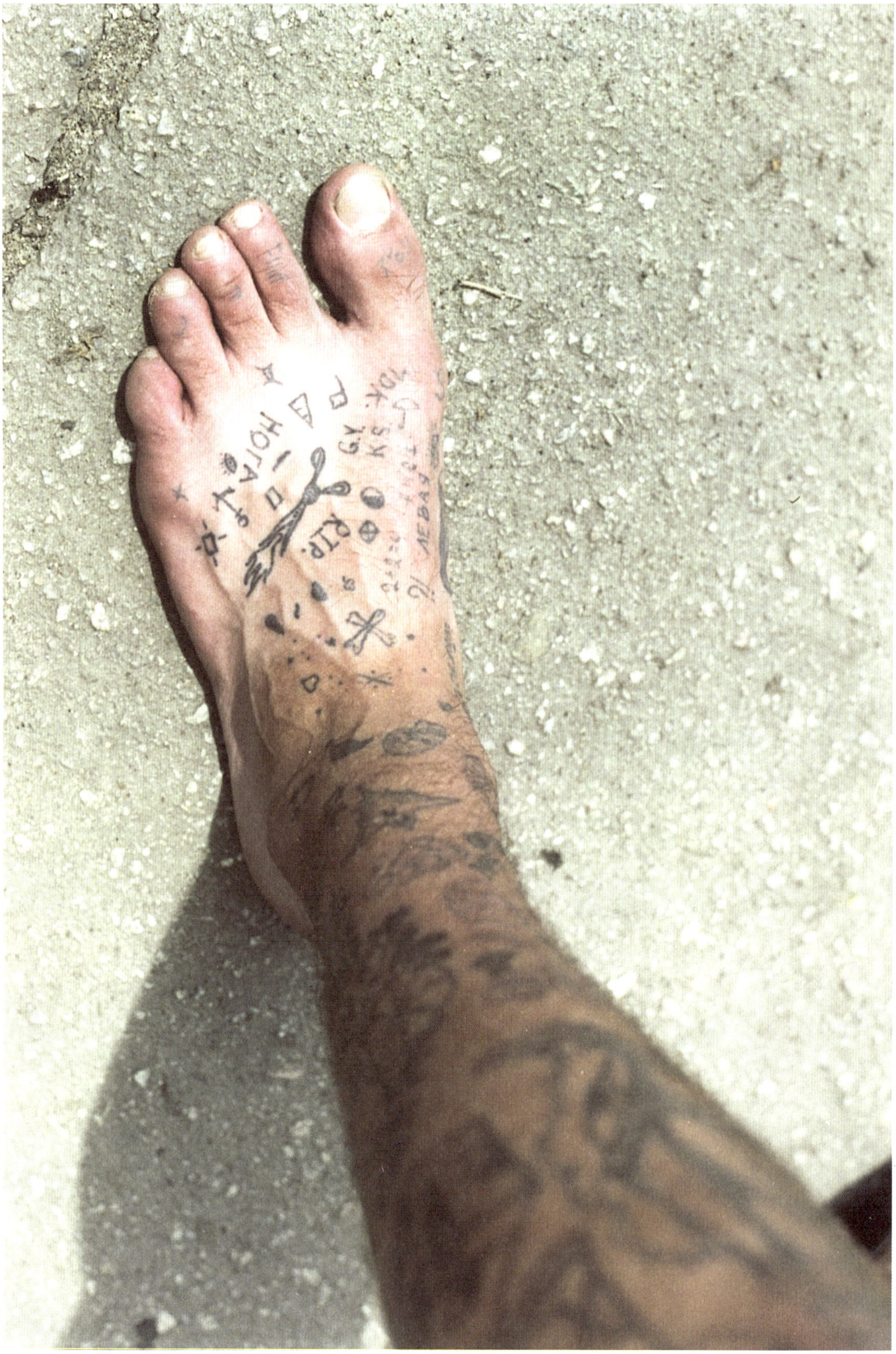

All I'm thinkin' is Sugar,
African me till you African't
leave every jaw

dropped, cocked and locked,
freeze the whole
homeboy corner crew:
Pope - Czar,
Metternich - Guizot,
French Radicals - German police spies

all sewing duodecimo editions
of New Jerusalem, this special organ appearing
to be the muscular apparatus of
old Europe's powers
in holy alliance to exorcise

this special organ appearing to need
my help. I do what I can. "Hola' hotty!" I holla –
when what I really mean is,
"Baby got back!" as here
and there among the spindly trees the contest
breaks out into riots: What does it mean when we say

making something conscious? Have not
the Christians already declaimed:

Underneath this thug armor: a corn ear of nuclear cornea fission.
It fuels my new clear cornrow vision.

All fixed frozen relations,
their ancient
and venerable trains
swept away,
all new-forms
antiquated before
they can ossify? Sho' 'nuff,

at fifty feet your party smile puts a wrinkle
in a salt fish patty substitute for longing for the father,
the germ religions spawned. By days, by degrees they
sink into their fanatical, superstitious belief
in the miraculous effects of their social science.
And you thought I was a player

'cause you heard some other guy lace that last line
to your little sister? Little did you know he wasn't nothing
but a biter, player-hating cause the ladies
love me despite the fact my hair is nappy—

the annexation taking place as when a foreign language is appropriated, namely, by translation—

unlike
"True" Socialism, which appears to kill
with one stone,
spreads like an epidemic,
and is fore-most a body-ego.
Of course this is only hypothesis,
there's no museum space
to offer – exhibit A:
the ever-mean talk show hosts,
bitter preachers, dirty rappers,
all up in my shit,
running their mouths
like they was me,

but winding up lipping blisters:

Whereas the Communists have no need to introduce
free love; it has existed almost from time
immemorial, and on and on to the break
of dawn, to let us now
take wage labor:

clinical observation showing
circumstances where hate changes to love,
love to hate and

our bourgeoisie taking great
pleasure in seducing each other's wives.
Real real soon,
as in yester-after-noon, I need to step to
your crib, and tell you how I feel the proletarians
have nothing to lose but their world to win.

Be ready chula,
I'm a move the mood up.
You gonna call me "Vision master,"

Ergo, those who work, acquire nothing and those who
acquire anything, do not work!

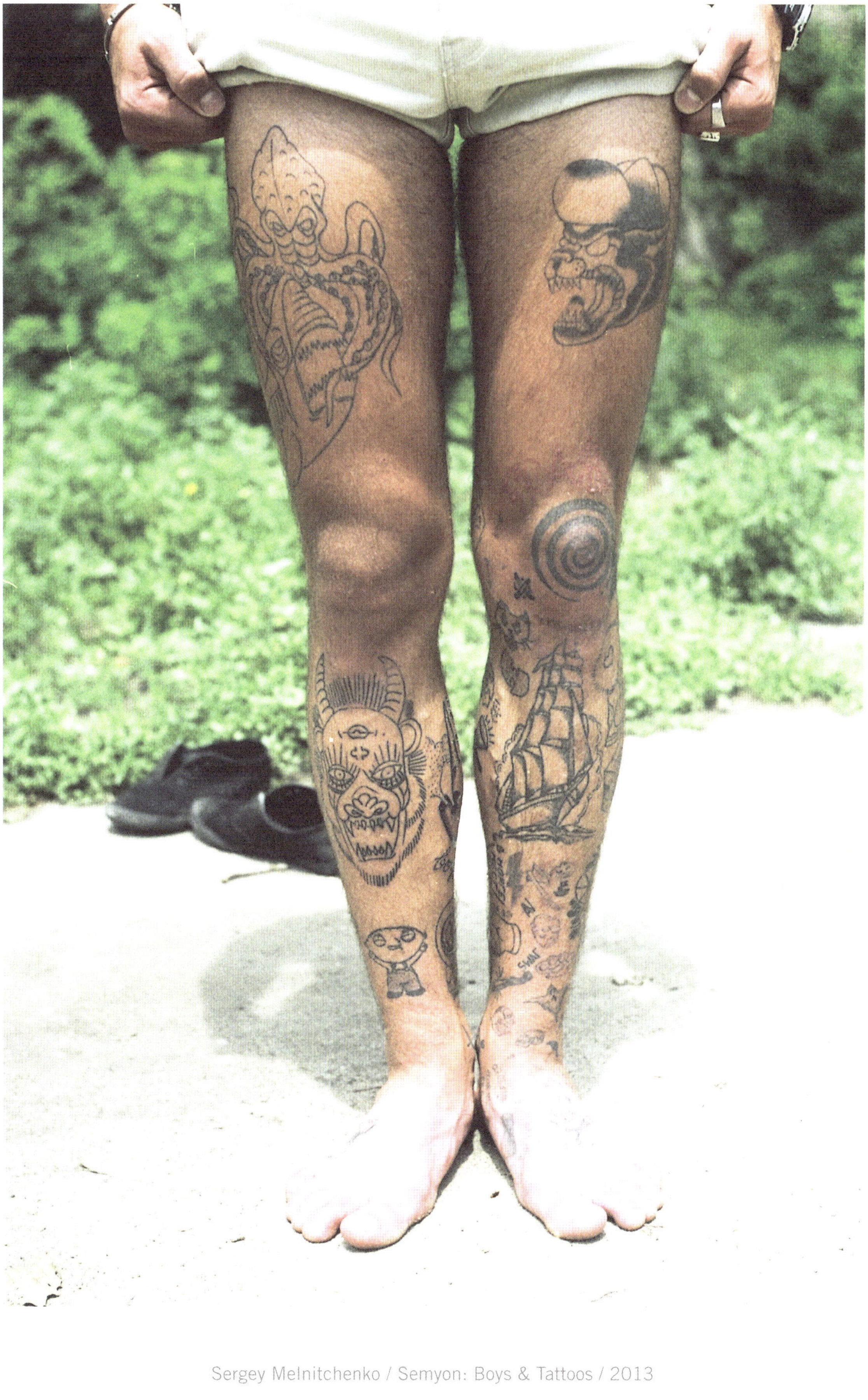

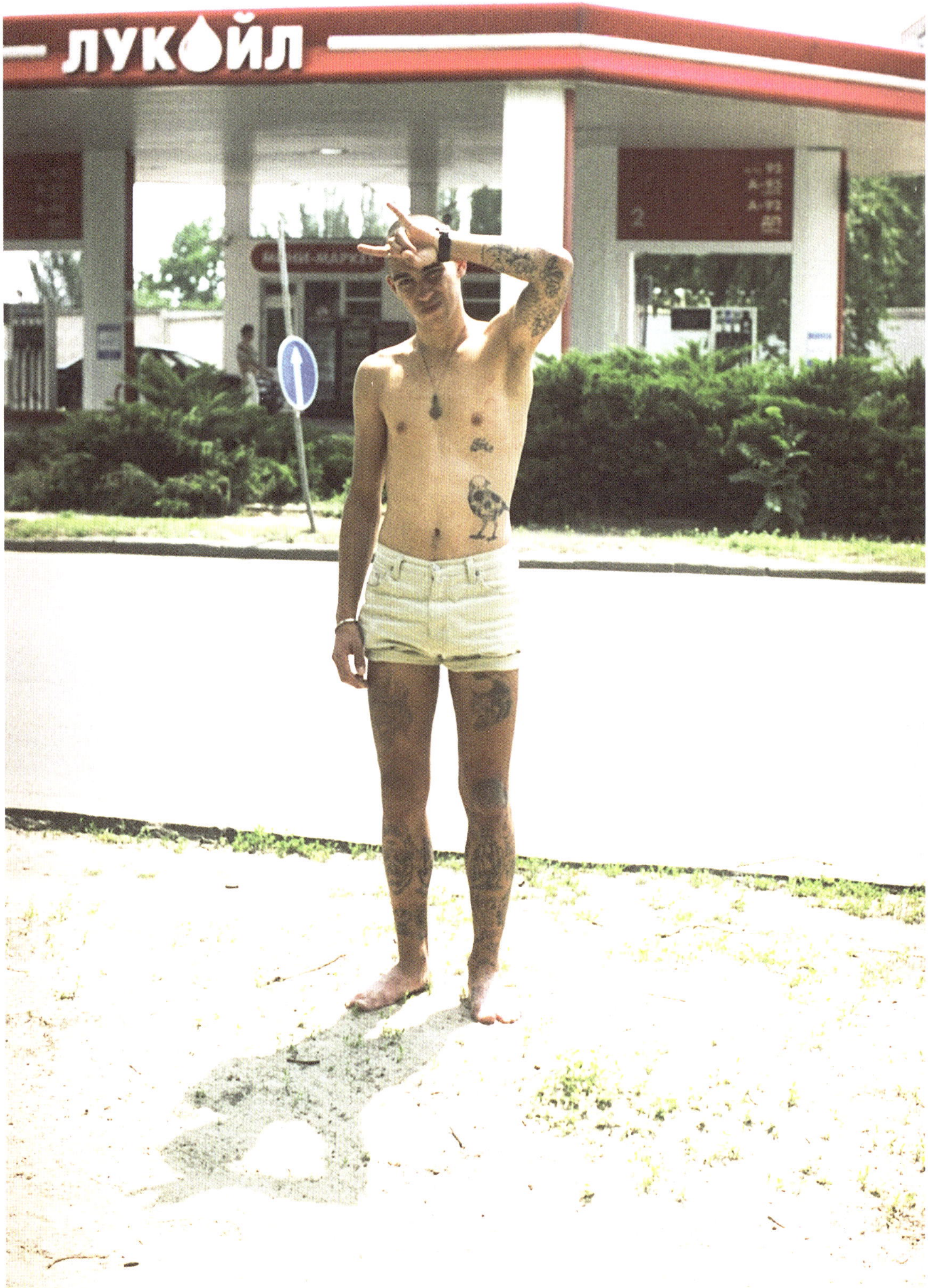

Sergey Melnitchenko / Semyon: Boys & Tattoos / 2013

Ain't it all good,
ain't it morning before you know it,
ain't my suits crazy insulated
with gold leaf history

in which free
development of each
is the condition
for free development of all.

Likewise it has to feed a man,
instead of being fed to him. He
becomes an appendage of the machine,
but it is only simple yak fur
lining my boots
that I need if I got you...
I'll make
all that is solid melt into air
all that is holy profaned

Sergey Melnitchenko's Body Language

"My name is Semyon. I'm 18 years old. I work as a sales representative in the company which sales household products. There are 68 tattoos on my body at the moment. A lot of tattoos on my left leg from the knee to the ankle were made when I was drunk. Some of them were made by tattoo-masters, some – by me, and there are even some tattoos that did my friends who were holding a homemade machine for the first time in their lives. Few masters trained on me, when they were starting their careers. I dedicate my tattoos to nothing and nobody except the one on the right foot – the cat and the number '13'. I dedicated it to our relations with my girlfriend. It symbolizes the day we met, and it's our pair tattoo, she has the same one. In most cases, it's just the memory about some parties, hang-outs, movements. The whole left foot is covered with small tattoos. I made them myself, being under the strong alcoholic intoxication, at the time of a stressful situation. On the left hand, between the tattoos, I have 1,020 dots. I remembered this number very well, because after three hours of work over my sleeve tattoo, dots were really painful, so every time the needle touched me, I shouted the number of the dot. By the way, it was two in the morning. How do my relatives accept such hobby? My mother got used to it, sometimes she even asks me if I did something new, and asks to show her. Father doesn't live with us, he even doesn't know."

Semyon is one of the young men that Ukranian photographer Sergey Melnitchenko set out to photograph in his native city of Nikolayev. As if he had stumbled on a strange new language being spoken on familiar streets, Melnitchenko noticed a profileration of tattoos among the young men he encountered and felt compelled to understand what they communicated. Drawn as much to the men themselves as to the images on their bodies, Melnitchenko became focused on the environment in which the tattoos were made, especially for those who couldn't afford to have them done professionally: "I knew that I wasn't going to photograph guys with well-done and high quality tattoos—it's not for me. I decided that I would do a project about the cheap, funny and trash ones... I was interested in finding out what influenced the choice of the sketch, how did they make a decision and in what conditions it was happening." The images of Semyon capture the spirit of Melnitchenko's project. Semyon's body draws attention to itself, like an object of visual display, offering both a reason and an excuse to look. Yet instead of serving to objectify him, his tattoos give us an opening to know who he is, a chance to get under the skin.

-Keith Newton

COMMENTARY

by Marcelle Sauvageot

Marcelle Sauvageot died of tuberculosis in 1934, at age 33, in Davos, Switzerland. She had been a literature teacher in Paris, where she was connected to many artists and poets, particularly among the Surrealists, yet she published only a single work of her own, variously titled *Laissez-moi* and *Commentaire*. This groundbreaking book—part-memoir, part-fiction, written as the narrator journeys from Paris to a sanatorium in the Swiss Alps—is a brilliant investigation of a recently ended love affair. The excerpt that follows is from Christine Schwartz Hartley and Anna Moschovakis' translation (the first to appear in English), published as *Commentary* by Ugly Duckling Presse in 2013. —Editor's Note

14 December, 1930

Some ballads begin as your letter does: "You, whom I loved so much..." This past tense, with the present still resounding so close, is as sad as the ends of parties, when the lights are turned off and you remain alone, watching the couples go off into the dark streets. It's over: nothing else is to be expected, and yet you stay there indefinitely, knowing that nothing more will happen. You have notes like a guitar's; at times, like a chorus that repeats: "I could not have given you happiness." It's an old song from long ago, like a dried flower... Does the past become an old thing so quickly?

Happiness? It's a term of complaint. You—you embodied it, you identified it, you define it. Can one really speak about it as you do?

When you like a perfume, you try to hang on to it, to find it again; you don't let yourself become completely intoxicated by it, so you can analyze and soak it up little by little, until the mere memory of it can produce the same physical sensation; when the perfume returns, you inhale it more slowly, more softly, in order to perceive its most tenuous emanations. A brutal whiff of perfume makes your head spin but leaves an irritatingly incomplete, unfinished sensation. Either it's an unpleasant, suffocating feeling you'd like to be rid of so you can breathe freely, or it's a brutal intoxication, over too soon because only the nervous system has been touched. To be turned upside down and no longer know anything—that is happiness. But to hang on to a little corner of consciousness that is always aware of what is happening and that, because it is aware, can allow the intellectual and rational being to also enjoy, fully, with each passing second, something of the happiness that arises—to hang on to this little corner of consciousness that appreciates the slow evolution of joy, that follows it to its farthest reaches, isn't that happiness? There's a little corner that does not stir, but that remains witness to the joy being felt; that remembers and can say: I was happy, and I know why. I don't mind losing my head, but I want to capture the moment when I lose it, to push my understanding of my abdicating consciousness as far as it can go. We must not be absent from our own happiness.

This corner of myself judged you, measured you; and in judging and measuring you I saw your weaknesses, your insufficiencies; where is the harm in my staying, in my accepting these insufficiencies, in my loving them? O, Man! You always want to be admired. You do not judge, you do not measure the woman you love. You are there, you take her; you take your happiness, she seems not to belong to herself anymore, to have lost all sense of anything: you are happy. To you she cried: I love you, and you are satisfied. You are not brutal; you are gentle, you talk to her, you worry about her; you comfort her with tender words; you cradle her in your arms. But you do not judge her, since you are asking her to be happy through you and to tell you that she is happy through you. But if you notice two eyes watching you, then smiling, you revolt. You feel that you have been "seen" and you don't want to be seen: you want only "to be." Nervously, you ask: "What are you thinking?"

I am thinking about you. You have a small, throaty laugh and teeth I do

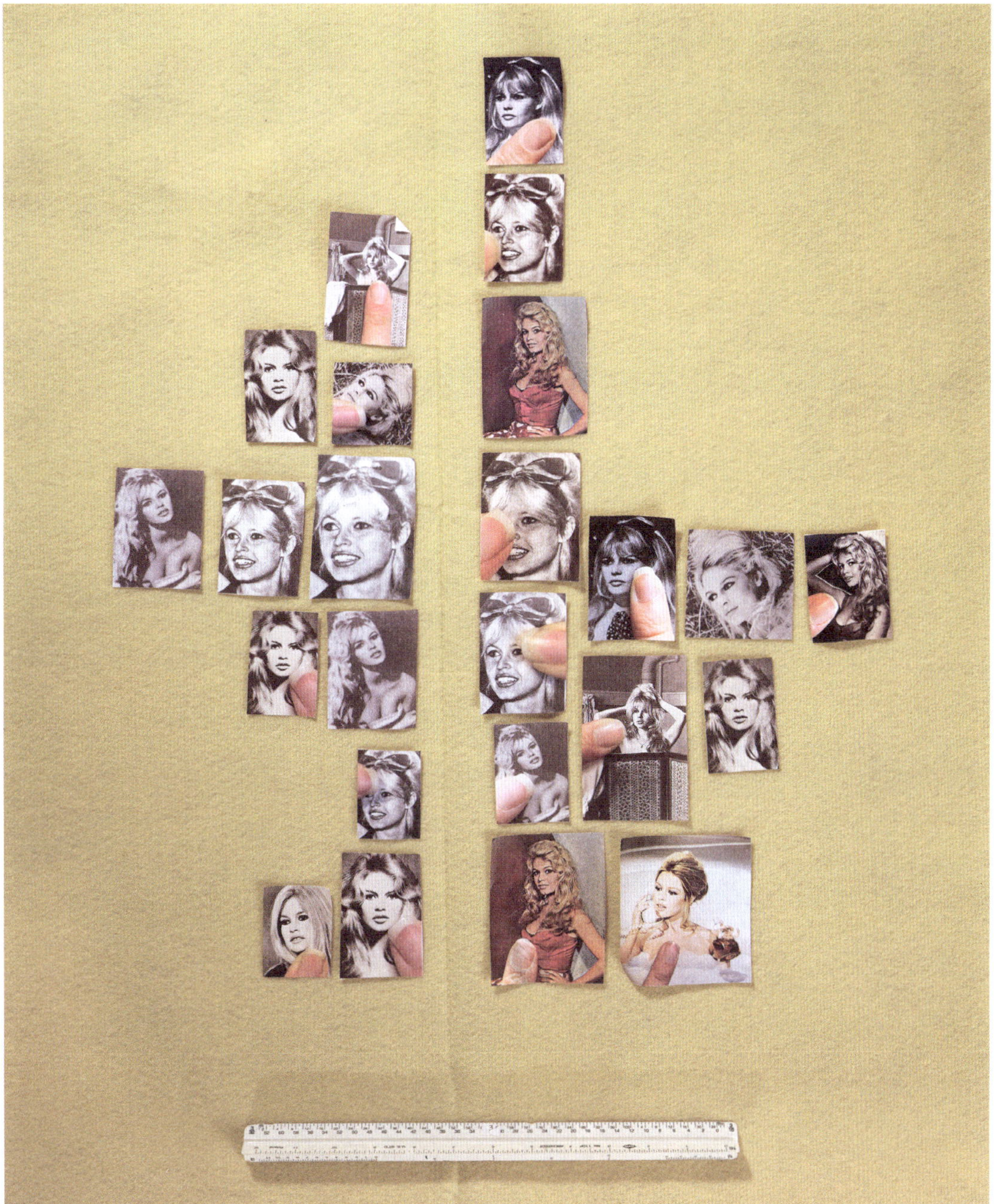

Sara Cwynar / Encyclopedia Grids: Bardot / 2014

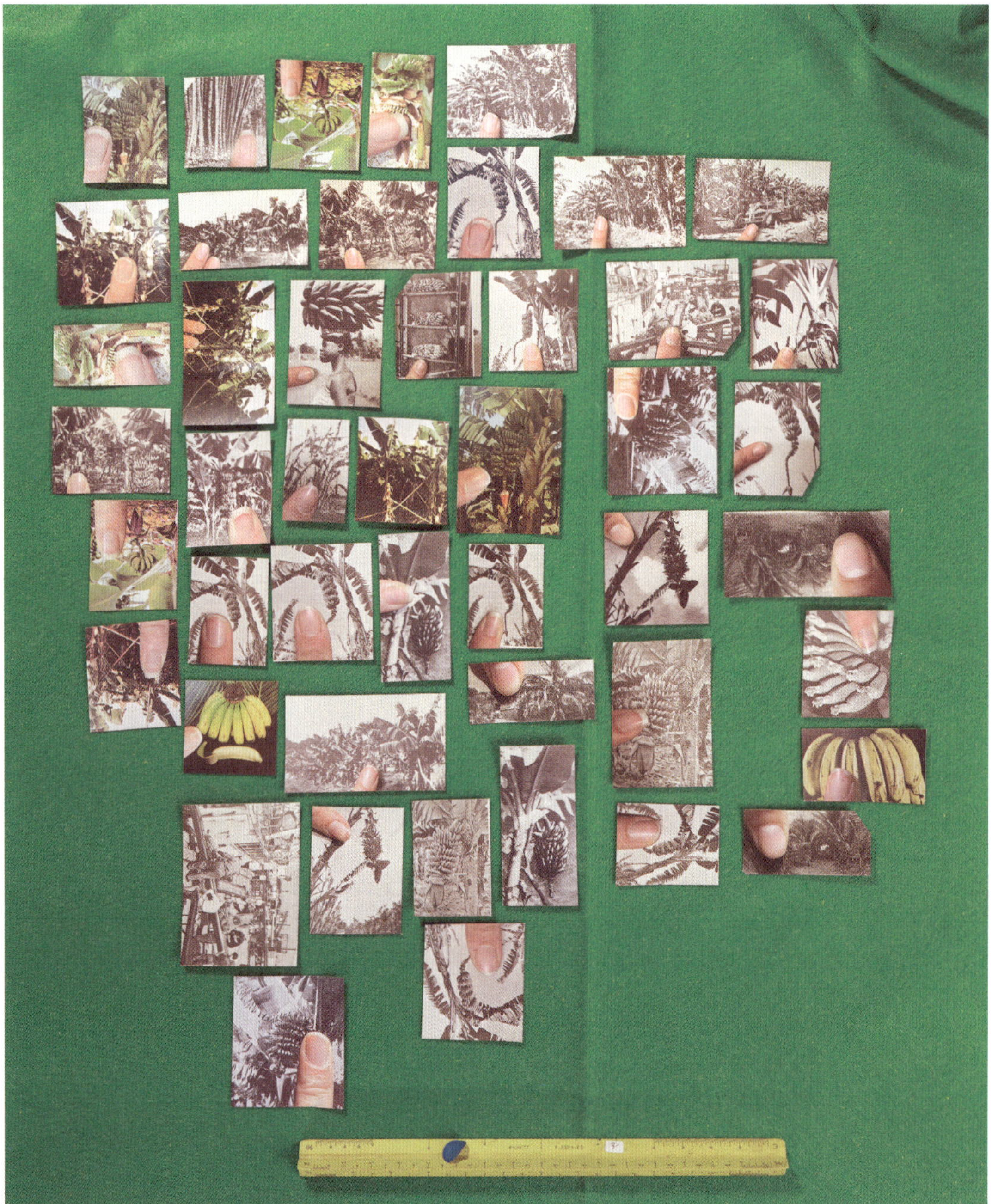

Sara Cwynar / Encyclopedia Grids: Banana / 2014

not like. Your eyes close slightly, as if to penetrate the mind of the person you're speaking with and show him that you have seen clear into him. Your lips recede somewhat over teeth that appear black, and your whole head strains forward. You assume this air when you are expounding a brilliant theory you have just discovered, or when you have found a way to reduce what someone had believed to be a beautiful thought to a mediocre sentiment. You look like a shopkeeper who won't be pushed around. I am embarrassed when you are like this: it diminishes you. But no one had better take notice of this minor flaw and say something: I would be very mean. You have odd judgments sometimes, in fields you claim to know nothing about. You take down a painting, a piece of music, a poem with your words: it's facile. It's as if you want to recover your stability, compromised for a moment by something greater than you; and you are so afraid of snobbism that you reject what you have experienced as beautiful. I see it, and I don't like it. But were others to intimate any doubts as to your taste and your intelligence, I would reply sharply, as if I were being insulted. You are a bit vain: you steal satisfied glances at yourself in mirrors on the sly, you straighten up when passing by a woman, and you stare at her while maintaining an attitude of false indifference; if she glanced at you, surely she found you handsome; if someone tells you about a woman, you interrupt to ask: "Is she pretty?" I find you amusing, and I feel like smiling derisively. But let no one tell me you're a "ladies' man"; your weaknesses are my own. I discovered them little by little, by examining you without rest. I suffer from these faults of yours, but I wouldn't want you to change. I sometimes talk to you about them, smiling. I wouldn't want to offend you, or to give you advice. I would like for you to know what I know; and I wish that instead of trying not to show yourself as you are, you would reveal all your little uglinesses to me. I would love them, because they would truly be mine. Other people wouldn't know about them; and this is how we would find each other outside this world. Nothing is more endearing than weaknesses and faults: it is through them that one penetrates the beloved's soul, a soul perpetually concealed by the desire to seem like everybody else. It's the same as with a face. Others see only a face; but we know the precise moment when, instead of continuing along its ideal line, the curve of the nose breaks imperceptibly to delineate an ordinary nose; we know that, up close, the texture of the skin is coarse, with blackheads; we have discovered the blemish in the eye that sometimes dims the gaze, and the extra millimeter that keeps the lip from being elegant. These small irregularities, we feel like kissing them more than the perfections, because they are humble, and they make this face not be that of another man.

> **I am thinking about you. You have a small, throaty laugh and teeth I do not like.**

Do not complain that I am judging you and measuring you: I know you better, and that is not to love you less. It was not I who was unhappy, but you. You should have rephrased the sentence in your letter to say: "You know quite well that you could not possibly have given me happiness, because even in the moments when we were closest, you always withheld a corner of yourself… that did not stir… that was judging me."

For that matter, was it you I was judging, or myself? You know full well that I am always watching myself as I live, that I make fun of myself, that I belittle myself, that I laugh at my impulses and my enthusiasms, that I deny myself any self-confidence. So I had no confidence in you either. I wasn't sure, despite all your love. You had many woman friends: I did not reproach you for this; I would have liked for you to tell me about them, so I could know what drew you toward them, away from me. But you told me very little. I thought you did not love me and didn't dare question you, when I wanted so much to know. I worry over a glance, a word, a silence … but I say, "You are free," because I don't want a person to stay out of obligation and I would like for him to stay nonetheless. The thing is, I understand so well when someone does not love me anymore that I find any effort to fight or hold on foolish. Such effort would be so pointless, I laugh at my least inclination to protest: "You, jealous? Oh no! That isn't your style: don't say anything. All you would elicit is a smile, a few painful words of appeasement... And he would leave anyway, just as fast, not any faster... So: you are free."

I tried to hold onto a small support separate from you, so I could cling to it the day you would no longer love me. This small support was not another man, it was not a dream, nor an image. It was what you called my egoism and my pride; it was my self that, in my suffering, I wanted to be able to find again. I wanted to be able to hold myself tight, alone with my pain, my doubts, my lack of faith. When I am in distress, only my sense of self gives me the strength to go on. When everything is changing, when everything is hurting me, I am me with myself. To have lost myself, I would have had to be sure I no longer needed myself.

You describe your fiancée in a periodic sentence whose rhythm conforms to the evolution of your feelings; it draws itself out slowly, tilting progressively toward its terminus, where it stops for good without a sound, lacking the strength to go further: it is there, stopped forever, just as you are there close to Her.

If I were very vain, I would think you still love me and that it is out of a sense of obligation to avoid injuring a young girl who believes in you that you are distancing yourself from me to marry her. But rest assured: I am not at all vain; I only smiled at a few words: "compelled," "fear of disappointing her." I also thought that if I were your fiancée and if I read this sentence, I would be saddened. I wouldn't like for a man to marry me so as not to disappoint me; so as not to show me who he is. This half-lie, as the basis of a union, would offend me; I think I would prefer to leave. But these are my own ideas. In any case, your fiancée did not read the sentence: she doesn't know "what you are." And if she knew, she would probably be happy to have such an homage paid to her love. Is a woman in love not delighted when a man chooses her as a reward for her total love? You enrich your feelings with a confused and happy gratitude for the contentment She is giving you, of which you are not worthy and which you will not be able to return. All this, with a touch of superstition, sets "my teeth on edge" slightly; I don't know why, because what you are saying is the eternally idiotic, but eternally true, song of those who love and are loved. I am not making fun. What you are saying in this sentence, underneath all these words, is that you love, and that you love a woman who is different from me, that you love her for all she is in opposition to me, that you have loved her for a long time without ever wanting to tell me.

Last year, in the country, the day after you arrived, we climbed the path halfway up the slope; sitting in the tall dry grasses, we were looking out at the prairie and I'd seated myself right next to you. Softly, I talked to you about your friend: you didn't answer. I insisted, and you said somewhat dryly that it was a part of you I didn't love and that you would rather not show it to me. Your gaze became distant; you made a gesture, with your hand, of someone who wouldn't be understood; then you looked at me with the superiority of one who will not speak. You talked about something else. I fell silent; a dark veil had fallen over the joy I'd felt on seeing you again. For six months, I had been sick, far from you. You hadn't forgotten me, but someone was making you see me differently from the way I was. You reproached me for my character, my tastes... You became partial to the things I disliked: I had the disorienting feeling that you were thinking about someone who was the absolute opposite of me and that you were making a constant comparison. You had a fixed idea of who I was; and in my words and gestures you were looking for anything that could be attributed, one way or another, to this idea. You credited me with petty feelings, a monstrous egoism, demands... And I gave up telling you that you were mistaken, because you had the self-assurance of a man who knows how to say "that's not true," and how to laugh with the kind of laughter that precludes all protest, because one gets the sense that nothing could puncture "his truth." You approved of what you had once found idiotic; you ruined what had seemed to be your most intimate

Wherever I was, you were within me.
You placed yourself in the way of my feelings.

thinking. It was as if you were trying to kill me inside of you. I was in pain; the faults you held against me and the qualities you acknowledged I had mattered little to me: you no longer wanted to see me as I was; and I wept to see myself destroyed in this manner.

You explained how you recognized the love of a woman "without prerogatives and without demands."

If you feel like spending an entire day spitting into the water to make rings, the woman who loves you will spend an entire day, without saying a thing, watching you make rings in the water: she will be happy because this pastime pleases you. And if you feel like making rings in the water every day, then this woman, every day, will stand there watching you do it. You added that I wouldn't be able to remain there like that. I feel compelled to confess that I would not. I would first attempt to sleep, or else do something myself; and, if that weren't possible, I would not be able to resist telling you that you're a fool and you'd be better off kissing me. Then I would come stand beside you to make rings in the water too, to do what you do, and I would invent the game of the biggest rings and the smallest. Would you really have been able to stand next to me watching me make rings in the water?

In Corsica, after a long walk through the scrub brush, I came upon an open path. I held my horse by its bridle; its head was above mine, and I was barely visible between two arbutuses: I was holding pink peonies against my breast. I wished you could have been there to smell the fragrance of the brush; you would have understood the taste I have for the wild sometimes; you would have been simple and wild like me and we'd have loved each other. I held my horse tightly in my arms and crushed the peonies. There was no one around to love what I loved.

On Venetian gondolas, at night, along the fetid canals where a raspy Sole mio is sung beneath tricolor lanterns, near the dead, sad palaces, I cried because I was alone and because I knew you wouldn't have let yourself be carried away with me by this morbid charm.

From the tops of mountains, gliding as in a dream down tall slopes covered in white snow, I thought to keep the marvelous vision in my heart, so that, back at your side, I could make you see it; I searched for words intense enough to make you taste my joy and give you the desire to come with me. But you quickly stopped listening to me and took on a somber look.

I wanted to take you to see dances and to hear special concerts. I did everything in my power to make you content, and my own happiness was greater when you were moved. But you resisted accompanying me, and you stopped wanting to come along.

Wherever I was, you were within me. You placed yourself in the way of my feelings. They were sad because you weren't there. I tried to preserve them in all their detail, to be able to bring them to you almost raw. Did you never sense the passion I put into trying to bring them to life for you? I thought about keeping you with me all the time so you could feel what I felt, so that nothing of my experience would occur in your absence: the glint of the sun in my eyes, the posture of my body in a dance... And I became impatient if I felt myself flourishing when you weren't there. A success satisfied me because I could tell you about it; a problem was alleviated because I could recount it to you. I wanted to do more things, always more things, in order to bring you the growing bounty of my enrichment.

You hadn't forgotten me, but someone was making you see me differently from the way I was.

And at night, in the streets of Paris where I always walked quickly without seeing anything, I tried to love what you loved. I timidly put my arm under yours like all the couples on the street, and, curious to feel what you felt, I liked the perfume of the fog, the brush of the crowd, the bustle of the shop girls. In the dark streets, athough I detest all public displays, I took pleasure—a forbidden pleasure—in returning your kisses, which weren't very "comfortable" but were sweet because you liked them. During hot summer afternoons on my bedroom sofa, we sang ballads, dance tunes from ten years back; the lyrics were silly and I am not sentimental; but next to you, whose soul is more romantic than mine, I let myself be swept away by the simple melodies, evocations of the masses who are moved and captivated by the crude song of human tenderness. The "tango of dreams, tango of love" helped me get a bit closer to you... I would have liked to read what you'd read and see what you'd seen. But you said only a few quick words, as if none of this was meant for me.

When people talked about love around me, I thought of yours, and I smiled: when they talked about "men" and the harm they cause "women," I kept on smiling, because I thought you weren't one of those "men."

But that wasn't loving you, because I still wanted to enrich myself, because I didn't want to destroy myself in order to become an acquiescent form with no desire left for self-improvement, that instead falls asleep in childish admiration of the man it loves and lets itself be guided by him.

It's curious how frequently a man, the moment he thinks about marrying the woman he has loved for a long time, becomes obsessed with moral and societal principles. This woman he loved because she was strong, independent, rich with personal ideas—when he thinks about marrying her, his instincts of domination and pride, and his preoccupation with "what people will say," transform strength into rebellion, independence into pride and bad temper, personal ideas into egoism and demands. He points out that life is made up of small daily incidents to which one must adapt and for which one must prepare by adopting an average "mentality." One ought to specify each party's role in advance, because this is no longer the time to act like children. Toward his wife the man will be respectful, loving; he will say in a soft voice that one should not go here or should not go there, that one should behave like this and not like that, because it's everyone's custom; the wife will say, "yes, my darling"; and when in the company of her friends, you will hear her lend her voice to the universal chorus that proudly repeats these words: "my husband." She pronounces the word with a delight imbued with arrogance, astonished as she is to now be among the elite who can say: "my husband." Each of them in turn outdoes the others with tales of what the "husband" does, what the "husband" says; all the loving gestures or reproaches made by "the husband" are revealed beatifically, like so many jewels brought as an offering to the young woman. With every question asked or subject broached, you are sure to hear: "I will ask my husband," or: "My husband told me..." As I write these lines, I can hear, on the terrace next to mine, a group of young and pretty women conversing with animation and good cheer. I cannot understand what they are saying; but I can clearly make out, as a constant and frequent refrain, "my husband"; when I come across them during a walk or at lunch, if I catch a few words of their conversation, these words are always: "my husband." Is it really necessary to become like this, and can a woman not think except with the husband's ideas? This might make you smile, lead you to think that resentment has made me sarcastic. But I am so bored with all these women who talk about their husbands!

Many a sentence in your letter aroused these "feminist" thoughts in me. Was it intentional that you didn't understand why I asked you to return my photographs? I am not so vain as to think that they would remind you of me and that this reminder would be a nuisance in your new life: daily life will quickly wear away the vividness of things past. Nor did I want to make the traditional gesture that lovers make when parting ways. I would gladly leave all these things from the past with you, because they no longer have any meaning or importance. The thing is, I thought about your wife. That you wouldn't tell her about me, I understand; but then you must not keep anything of mine in your house: it would be a cumbersome secret she might discover. If you tell her about me, I feel a certain unease thinking that it will perhaps be in the tone you used when telling me about other women you had loved. There is one about whom you said, to explain your breakup: "I'd had enough." Your eyes hardened; you spoke in a husky, hoarse voice, from deep in your throat, and for a moment your eyes became fixated on a point in the distance. This was a reason without chance of appeal; one says as much, upon leaving the table, when one has lunched well: it would be wrong to insist. A few seconds later,

> Happiness? It's a term of complaint. You—you embodied it, you identified it, you define it.

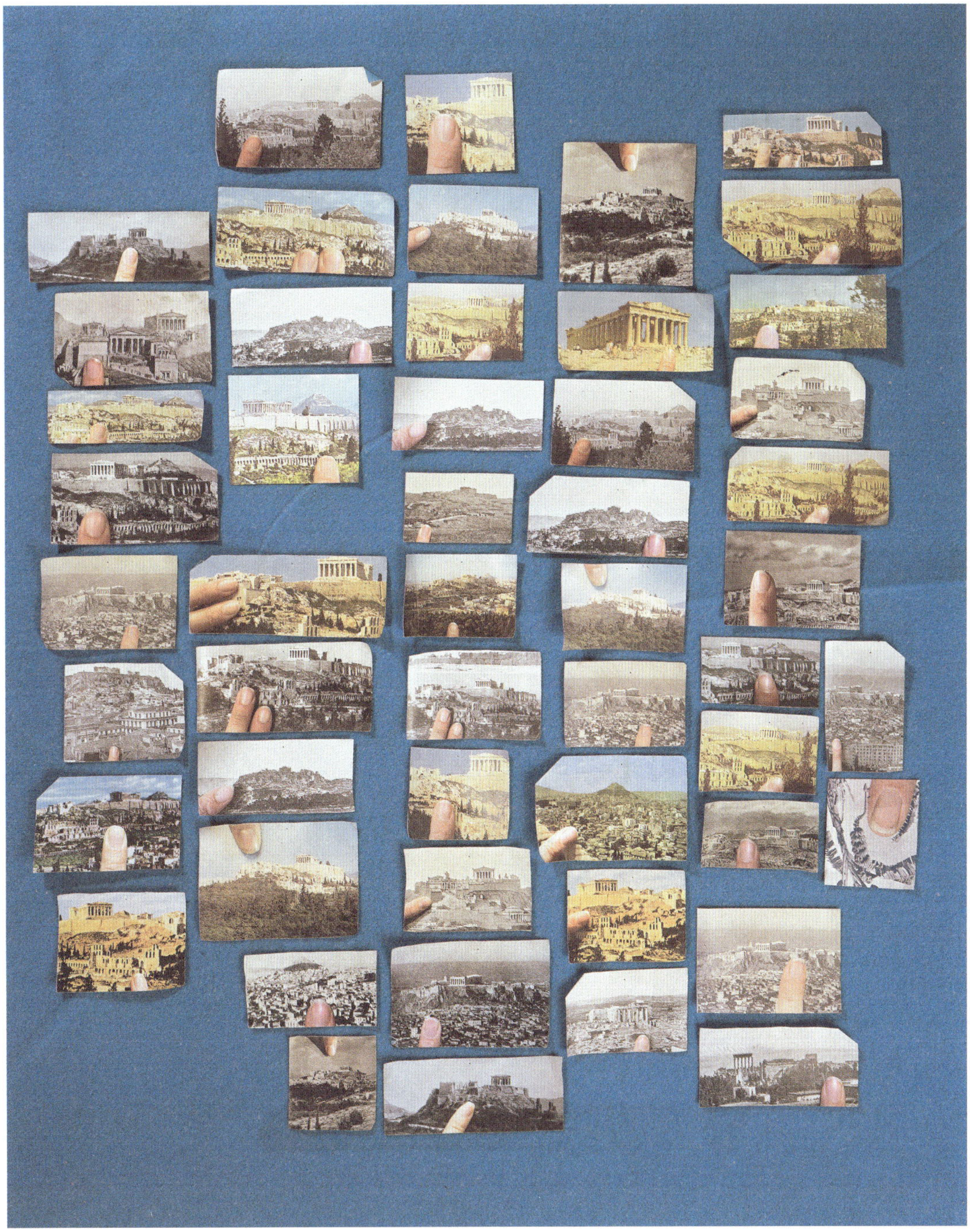

Sara Cwynar / Encyclopedia Grids: Acropolis / 2014

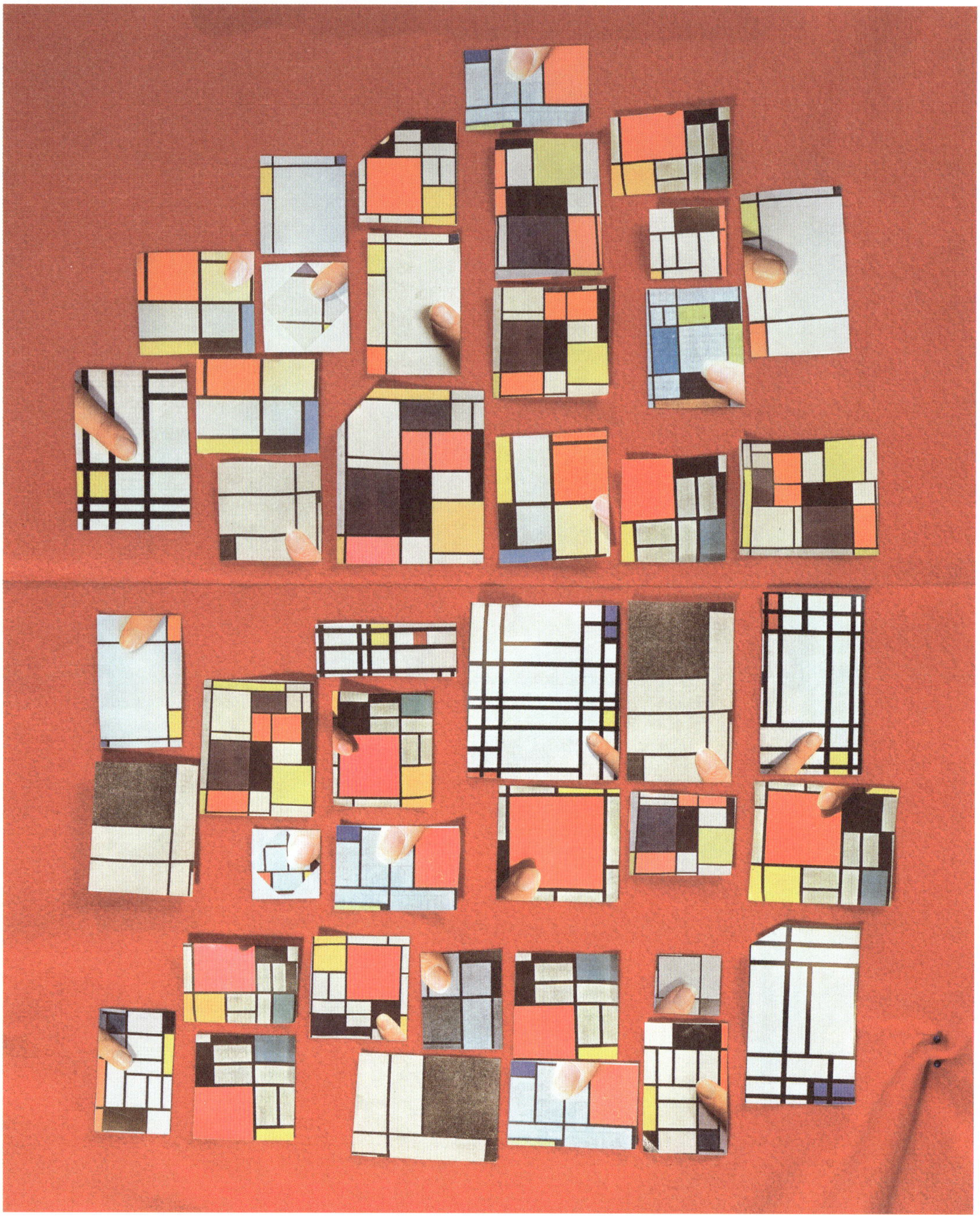

Sara Cwynar / Encyclopedia Grids: Abstract Art / 2014

you rubbed your eyes for a long time, and added with a sigh that came from deep in your heart: "She is married: I sincerely wish her all the happiness in the world." I don't know why we ascribe any importance to what a lover will say about us later. Is it pride? We don't want to be treated like the others. So, for now, I would rather be able to tell myself that you will never speak about me. But there are my photographs, which your wife can find. You'll tell me that you will "handle" the pain this discovery may cause her. I wouldn't want you to "handle" it. That offends a certain, very deep feeling I have of feminine self-esteem. I imagine you will console her: you will be much more tender, more affectionate, more attentive; you will make her questions vanish under caresses: you will "make do." Don't you realize how humilating that might be, and the hatred it might spawn? I don't want you to have to "handle" this consolation because of me.

Why do you ask me: "Does he exist, the man you were made for?" People say to a woman: "The man you were made for," and to a man: "The woman who was made for you." Can they envision: "The woman you were made for"? A man is: everything seems to have been made available to him... even, somewhere in the world, a woman who suits him, whose union with him existed before her birth. These words—"you were made for"—imply an obedient and submissive adaptation on which a woman's happiness will depend. Strange thing: the woman is made for the man and it is she who will be made happy. Can the man not be made happy, or does his happiness reside in feeling the consenting pliability of the one who is made for him? Is the man caressing a beautiful Siamese cat hoping to find out what the animal's light eyes are saying? Or does he think that the caress itself is the only thing that can cause the animal to be moved?

I find this idea of the pre-existence of a union very pretty. A Japanese legend, I believe, has it that at birth, the moon attaches the foot of a future man to the foot of a future woman with a red ribbon. While they are alive, the ribbon is invisible, but the two beings look for each other and, if they find each other, their happiness will be on earth. Some do not find each other; as a result their lives are restless and they die sad: for them, happiness will begin only in the other world; they will see the one to whom the ribbon attaches them. I don't know if I will find the red ribbon that is attaching me in this world; I think this legend is, like all legends, a poetic comfort. Isn't the man for whom you are made the man for whom you accept you have been made? That man, for me, could have been you.

Sara Cwynar's Encyclopedia Grids

Patterns are both emergent and elusive in the photographic assemblages of Sara Cwynar. Raised on glossy magazines and blogs, yet also drawn to found photographs, vintage snapshots, and kitchy reproductions, Cwynar repurposes seemingly outmoded images for her own photographed installations. Like an archivist, she collects and catalogues, but like a builder she constructs new forms in space, and it is here, in the mixing of these two potentially contradictory instincts, that the patterns in her work surface and then recede. Her works have a sharp-eyed formality along with a playful spirit of misdirection, allowing the shapes she makes out of old pictures to be both more and less than what they seem. By encompassing images within images, by photographing photographs, Cwynar ensures that the theme of artifice is ever-present in her work. Yet from the bits of finger included in the base photographs of her 2014 series *Encyclopedia Grids* to their particular alignment on the walls, there is never a question that a person selected, organized, and executed each arrangement—and did so for reasons that may be unfathomable because they are so personal.

It is in the meaning of these acts themselves—of finding, of archiving, of choosing, of arranging, of placing—that the works in *Encyclopedia Grids* turn us from the beauty of the layouts, with their shifting rhythm of symmetries and asymmetries, to the personal vision that both creates and beholds their display. The four pieces here—"Encyclopedia Grid (Bardot)," "Encyclopedia Grid (Banana)," "Encyclopedia Grid (Acropolis)," and "Encyclopedia Grid (Abstract Art)"—each exploit a different style of kitch (the celebrity shot, the nature shot, the tourist shot, the art shot) to create recurrent visual patterns that both attract and frustrate the eye through their constant fragmentation and resistance to logical sequence. There is nothing actually "encyclopedic" in these works, and in fact any indication that there is (the "Abstract Art" piece, for instance, appears to only include images from Mondrian) seems willfully misleading. What there is instead is an almost palpable love for images, their power to capture our attention, to alter our thinking, to influence our desire. By using the scientific language of archival cataloguing and historical investigation, Cwynar is slyly baiting us to think of art as other than what it is: a private dream world of pleasure and obsession.

-Keith Newton

OF RECOVERY

by Julia Cohen

The mental hospital takes: your shoes, your pens & pencils, your belt, your computer, your iPod, your cell phone, your wallet, your passport. For 10 days I keep N's brown wallet in the front pocket of my backpack. I take it out every night, hold it in my hands like a dead starling. I look through his IDs. I look to see if he left a note. Nope.

Born in a deadlight? Stop teasing. Furnace full of patient stars. Here because I could not abandon love: coffee grounds, a box of opened cereal, cherry magnets. My bed unburdened by sex? To hold nothing against nothing. To hold nothing against.

*

In 10 days I visit 19 times.
In 10 days we play 26 rounds of Scrabble.
In 10 days I tell almost no one.
In 10 days I bring N 17 meals.
In 10 days I cry at unexpected times.
In 10 days I do the laundry once so I can bring N clean shirts. I bring the blue & white striped collared shirt, it's his oldest & feels like worn pajamas.
In 10 days I wash the kitchen floor.
In 10 days I meet N's social worker, young & chipper.
In 10 days I buy Clorox & scrub the bathroom. Even the shower.
In 10 days I clean out the fridge. Shriveled peppers. Salsa with a moldy lid.
In 10 days N's doctor asks me if I plan to stay with N. Of course, I say.
In 10 days I vacuum the living room & hallway.
In 10 days I wait until the ninth to throw out N's noose.

Light could not look. Inside my lung, the night. I'm not dry land. Pages stuck together. So creeping so day. Origin in simile. To subdue exploits. If I thought fruit could impart, I would sample from each seed. Untidy summer. Not afraid of childbirth, afraid of sex after childbirth. Firstlings cling or canter with help. A city named vengeance. In tents, years blink out like seeds crushed from a lemon. To make room by reduction: sink. This one is taken? Bite of fig & ice-cream. A living. Out of architecture, "Dibs."

*

Questions I can't ask: Why weren't you going to leave a note? What other methods of suicide did you consider? You were going to leave me without knowing how to cook collard greens & black-eyed peas? Without knowing how to make tofu-scramble? How many lies did you tell to sustain this deceit & what did they feel like? Who would identify your body? I once watched a TV show about how dogs won't accept the death of their owner unless they see/smell their owner's dead body. Otherwise they'll keep waiting at the door. I'd have asked permission from the police to take our dog with me to the morgue, to accept.

*

Remember: N reads to me in the bathtub.

*

Therapy Session #7:
J: Last week we were talking about external experiences that test or...within seconds transform how you conceive of yourself. But I walked away from the conversation not knowing what to do with that information. Like, letting outside things have such a strong effect. I guess? Reading a book about questioning gender when I was twelve & then letting that obsessively take over or dismantle my positioning of self...
Dr: That sounds like you're choosing for things to go that way, which is not quite the way it seems it went. But rather, it happened automatically. Jumping back to your first point, I don't know if we got to necessarily what we were supposed "to do" with it, but simply understand what hap-

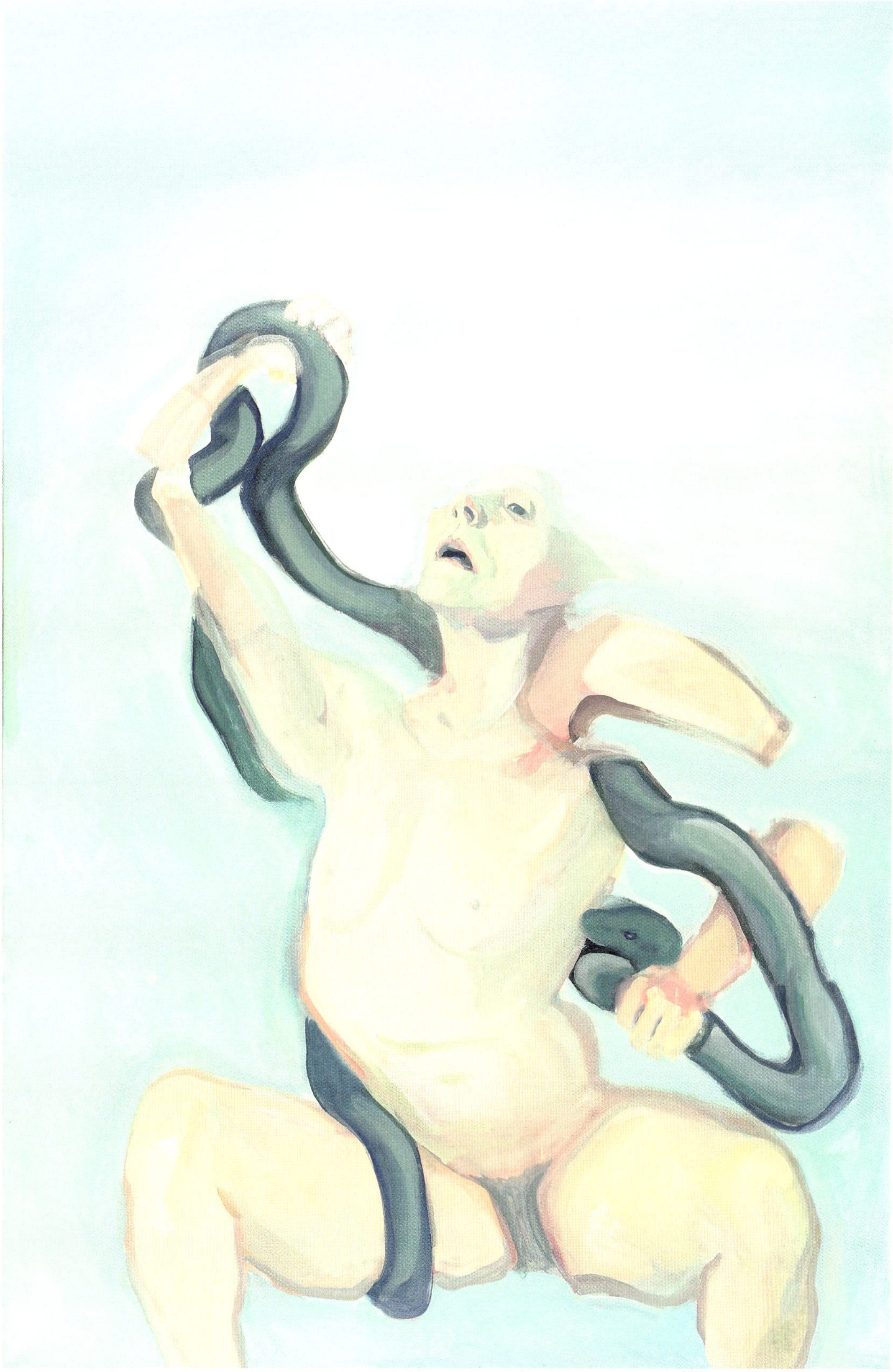

Maria Lassnig / Woman Laokoon (Woman Laocoon) / 1976

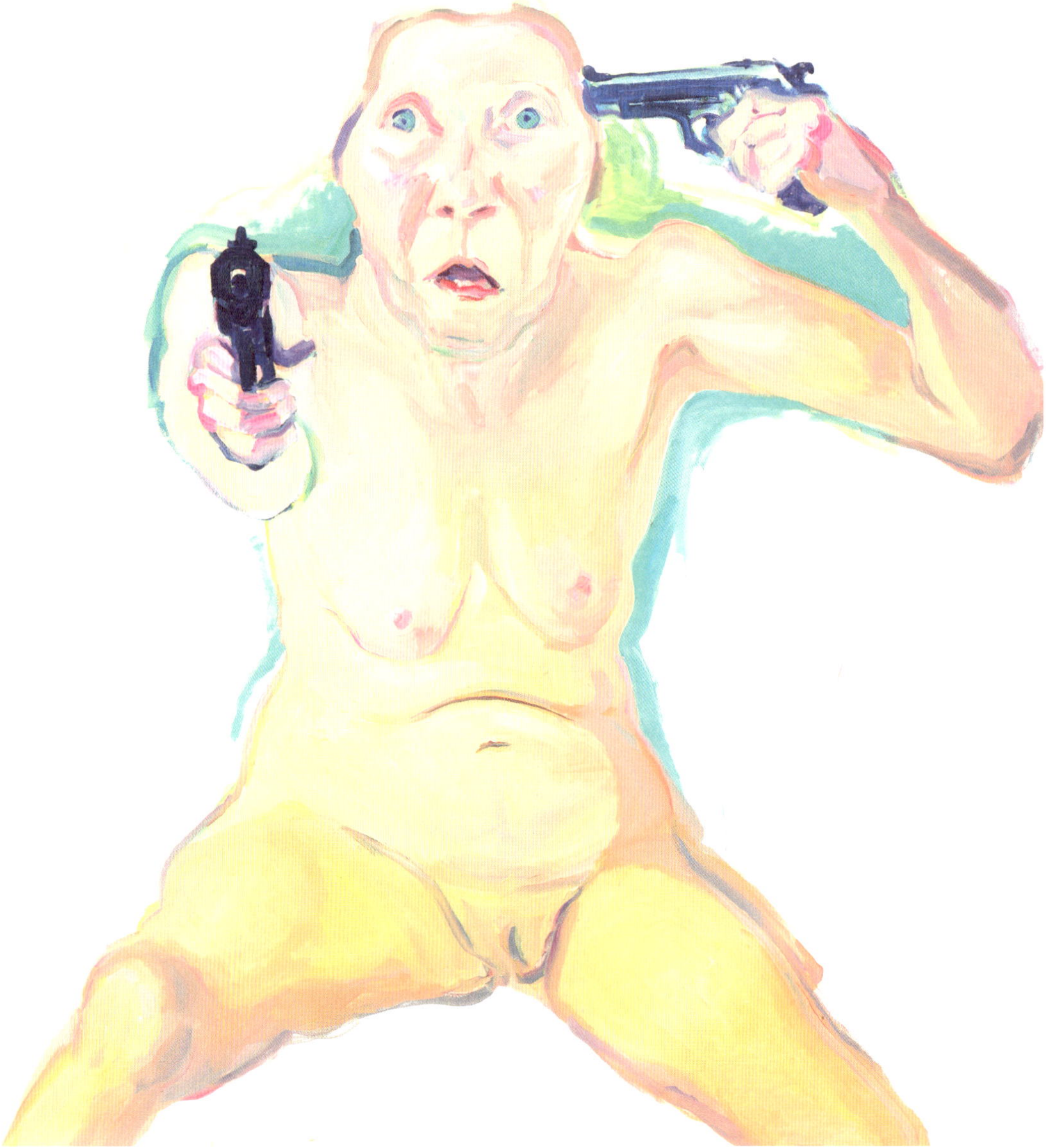

Maria Lassnig / Du oder Ich (You or Me) / 2005

pens. You described this experience at an all-girls school of stumbling upon a book that questioned sexual orientation, that first was a notion & then became a preoccupation, & then you weren't sure what you were supposed to hang onto about your own orientation.
J: Right, yes. I mean, that was one of those larger moments, but I have the tendency to obsess about many things &, not that there is a proper place to put something or that one should compartmentalize, but I feel like I don't know how to quiet some thoughts down. Not that events happen all the time where I lose track or feel destabilized from who I am, but rather I'm socially anxious. I'll send an email when I'm tired & feel like I got my thoughts wrong, & then if the person I sent it to doesn't get back to me right away, I'll obsessively think about how he or she could have interpreted it wrong & I was accidently offensive. Then three days later they do respond & are like, "you sounded tired in your email..." so there is some sort of concern about how other people understand you that's healthy & then in certain instances I can take it to this other level that's unproductive & time-consuming. That's where I get afraid in regards to how I'm considering my relationship with N. I can't decide whether I'm thinking about this situation most of the time because it's what any one would do if her relationship was in a complicated place, or if I'm contributing to my own unease by having this take over my thoughts.
*
My calamine-blitzed child. Lucky licit, I claim a mountain & adjoining lake I know what's lunging. Tetchy water or feeble soil. Like a future roof, the fingernail un-creases aluminum foil. My makeshift. My lifelike.

Will someone string cold lights through the tulips? Will someone close grief's atlas & ship the salt to bookend the night?

Someone briefly touches my shoulder while I sleep. Moat, moat, moat. My arm like a drawbridge lowers to the grasses, an unstamped postcard, slight glances through curt branches, grey trousers, the hand-drawn airplane. Addresses. I pack myself with milkweed & thistle. Season of what?
*
Remember: We write poems together by email, by text message, on car rides, side by side at a bar.
*
The noose is longer than I thought it would. A surprisingly smooth cord, soft & glossy like a doll's braided hair.

For nine days I peek into N's backpack but don't touch it. Standing by the blue dumpster to decide whether to untie the noose, turn it back into knotless rope, or toss it in as quickly as possible. I'm compelled to destroy the evidence, to leave usable rope for those who pilfer our dumpster. N tells me he looked up how to knot a noose on the internet. I try to picture him researching this at Whole Foods or the library where I go to play Scrabble & check Facebook. He says the instructions were easy to follow. The cord, bought locally at Ace Hardware.

Remember: N writes for me, "I will warm your frozen hands / in my cold hands."
*
I cannot get warm. I cannot clip the syrup from the homespun tree. Cannot scrape the banquette into the baby swing. Blue leaves at last. I feel like I can feel.

Garden of babies? I planted the sun under the tongue of returns. A whimper winds the sound gears grind over. Foraged syntax. Who romps the ruins? To locate a glance in the forest, stride through the wild chives, the beehive swinging like a lantern. Honey & hiccups.

Success in stems. Success when the nod. Success after soft cashews. Success of preservation undermined by owners. Success of passing the feeling-baton! Outside of family. Holding your bear by the ear. To plump the scrawny feeling.
*
Therapy Session #7 continued:
Dr: When you were describing that e-mail piece, it sounds like you were saying that not only do you worry about the other person's experience of you but that you spin out the worst-case scenario that the other person might have of you, to detailed & negative places. So it gets to be an involved process in your head.
J: Haha. Yes, more involved than the other person would ever give it time.
Dr: Right, they haven't been staying up at night. So that's also a process where not only are you obsessing about something & really taking up a lot of room in your head, but it's all stuff that's about your worries about other people's experiences.
J: Right.
Dr: Their experience of you. How your actions might affect their experiences of you. So these are ruminations of them, about you in relation to them. In that sense, it's the thing that takes space away from your experience of you.
J: That seems true. That doesn't sound good. It sounds not confident in how people...
Dr: Maybe it doesn't leave as much room for you to feel calm & comfortable.

J: I don't give myself that space... which is why I'm so anxious all the time!
Dr: Yes, & maybe it's a cycle that feeds itself. Obsessing about something makes it feel more important & central, which makes one feel like one should obsess about it.
J: Yes, I have these moments where I'm going through the same loop in my head that isn't getting me anywhere, where I can step back & tell myself this isn't productive & tell my brain to switch topics & get work done, or tell myself that there is no point in worrying about it, it's out of my hands, until someone actually responds to an email, until something external happens.

N naps & naps. I walk the dog, wash dishes, take out recycling. Don't cry in front of N. Instead, on the orange couch late at night or in the bathroom, while looking at myself in the mirror. To study the uncontrolled face. This is what it means to surprise yourself.

Unfaithful: when I divide our belongings in my mind. The nightstands, mine. Mattress, mine. The dishes & glasses, mine. Lamps, mine. Plants, mine. Trinkets & heirlooms, mine. CDs, his. Most of the records, his. 65% of the books, his. What of the book-doubles we threw out to merge our collections? Chapbooks, who knows. What of the artwork we bought together? Our dog?

Can't? "Because I'm afraid I'm going to hurt myself." One stoplight, three intersections, the choking floral scent of a Laundromat. I run the six blocks home to find N deflating on the couch. A noose in his backpack, a mind full of suicide. 31 tall buildings in Denver. 89 local bus routes to jump in front of. I would write about anything else if I could think of something other than N.

*

Therapy Session #7 Continued:
J: I mean, in the first session or two we talked about how in sixth grade my best friend stopped speaking to me & then therefore all of my friends stopped speaking to me— how jolting & horrible it was.
Dr. Yes of course.

When you came home after failing, when we had sex, were you at all glad you'd failed to jump?

Dr: Say one more time what the piece is that you need to break the cycle.
J: I just remind myself of what's fairly obvious: obsessing about what's on my mind isn't going to get me anywhere because there is nothing I can do about how this other person is experiencing me. Or, well, I mean, I guess about that particular interaction. Or I tell myself that either way, it's not a big deal. Even the worst-case situation.
Dr: The feeling you're having is disproportionate to the importance of the issue.
J: That may be an uncomfortably accurate way to phrase it.

*

Thoughts fall into two categories. Faith:

*

Will someone skip over radio-regret on the crumbling wave? Slinking mischief cracks open an egg or loosens the pinecone. Wrapping-paper grip? A leveled statue releases.

I'm trying to be here. Here & not sad. Sometimes a coffee table equals endless. A feeling tramped into route.

Remember: N introduces me to black metal, to Levinas, to Hannah Weiner, to Alice Notley, to nutritional yeast.

*

The reveal: I miss two calls on the bus ride home. As I step off to meet him in the park with the dog, I return the calls to hear he can't make it.

J: But that was based on nothing other then the whim of a twelve year old. There is an anxiety that comes from that which is: I can just be doing whatever I normally do & then all of a sudden my friends will decide they don't like me anymore. I totally know that's a sixth grade thing, but I see that anxiety rooted in situations like emails or miscommunications with friends. But I don't see that same thing when I think of my relationship with N. My anxiety is more about what's happening to our relationship with me in it, although clearly a lot of it is out of my control right now.
Dr: Is it possible that your relationship isn't exactly like the former dynamic because it's not so much that you

think N is experiencing you negatively, but is related, perhaps to one of the byproducts of obsessing about how the other person experiences you: that there is very little space left for you to tune into your own experience of what's going on, because a lot of your energy is focused on the other person's experience. Could that be contributing to the anxiety in your relationship? What I mean is: if the process you find yourself stuck in is a process the results of which is you have had less space to feel clear about what you're really needing & wanting because your anxiety has caused you to focus more on the other person, then gathering data about what you want or need is not a process that is accessible or with N.

Dr: What are those feelings?

J: I feel sad a lot. I think a lot about the attachments that are missing right now, the camaraderie, the immediacy of attraction & spontaneity when both partners have energy. Or, sometimes it's the opposite: I'm happy & comfortable with this person, but then I also know that it's the same person who, when he's sad, can't physically hug me back. He just stands there with his arms at his side. Feeling happy but then knowing that there is all this other stuff swirling around it making any easy & comfortable moment more complicated.

Dr: So you're aware in a very clear way of what you need to feel good. But house surrounded by the life we've created together, much of it feels so good & positive. We want the same things for the future, although for a long time he hasn't believed that this future would come to him. But we care about the same friends, we want to write, to pursue academic jobs, to settle down & have kids and so on. But when I step away from that, I'm faced with the lack of camaraderie & the very clear reality that N does not yet know how to rely on anyone else to make himself feel better. He does not have the foundation to trust others to help him, & that's terrifying. And he's just learning how. He never learned those things, which is not his fault, but is also the situation we're both

I would write about anything else if I could think of something other than N.

easy to you. In so far as that's true, in a relationship that's troubled, it could lead you to be quite anxious.

J: I feel like that's true. But when I view this relationship with N, I still feel like I'm very much concerned with how I'm feeling. But...maybe I'm just feeling things incorrectly! Ok, this is what I mean: if you're in a room with someone & you're trying to experience what that feels like, it should be a sense of community or connection, & I feel that community, but at the same time, thinking about how I'm feeling creates a distance. Like I'm no longer in the moment, I'm removed through thinking about my feelings. Does that make sense? I do feel like I spend a lot of time thinking about my feelings maybe part of the trickiness is that you just don't know what to make of this.

J: I might be having trouble with that in terms of the larger context. Part of it is that there are things in our relationship that make me sad but I don't know now how to express them to N because they center on N & where he is with himself, that really can't be rushed. He's working so hard & it's a slow process. But then there is the larger context of where I see/feel this thing & ask myself "what does this mean for our relationship?" I never have an answer. Or when I'm away from N the answer is I should probably get out. But when I'm with him, it seems like there is an immensity to fight for. Proximity, when I'm in the dealing with.

Dr: So why is it when you have distance you seem to feel more clear about what isn't okay about it?

*

Will someone kneed the humming-
bird that despairs the tulip's chalice.
Who in the leaf-lavished air will stick.
Belly-ached into an album. Light lifts
nothing. Forged opacity. Face.

Questions I can't ask: The week of your suicide-deadline, did fucking feel different? Did you think each time that week was the last? When you came home after failing, when we had sex, were you at all glad you'd failed to jump?

That Tuesday, N fingerbangs me in the middle of the day & I think, maybe things are changing. Thursday I walk him into the mental ward.

Remember: He ties a red bandana around our dog's neck. N wrestles with the dog, lets the dog sleep between his legs, in his armpit, on his chest, when all I can do is curl up & read. Watching this playfulness makes me feel sure, warm.

*

Will someone continue the bleached rhythm of sand? Will someone impeach the lighthouse? And if I sink my lilac imitation in night's wool to vase grief? Call. No, call. Moss traps in a necklace clicking at the gate. Flashlight. Canteen. Instructions for temperature. & you, will you incline the lemon shore?

*

Meaning: One Act Play

(N slumps on an orange couch with hands covering face. J runs down outside steps & enters living room.)

J: What's going on?

N: I didn't buy my plane ticket to the conference.

J: Oh, well, that's okay. I bet we can still get you a redeye ticket if we look right now. Is that why you're upset?

N: I mean, I didn't buy a ticket because I didn't think I'd still be alive to attend the conference.

J: What? What do you mean?

*

Faith: Come on my tits. Come in my mouth. Come in my ass. Come on my ass. Come in my hair. Come on my thighs. I am not absent in body. A new batch.

Unfaithful: When I think I wish you had jumped, I mean, this is uncertain, exhausting, I resent that I no longer imagine my own future. Silly halo, the opposite of slander. As if present. I have so much faith in N & so little I can do with it. My glasses like crossed arms in the crevasse of our hand-me-down mattress.

*

Mostly I think of N.

*

Bookshelves sway & N travels on airplanes with me to reduce the fear. He hate flannel, flaneurs, plaid. Anaconda coffee mug stumbling into laundry. Dirty keyboard. Scarf on the bedroom door handle, towel draped above like a Botticelli. The precision of parting wet hair. N wishes for a desk & then an annex to place it in. We don't need a bigger house, just more walls for the books.

Remember: I peel garlic while N prepares my favorite meal. Black metal growls on the warped record player.

Questions I can't ask: why didn't you break up with me when you decided to kill yourself? It seems selfish. Or, what does it mean that you didn't? To fight for hope?

Often I find N reading in the dark, he seems confused when I ask him, should I should flip the light on? We're surrounded by Stein, Zukofsky, Celan. Earphones cramp on the carpet.

*

Therapy Session #7 Continued:

J: Because what I love is immediately in front of me, & I have no distance to think about alternatives.

Dr: What do you make of that?

J: I don't know. The distance also makes it seem less real, like I would be losing less.

Dr: Why would it make less real what you're losing & more real what the bad times are?

J: That's just how it is! I'm not surrounded by the good stuff—ways of living together I can't imagine losing.

Dr: But you're also not surrounded by the bad stuff.

J: That's true. But the sadness is part of the daily life; it's not just something that happens when I'm away traveling. It happens when I'm sitting on a couch with him & watching a movie, knowing that there used to be more of this physical contact I don't get anymore. Feeling like we're talking about our day, but also not...I don't even know, something feels off. Partially shutdown or like we've forgotten how to latch onto each other, to look forward to that.

He's taking care of himself, but at the same time, able to be less present & to give less to me because of the consuming depression, & I'm afraid I'll adjust to this, expect less, and in turn give less myself. So that even when he's in a better emotional place, things will have irrecoverably changed. Despite this unceasing love.

*

Will someone tuck salt in the mailbox? Cursory lilacs. Will someone visit the false river, its spellbound child. A coast widowed into desert. Morning enemy? Take flattery out of response to sweep a face into a face. Descendant stars or marzipan feelings. Pangs, tambourine, rivals kidnap a keyboard to spool your note. Labor? Endemic split ends.

*

Remember: A prisoner, N, the offspring of religion.

*

On the 10th day I am afraid. Of N's release. The social worker asks if our house is empty of pills, alcohol, weapons. Yes, except for beer. I giggle. Maybe some cooking wine? N doesn't know I threw out the noose. Afraid of not knowing how to act with N. Will we have dinner & watch a movie? Which routines are okay & which hide us from each other? N, release to me N.

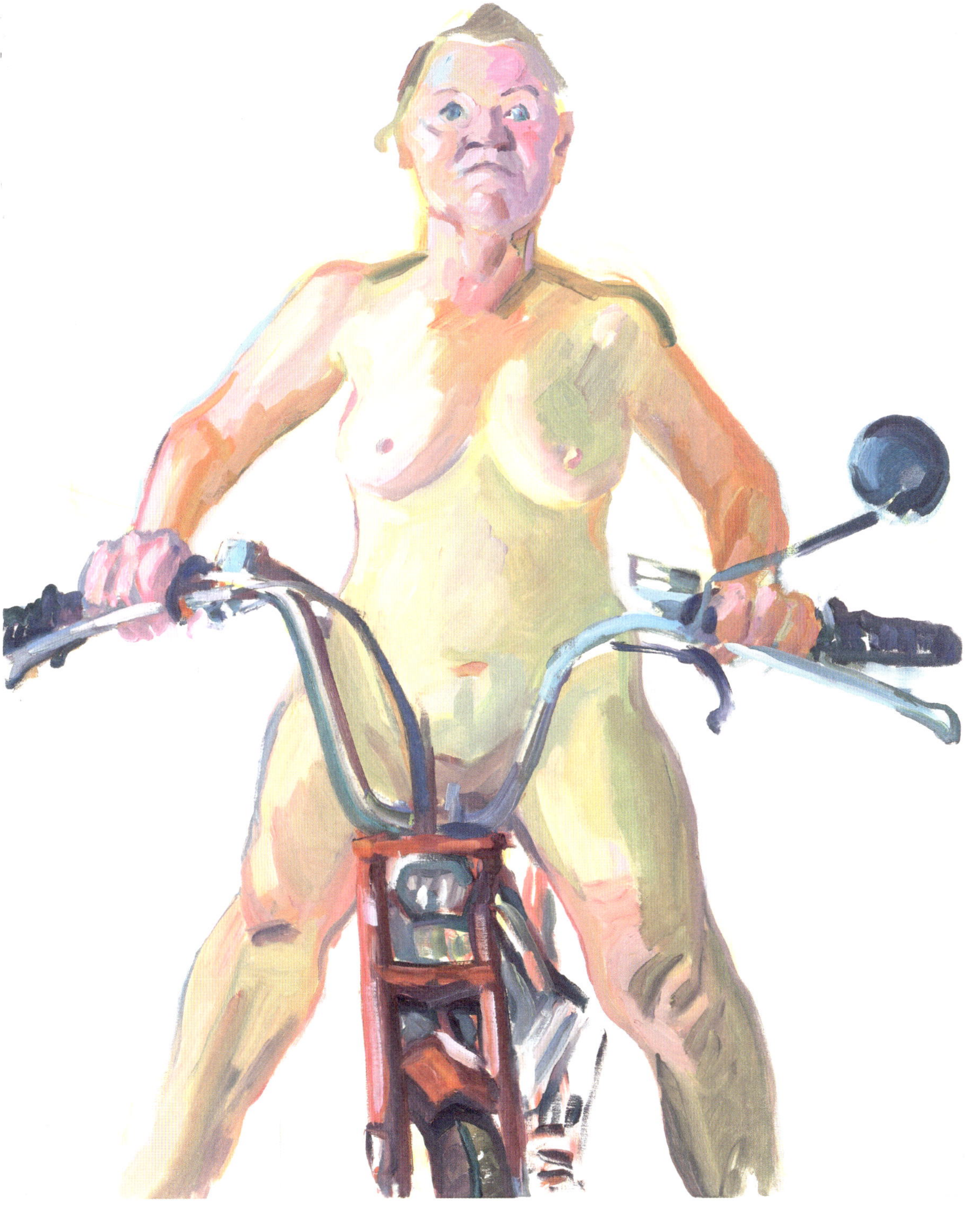

Maria Lassnig / Landmädchen (Country Girl) / 2001

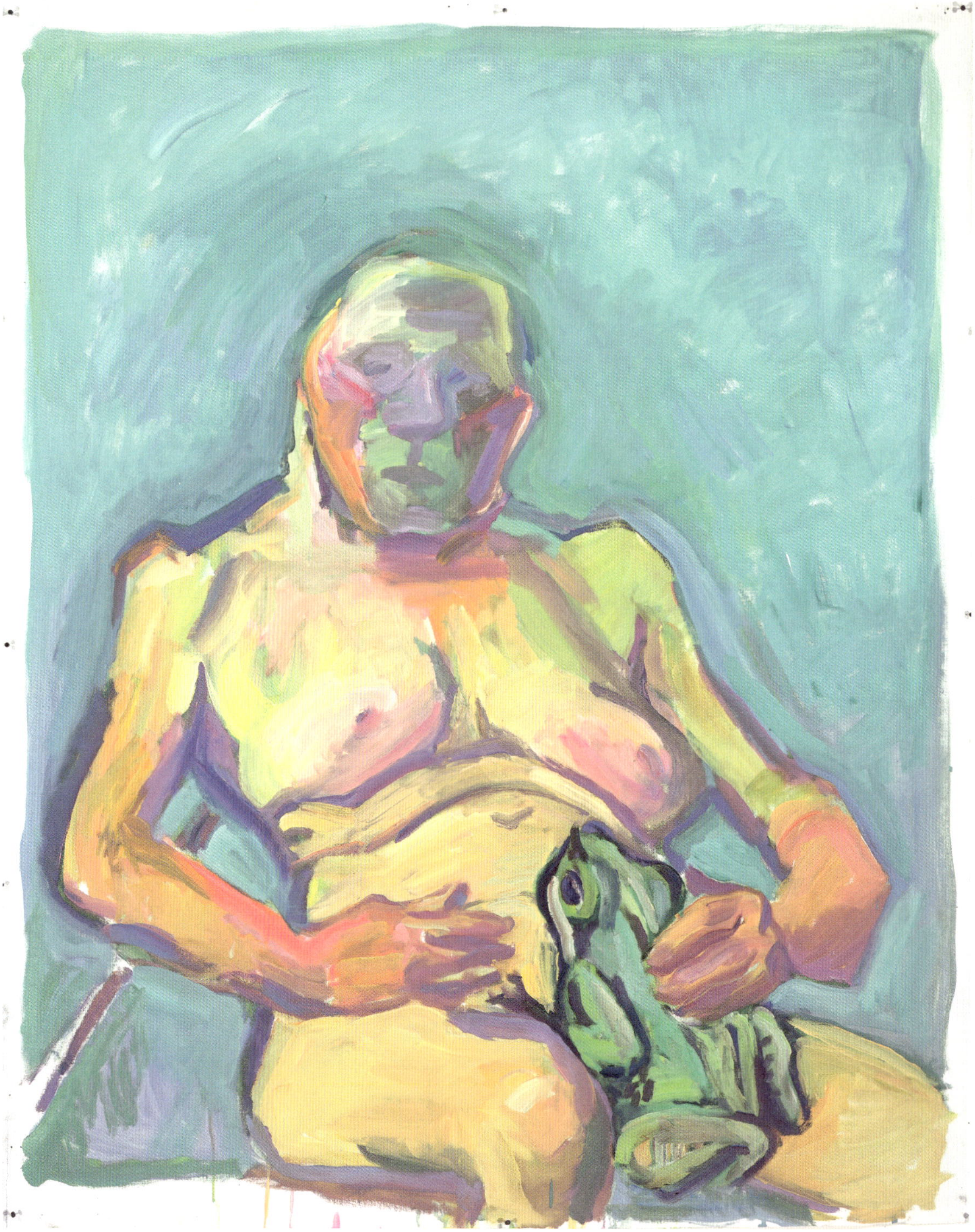

Maria Lassnig / Froschkönigin (Frog Princess) / 2000 / © Maria Lassnig Foundation / Zabludowicz Collection

*

Hush little humming humming hummingbird.

*

I thought to adopt a second dog when my first child could handle the feeding & walking. Now I don't know when that will be. I had thought within the decade. To lose this projection, a hallway full of splintered frames. Familial hologram.

To recover your wallet?
To recover trust?
To uncover a terrified boy looking for after-school snacks in the fridge?
To cover N's naked back when he sleeps?
To recover from Coltrane's A Love Supreme.
To recover alliance?
To recover the carpet, dismantling anthills of clothing.
To recover from a case of The Wine-Dark Seas.

*

Will someone ransack the shelves? Canine assurance, coins, thin leaves.

Remember: N introduces me to H.D. & Deleuze, to riding a bike as an adult, to multiple orgasms, to broccoli rabe sandwiches & homemade sauerkraut.

*

A "no touching" rule at the hospital. Afraid visitors smuggle in drugs or weapons. The nice nurses let N & I hug, touch each other's arms as we play Scrabble. "You can't touch," says the mean nurse, watching us separate before swishing down the corridor. Try not to cry. Rules betray need. Shifts end.

Faith: I stay busy with distant friends & packages. Fill glass vials with white beans, maroon ribbon, miniature books, a red tricycle. Cork. Bike to the post office. Only service dogs allowed inside.

Unfaithful: N asks me to scrape out the bowls & plates more thoroughly before stashing them in the sink. To prevent drain-clogging. In return I think, I had to throw out your noose. Of course we don't want to clog our drains with oatmeal & black-eyed peas.

N's shrink calls me back. Question medications. 10 months & I doubt his nurse practitioner who dubs N "treatment resistant." What could that mean? Higher dose? A different kind? Prescription bottles line the butcher-block like rooks, I sponge around them, toss out lost cashews. I say to his shrink, this is the only life he has. I used to say this about myself, detached from meds, as in, atheism, as in, don't laze.

*

Questions I can't ask: Which parking garage were you trying to jump from? Why where you listening to Coltrane, to convince you to jump or to convince you to stay? Did you say goodbye to our dog? How could I be better off without you? What did you think would happen to me?

*

Remember: N tenderly soaps my armpits in the shower.

*

A bowl of coins lunges for the sun & an unseen squirrel steals tomatoes. Do I live the way I read? The you's face blurs, a sandcastle blown into the sea by a greedy umbrella. A bellow. Will someone clutch the outside lung? To hum into a bird's belly.

*

Therapy Session #7 Continued:

Dr: This may come across as pessimistic but maybe also useful: maybe when you're in the relationship, in the moment—& it's often this way for many of us—uncomfortable to be in full contact with what isn't okay. It creates a sense of dissonance that prevents us from fully understanding what isn't okay. When we have distance, it can be easier.

J: Right. Yeah.

Dr: What do you think about that?

J: I think that's part of the push & pull of how I'm feeling. I know all the concerns I have are more than the limit, but...

Dr: You said you're sad a lot of the time and that there are pieces that are missing, & that an aspect that's missing terrifies you.

J: But that aspect is also something that could theoretically be learned, which N is trying to learn. I think that's also what makes this so complicated: it's not like I'm in a relationship with someone who isn't aware of these things & who isn't trying to change. ALL of what he's trying to do is learn & change. My faith in him.

Dr: Yes. When you start to feel upset about certain pieces of the relationship that are missing, when you say to yourself, "he's working on these things," does it sit well with you? Or is it a kind of rationalization that has to do with moving away from what.... is that what we were talking about earlier, about having the "incorrect feelings" & feeling guilty.

J: It's more that I can see him trying to change. I feel very sympathetic to this hard endeavor he's undertaking. It's exhausting for him, battling his history, his learned behavior, his daily suicidal thoughts. I don't feel like I'm using it as a device to keep myself optimistic or in this relationship. I genuinely believe he can make these changes. It's the timeframe—I know these changes will take a long time, & in the interim, it's really, really hard. For him, for me. I would need to either figure out a way to not be sad for the next five years or not to be accidentally collateral...I don't know.

Dr: Maybe part of the problem is that one never knows what someone else or even oneself will be like in five years. How far does that person have to move to be that person & what does that person mean to you, & how far would that take under ideal circumstances—five years is one figure, one year is another, thirty years is another.
J: Yes, ten is another.
Dr: The fantasy of that person—it's a fantasy in that the person does not exist right now—who, really, that person is in the fantasy is something we need to get more clear about. In time it will be clearer whether this fantasy will become available to you.
J: Fantasy N.
Dr: Yes.
*
Ace Hardware also sells almonds & faucets.

Is there joy between us?

Remember: we play air-swim. N on the bed, holding my body naked & above, his hands levitate me as I pretend to swim, stroking the bedroom air. Sidestroke, breaststroke, I dive into his dry chest. Skinnydip. Our dog barks at my ankles, trying to drag me to shore.
*
Faithful: This non-responsiveness, these three minute summaries of our days, this reading & grading in separate rooms, this avoidance of Feelings & Things Time, this automatic switching on of a movie as soon as dinner's served, I try not to take personally. Try not to see myself boring, flat, devoid, a receipt, a resurrection fern. Brittle.

Unfaithful: Drink coffee, check my email at Dazbog & then slyly cruise Craigslist for studios. I don't want to lose the library. To lose what I have faith in. I don't want lose-lose. That I write this, afraid to leave the document open on my computer? To feel a necessary secrecy.

Faithful: To believe the opposite of what N believes about himself: not a failure, not unfixable. To not wish for recovery, instead, to quietly wish N could accept his changes, these shiftings: how he can be sad in front of me, to unravel in the room, he lets me touch his leg. This, a new kind of uncovering.

Un/faithful:
J: I love you
but what are we doing?
N:
*
Will someone slap the light with mossy cheeks. A cut-up star. Reconcile to grief's thistled frock. Will someone hum when eating. The beehive waxes around a dog's bark. Will someone on the caved-in couch elect a broken feeling. Boxcutters. To leave the gift intact. Oh the baby's over there.

Maria Lassnig's Body Awareness

Raw, honest, angry, vulnerable, fearless – these are all words that suit the riveting paintings of Maria Lassnig, a prolific artist who passed away last year at the age of 94, and whose career spanned more than 70 years. Credited with influencing contemporary artists including Amy Sillman, Dana Schutz and Thomas Schütte, Lassnig does not create beautiful paintings for beautiful paintings' sake—though she does, unquestionably, create beautiful paintings. What she achieves with her work is to take the viewer by the throat and force them to look closer at what is going on in her psyche.

In an age where Instagram has made self-portraiture commonplace and often vapid, Lassnig's paintings, by contrast, appear more arresting than ever. The majority of her work features herself as subject (even those from her student days in Vienna, where she was expected to paint in the Nazi sanctioned style of academic realism), but instead of simply exhibiting herself, Lassnig portrayed her body not as it looked but as it felt at the moment of the painting's inception, in an approach she coined "body awareness." In her review of Lassnig's 2014 retrospective at MoMA PS1, Karen Rosenberg of *The New York Times* said "She paints in an exuberant, expressive style, unleashing gestural energy on the canvas while remaining carefully attuned to the action inside her brain and under her skin."

Just take her "Selbstporträt unter Plastik (Self-Portrait Under Plastic)" (1972), in which Lassnig uses thick strokes of pinks, blues and greens to render a woman trapped in her body and mind. Or Woman Laokoon (Woman Laocoon) (1976), in which a snake takes a bite out of Lassnig's body as she looks away from the viewer, an ambiguous expression – pain or ecstasy? – on her face. Lassnig's work became more aggressive toward the end of her life, likely as a response to her body beginning to fail her. Perhaps her most gripping work is "Du oder Ich (You or Me)" (2005), which greeted visitors to the MoMA PS1 retrospective. Lassnig paints herself with her legs spread wide, one gun pointed at her own head and the other at the viewer. It's almost as if she's saying, "Just try me." Those who take Lassnig up on her offer are rewarded with beautiful paintings which force us to reexamine our own selves.

-Rachel Kash

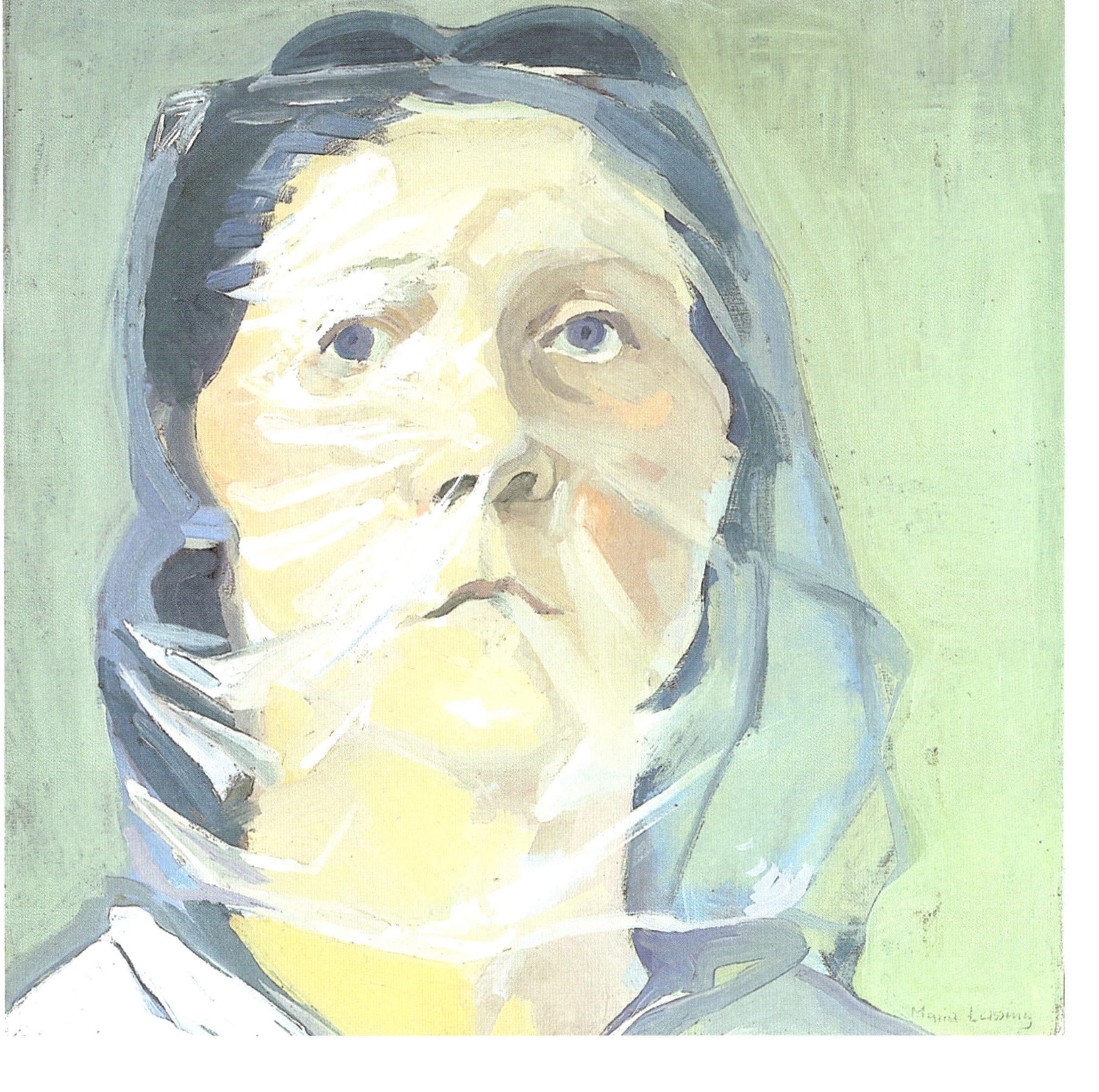

Maria Lassnig / Selbstporträt unter Plastik (Self-Portrait Under Plastic) / 1972
© Maria Lassnig Foundation / Collection de Bruin-Heijn

EXAMINATION

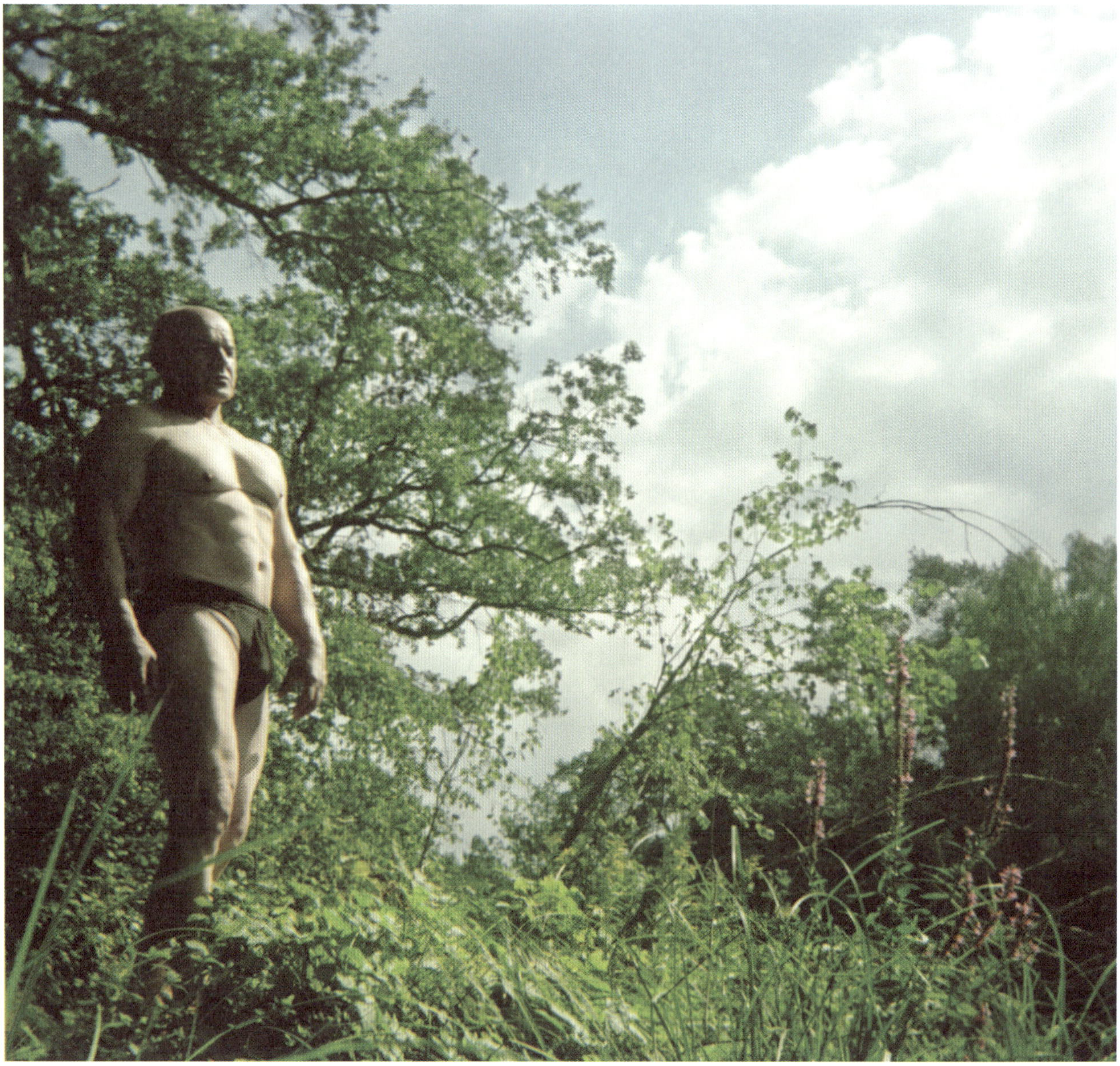

Aneta Bartos / Zeus: Dad Series / 2013

FATHER FIGURE

Aneta Bartos reveals her dad, the strongman

A close-up of bulging thigh muscles intersected by a high-cut black Speedo is not the first image that comes to mind when picturing an aging man, much less a 70-year-old father from small-town Poland. Therein lies the powerfully unexpected visual juxtaposition in Dad, a portrait series by NYC-based artist Aneta Bartos, featuring photographs of her body-builder father, Zbigniew Bartos.

Shot with a Kodak Instamatic camera and long-expired film, Mr. Bartos's chiseled figure stands out against the sun-blurred haze of Polish farm country, like a Greek statue dropped in the middle of a pastoral dream world. The idea for the series originated when Mr. Bartos asked Aneta to photograph his body while he was still in relatively good shape. Aneta eagerly agreed and later decided to develop a whole project around him, embracing the opportunity to document her father's impressive physique.

The final collection of photographs in Dad represents a mesmerizing study in contrasts. Mr. Bartos's tangible, fatherly vulnerability weighs softly against the sharp outlines of his imposing biceps. Attention is drawn to a flash of sunlight across a rippling abdomen or the framing of a distant, imposing silhouette within a border of lush greenery. Similarly, the series' nostalgically wholesome "family album" aesthetic offsets the titillation of his physical exhibition.

Aneta's intimate rapport with her father allowed her to photograph him in various states of undress without any self-consciousness on either end. She remarks, "Even though I grew up in a Catholic society, which made you constantly feel shameful about your body, my parents seemed to be disconnected from this rigorous mentality." In Dad, Mr. Bartos's extraordinary musculature is depicted as a source of pride, worthy of admiration. He poses and flexes with graceful confidence, embodying the ideal of a gentle giant.

Both of Aneta's parents remained open and unashamed about their bodies throughout her youth. Aneta reminisces fondly, "In our house my dad was always lounging around in his tiny speedos while my mom laid out topless in the garden... It was natural and fun with a great sense of adventure and playfulness, and it never felt like anything sexual or inappropriate." This positive perspective on the body as natural—never shameful—is evident in Aneta's photography.

But as much as Dad is an homage to Mr. Bartos's physique, it is also a poignant celebration of Aneta's close bond with her father. Aneta recalls how a childhood friend jokingly asked if she could imagine any other dad running around the forest in a G-string for his daughter. Aneta admits affectionately, "I honestly couldn't."

-Harling Ross

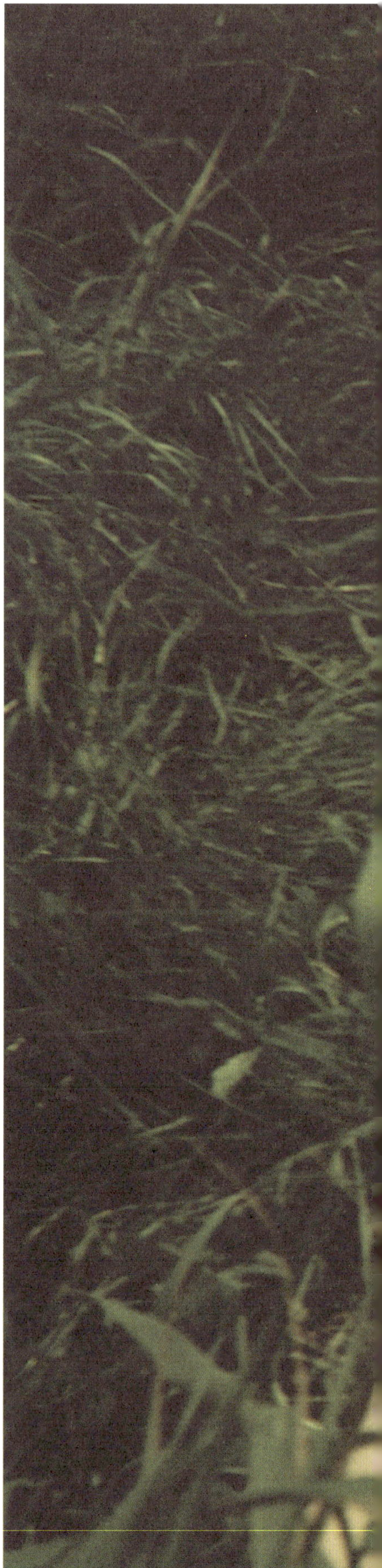

Aneta Bartos / Legs: Dad Series / 2013

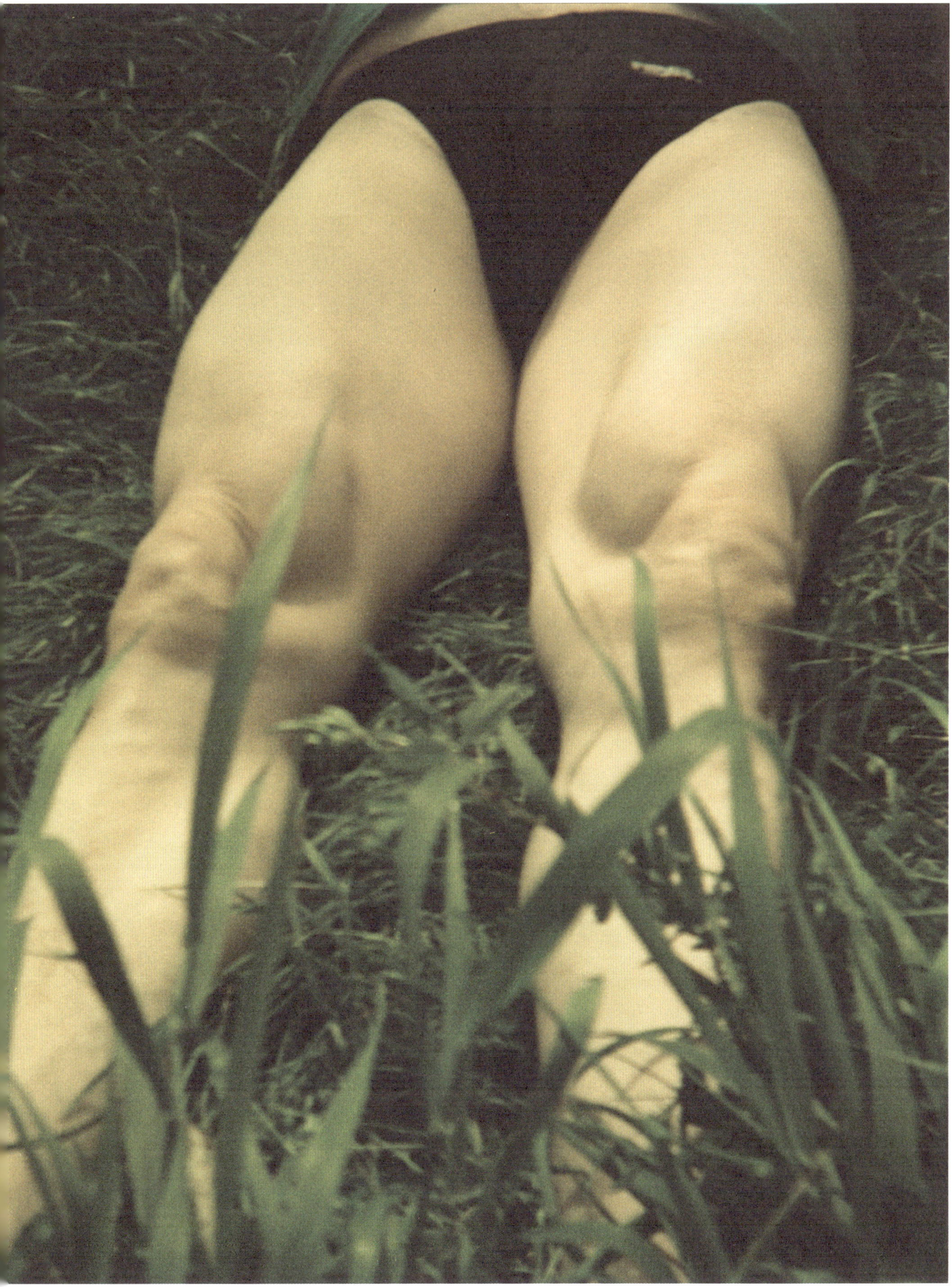

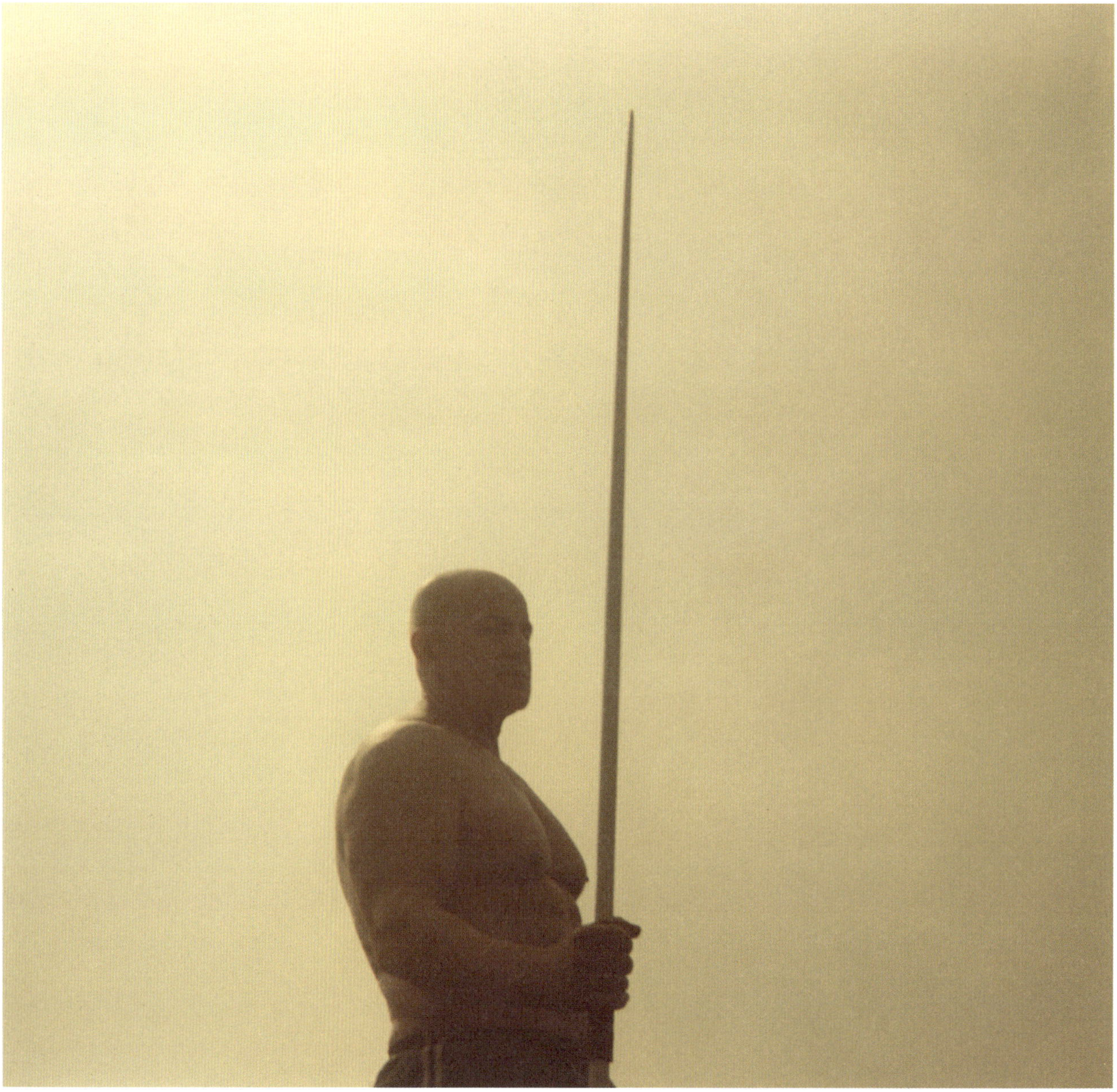

Aneta Bartos / Warrior: Dad Series / 2013

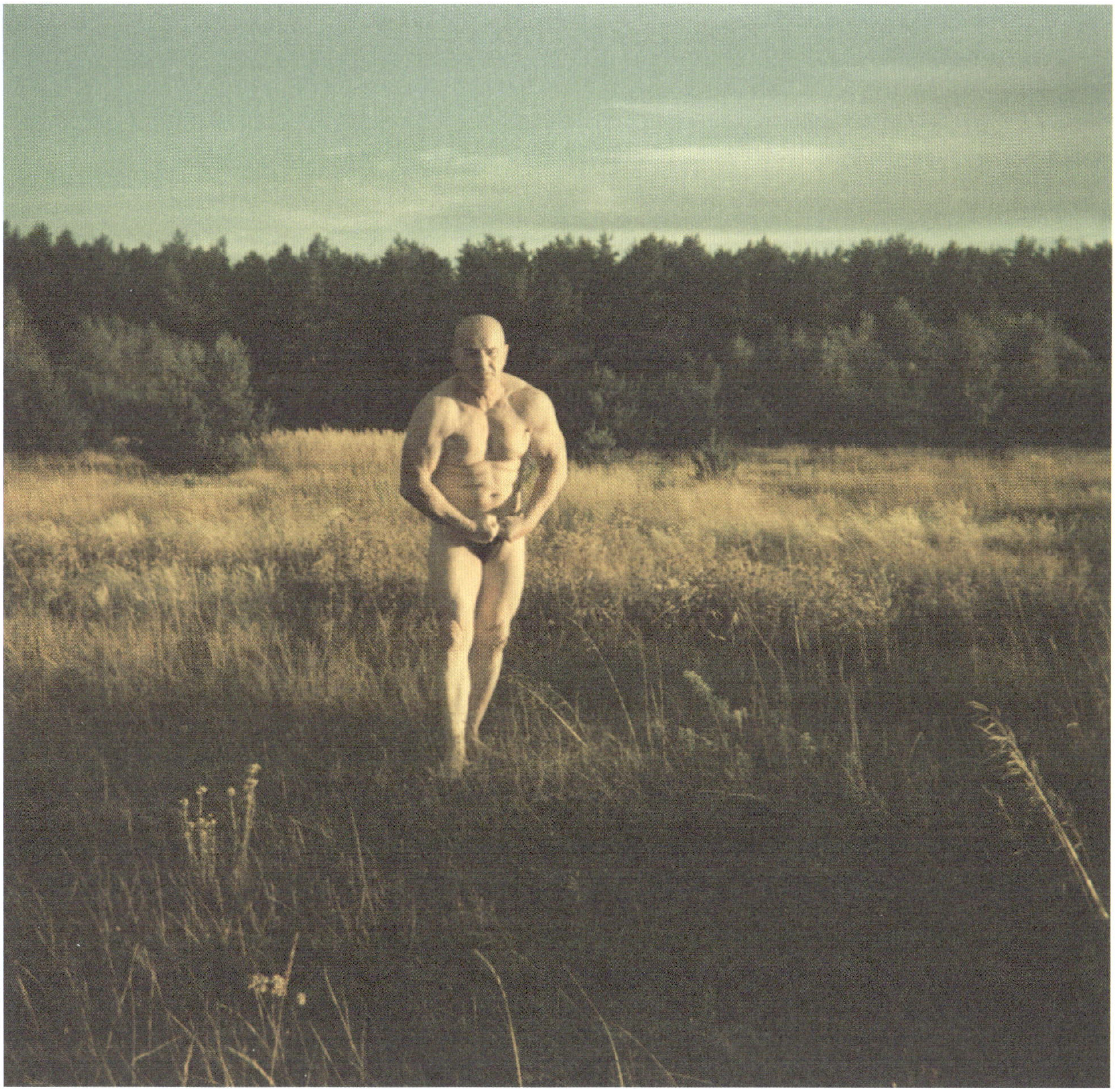

Aneta Bartos / Bronson: Dad Series / 2013

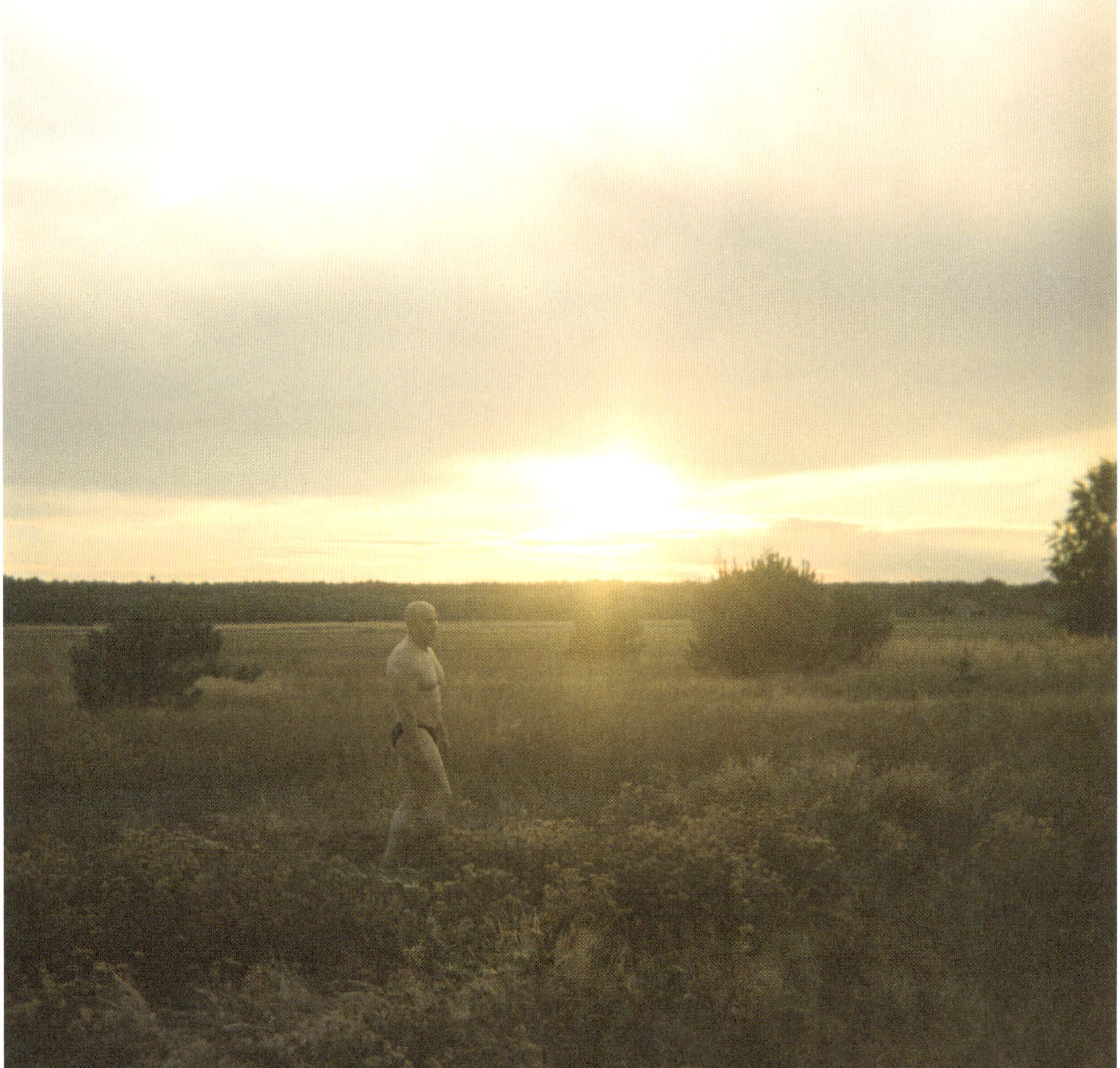

Aneta Bartos / Homo Sapien: Dad Series / 2013

HUMAN EXPLORER

Benjamin Frederickson photographs his community of strangers

At one time I had a fear of rejection. Social situations were difficult for me to navigate in a healthy way, especially when surrounded by people I didn't know. Once I discovered internet hook-up sites such as Adam4Adam, Craigslist, and Manhunt, my outlook on social interactions changed. These sites offered a new way of meeting strangers. Connecting through a computer screen helped to dissolve the feeling of isolation. On this journey I was lucky enough to interact with a diverse community of queer men. I first began documenting my encounters in Minnesota, and later, in New York.

Gradually my portraits began to include friends, and acquaintances; I received an email from Brian, he had seen my work online and wanted to meet in person. We met at the Wyndham New Yorker hotel in Midtown Manhattan. During our brief encounter, Brian shared stories about growing up in Boston with his mother, and the hospital that he worked at. The sexual tension was strong by the time I started to photograph him sitting nude on the bed.

The portrait of Drew was made in his bedroom in Northeast Minneapolis. The intimacy that we shared came from our mutual love for horror movies and thrift stores. I was drawn to his pleasant demeanor, photogenic face, and the story about how his boyfriend had punched him in his eye when they were both asleep. We remain connected through the internet.

The second time that I photographed Corey was in the bathroom of an E-Cigarette store in Minneapolis. I was back in town visiting and wanted to re-photograph people that I had originally photographed when I lived there. Corey looked just as angelic, and much more confident, than the first time. Our most intimate moments together were when he would take off his clothes and let me photograph him.

I've met a lot of people through Adam4Adam over the years. Many just come and go, Evan was an exception and unexpected surprise. When we met he was a photography student at Rochester Institute of Technology. His physical beauty paired with his passion for photography made the experience of photographing him fun and pleasurable. Since this first portrait was made, I've continued to shoot Evan once a year.

These are portraits of people I wanted to get to know. With some of them I was lucky enough to do just that, while others became intimate ghosts. The internet provided me with the source material, as well as a platform to share my journey. Using a camera, I became a human explorer and in the process I discovered my own vulnerabilities and my sexuality, along with a sense of community. Today the initial feeling of isolation no longer remains, instead it has been replaced with the confidence in creating the next portrait.

-Benjamin Fredrickson

Opposite Page: Brian, 2013. All images courtesy of Benjamin Fredrickson and Daniel Cooney Fine Art, New York.

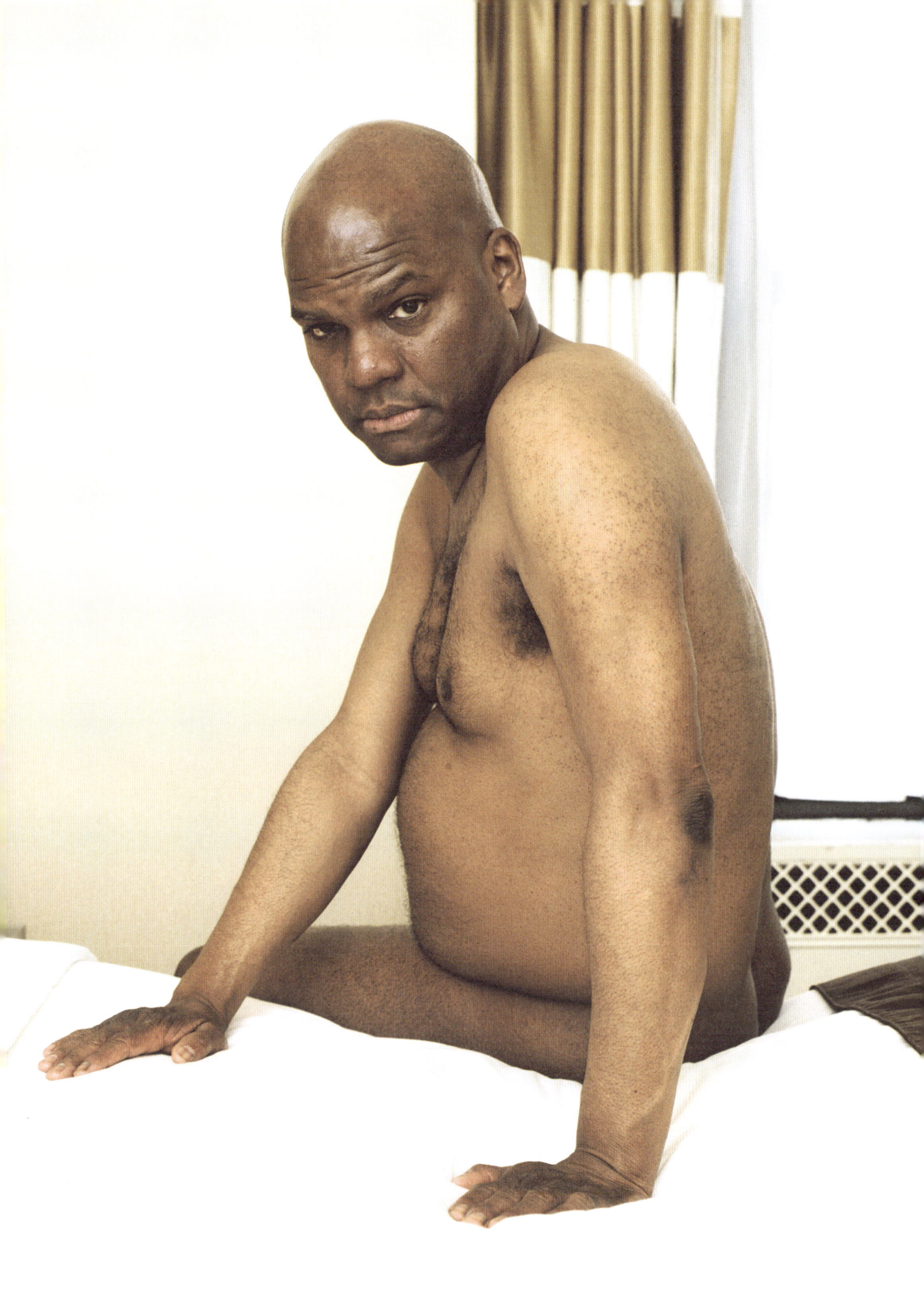

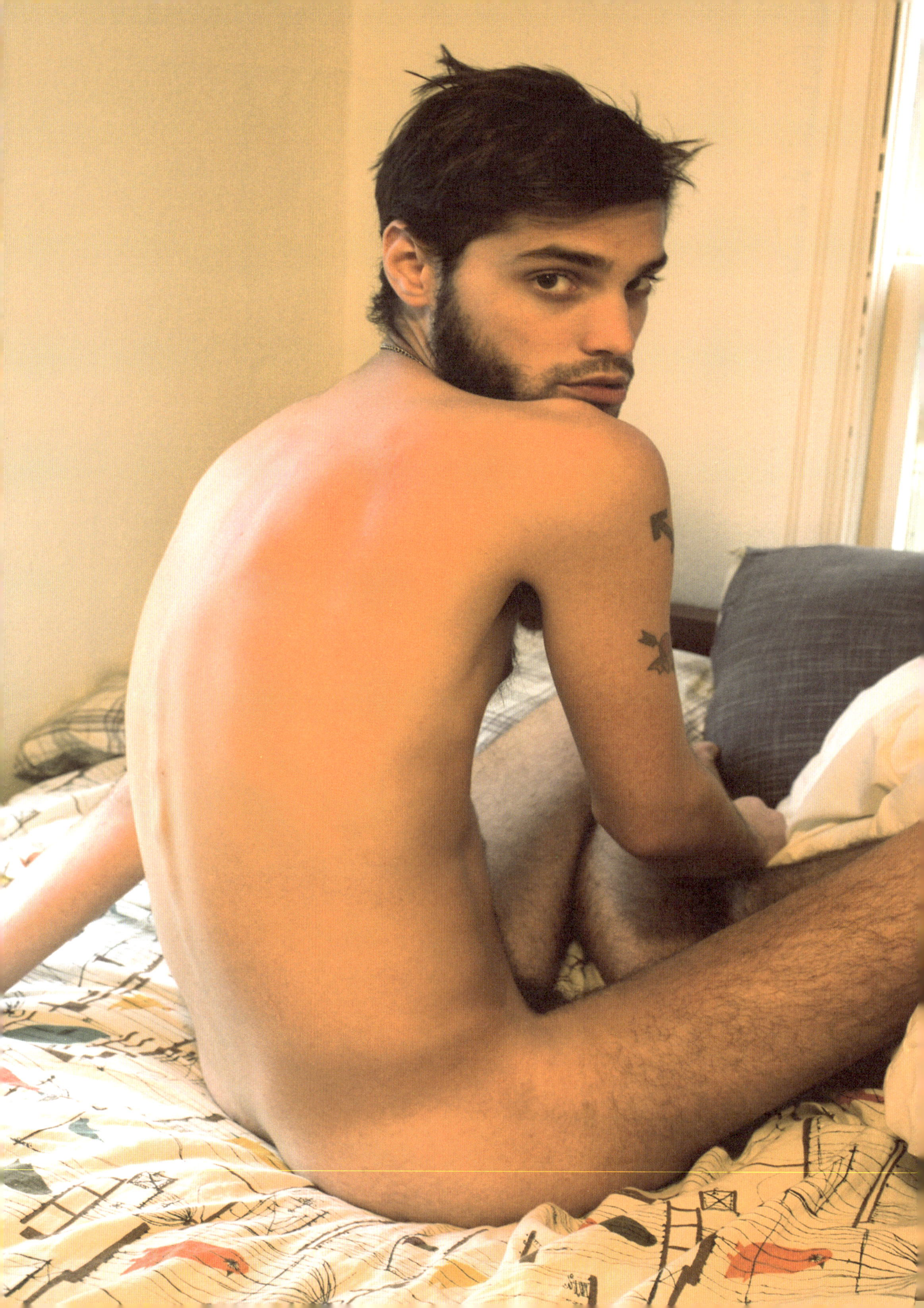

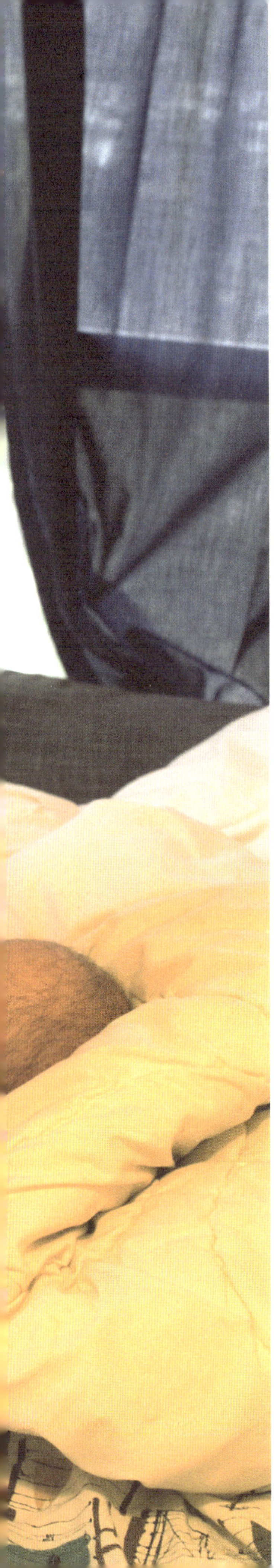

Benjamin Fredrickson / Drew / 2009

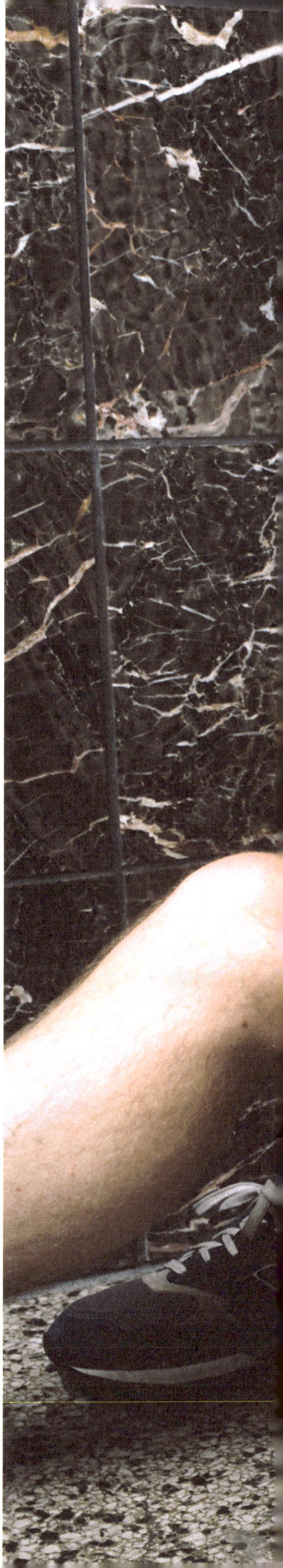

Benjamin Fredrickson / Corey / 2013

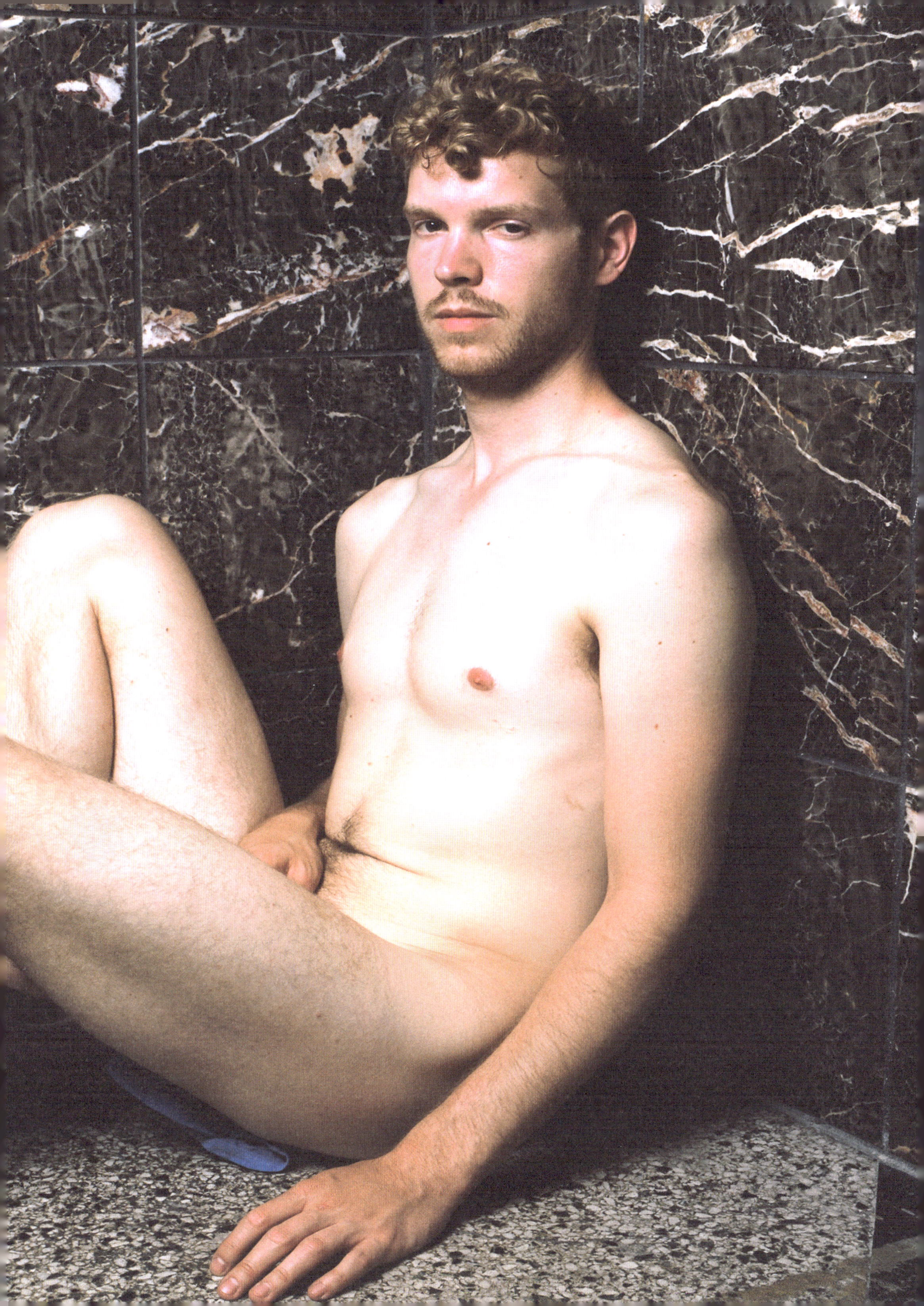

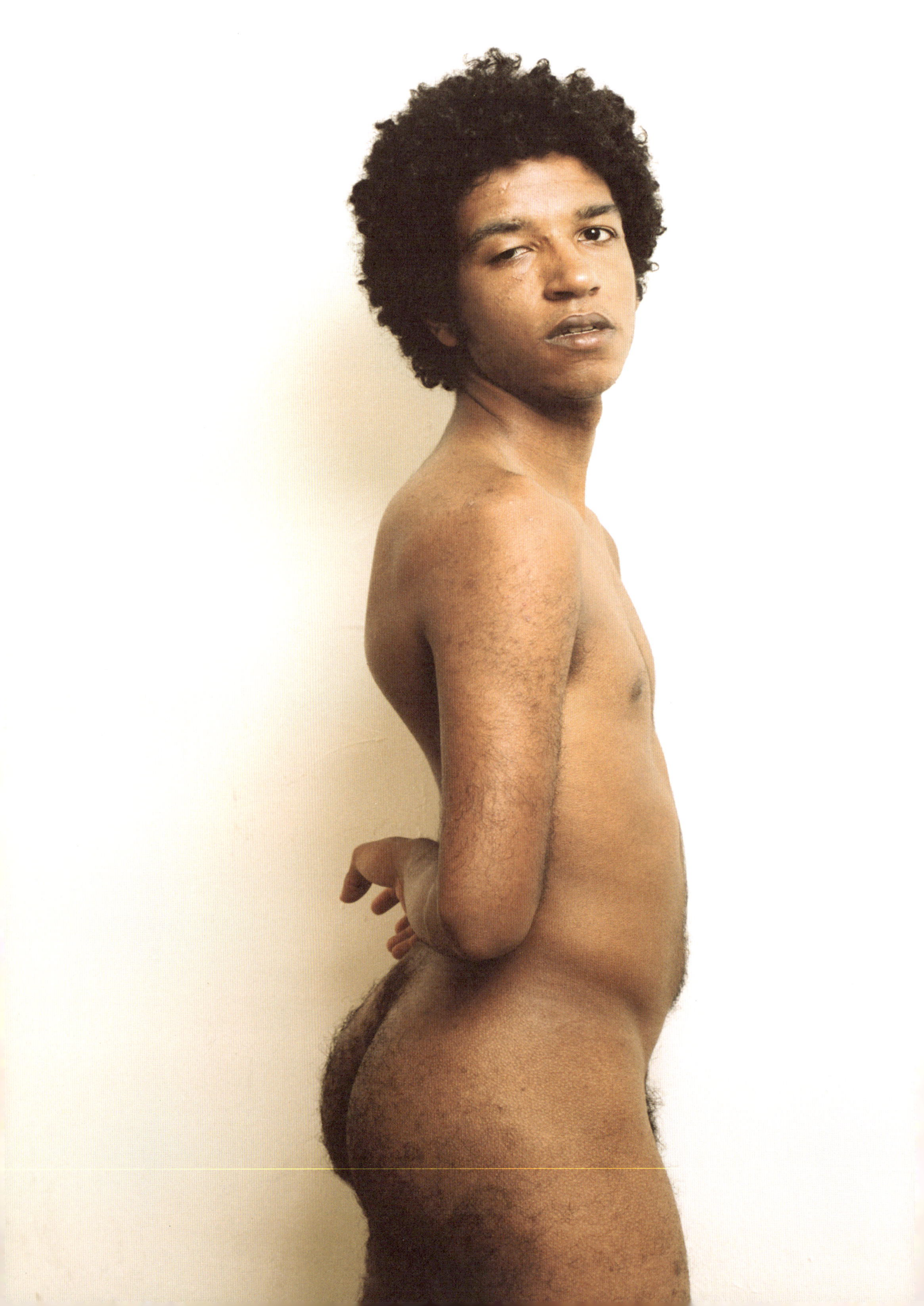

Benjamin Fredrickson / Evan / 2012

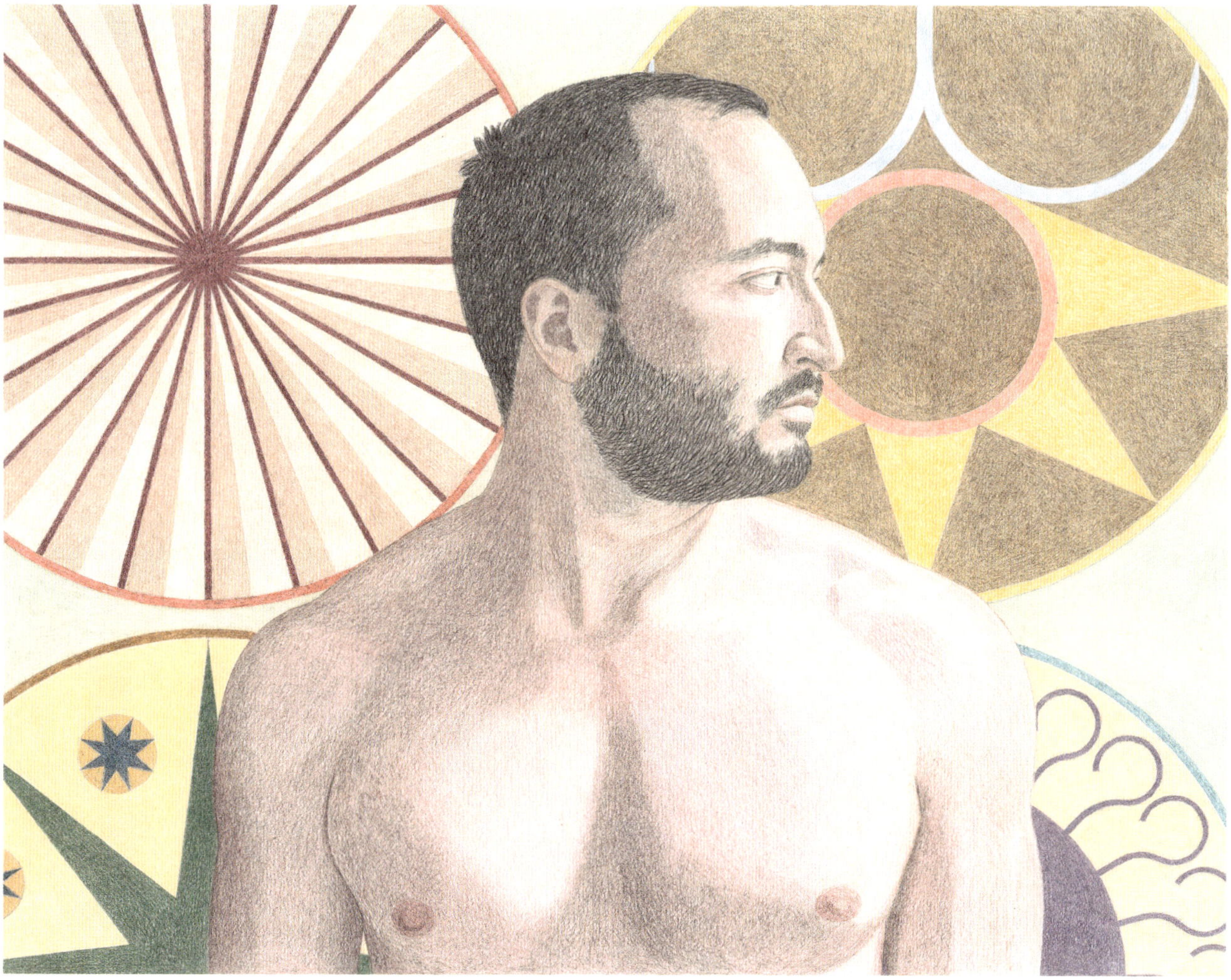

Bachelor with solar-anal emblems (Jonathan) / 2015 / Colored pencil on paper / 19x24"

SIGNS & WONDERS

Elijah Burgher's drawings invoke magic and desire

All images courtesy of Elijah Burgher and Zieher Smith & Horton. Photos: Mark-Woods.com

I first came to know of Elijah Burgher's art during a period in my life when several, now very prominent influences, began to tug at me, wistfully leading me down a path of small revelations. Burgher might say that these were signs, portents of fated things to come. Chief among them, my discovery of the Bay Area poet Robert Duncan, a visionary who tapped into the subversive currents of Beat Era San Francisco, while also channeling something far deeper, more acutely mystical. Duncan was the John Dee of Haight Street and his incantations of sex, magic, and the collocation of male desire with taboo were made manifest in piercing lyrical form. At a time when homosexuality was still "a love that dare not speak its name," Duncan created his own language to summon it.

It's not surprising then that Burgher, whose intricate color pencil portraits of men—usually naked—and his large canvas banners, dense with abstracted occultist symbols known as "sigils," would come to my attention at the same time. In Burgher's works, which draw upon a heady confluence of esoteric practices and a bent for the sublimated eroticism of male desire, I found a thread leading back to Duncan. And, as the magus-cum-poet had in his own lifetime created a circle of lovers and friends bound by their amatory and spiritual yearning, so too has Burgher with his "Bachelors of the Dawn," a fictitious cult of men for whom the bachelor is its archetype.

As with his 2015 series of portraits, "Bachelors," Burgher incorporates elements in his drawings that continue to evince his interest in the linkage between sexuality and Hermetic traditions. In Bachelor with solar-anal emblems (Jonathan), the profile of a bearded man is set against a backdrop of circular discs evocative of stellar forms and erogenous apertures, while in Bachelor (Paul), a naked young man grasps a cylindrical staff, bordered on both sides by vertical banners decorated with sigils. Indeed, Burgher's use of the sigil is a recurrent and elemental aspect in most of his works. Graphic forms produced through the abstraction and recombination of letters derived from existing texts —often spells and incantations—Burgher deploys the sigil as a means to subvert linguistic signification in favor of his own, cleaving expressions of sexuality from connotations levied upon them by cultural expectation. Love abstracted is, in many ways, love unbound.

In another of Burgher's drawings from the series, Bachelor (Anthony), a handsome naked man, gazing off into the horizon, stands in front of a banner of sigils. As my eyes wander over the fit body, taking in the broad chest and toned arms, noting — with a frisson—a dash of chest hair, a verse from Duncan's poem, "The Torso," seems fitting for Burger, too. "I have been waiting for you, he said: / I know what you desire / you do not yet know / but through me."

-Joseph Akel

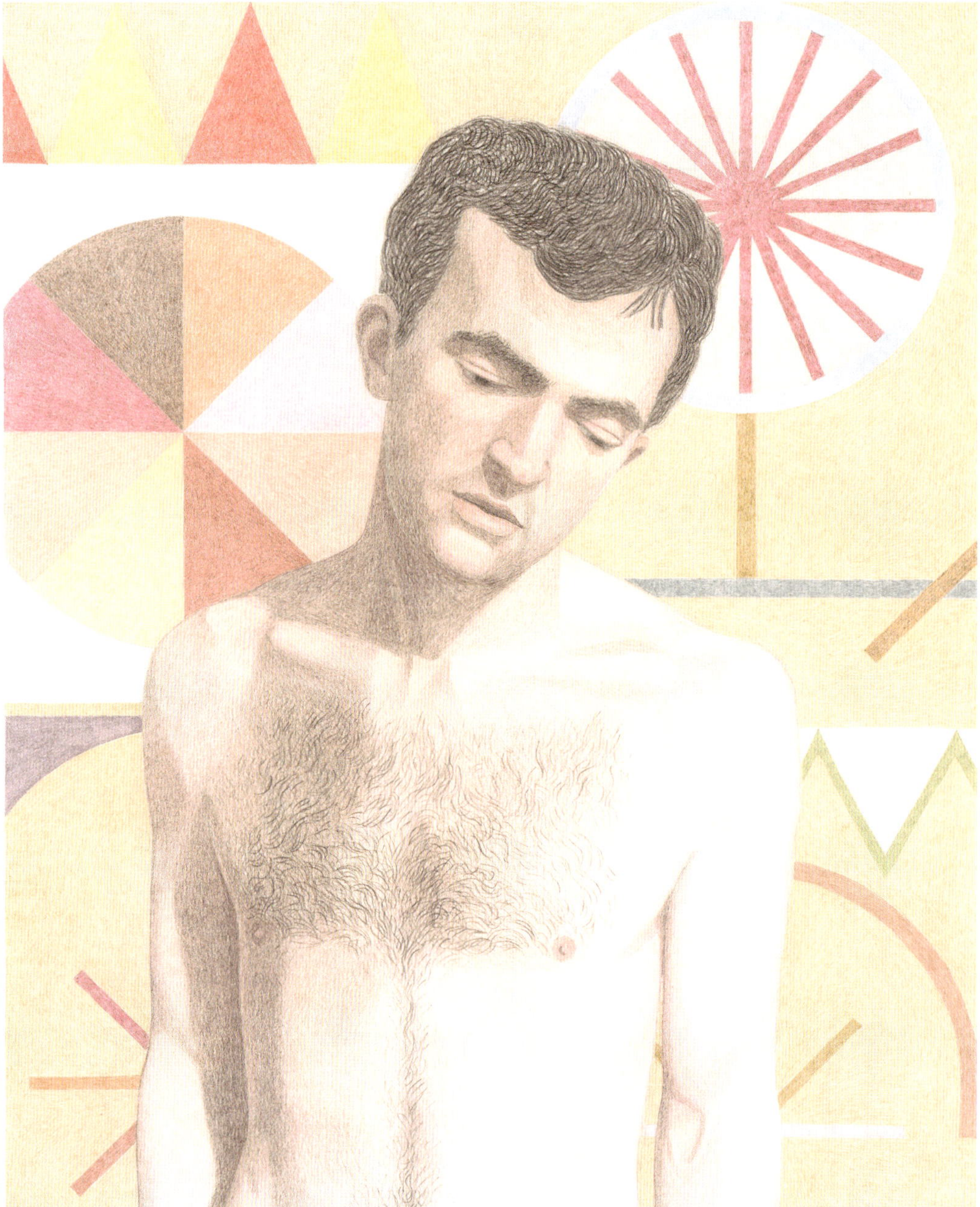

Bachelor with "demons" (Sleezy) / 2015 / Colored pencil on paper / 24x19"

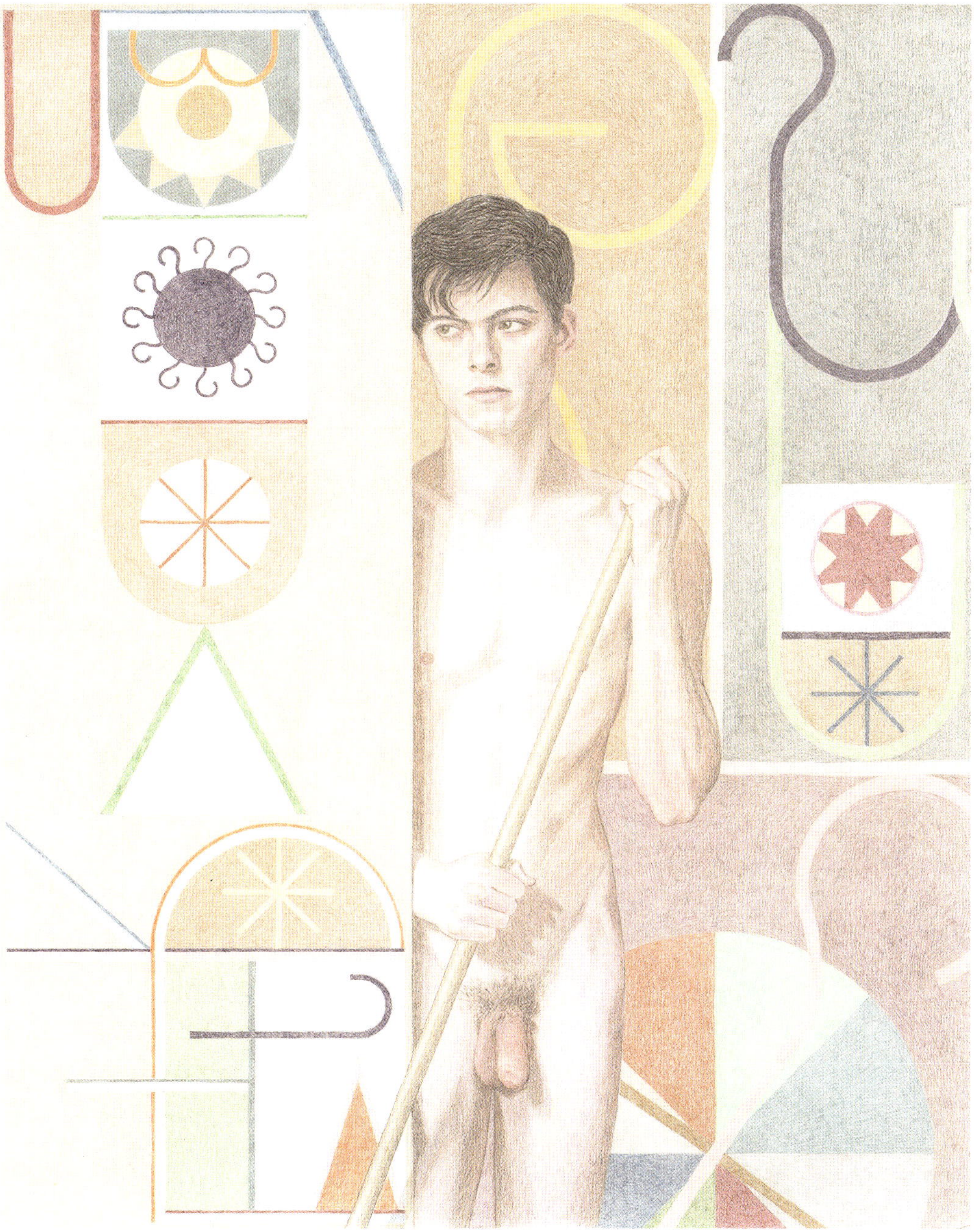

Bachelor (Paul) / 2015 / Colored pencil on paper / 24x19"

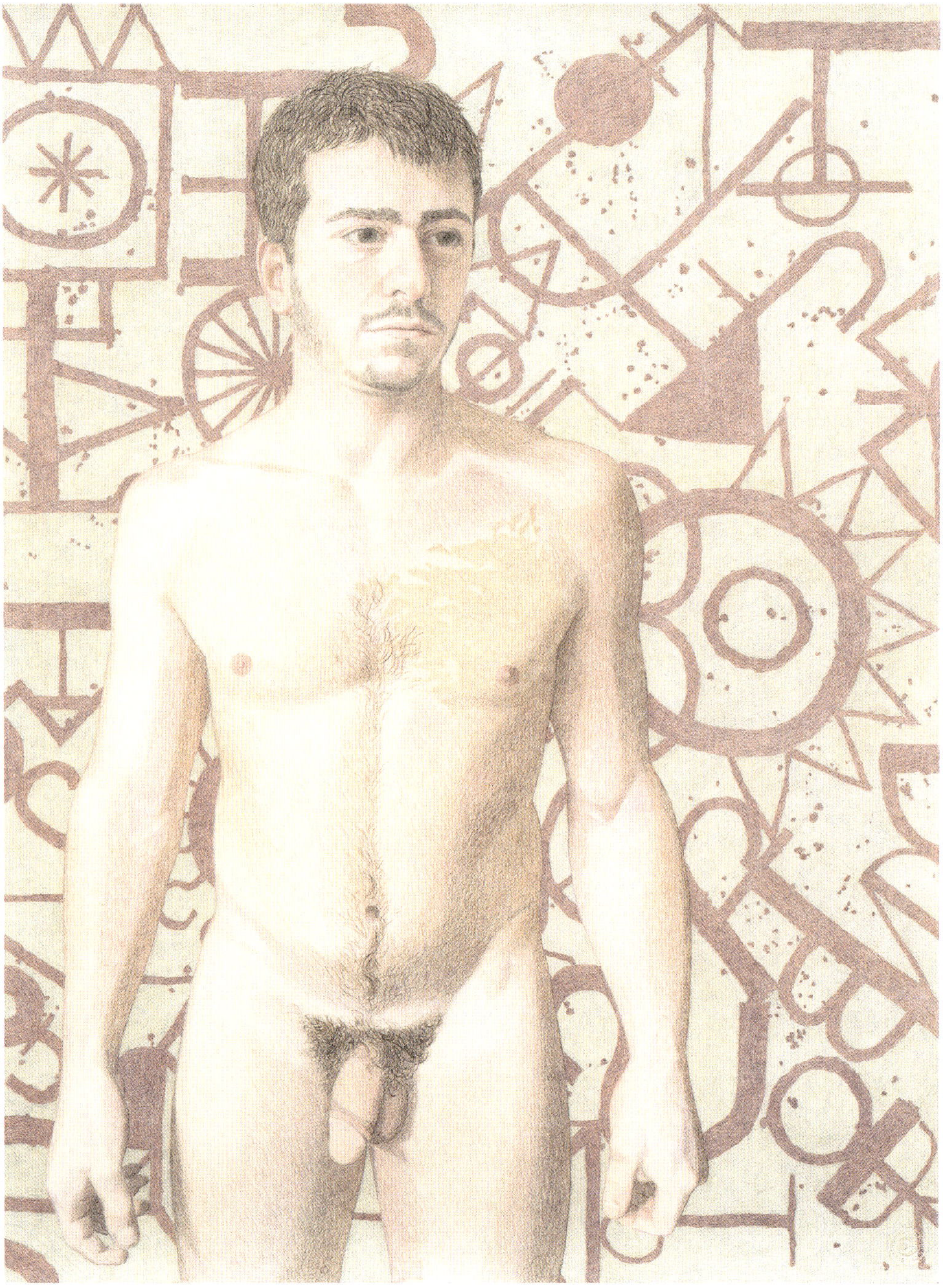

Bachelor (Anthony) / 2015 / Colored pencil on paper / 30x22"

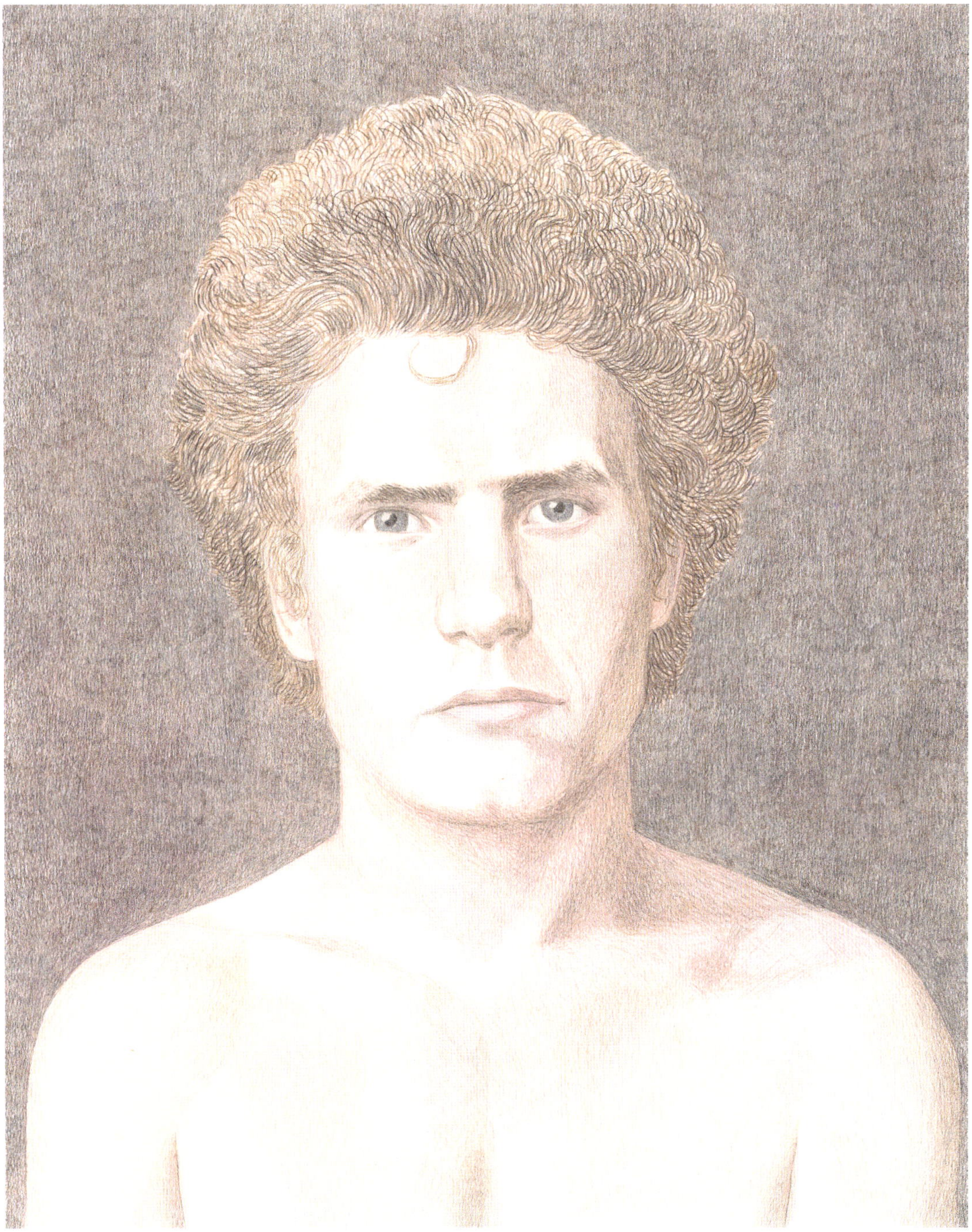

AOS / 2015 / Colored pencil on paper / 24x19"

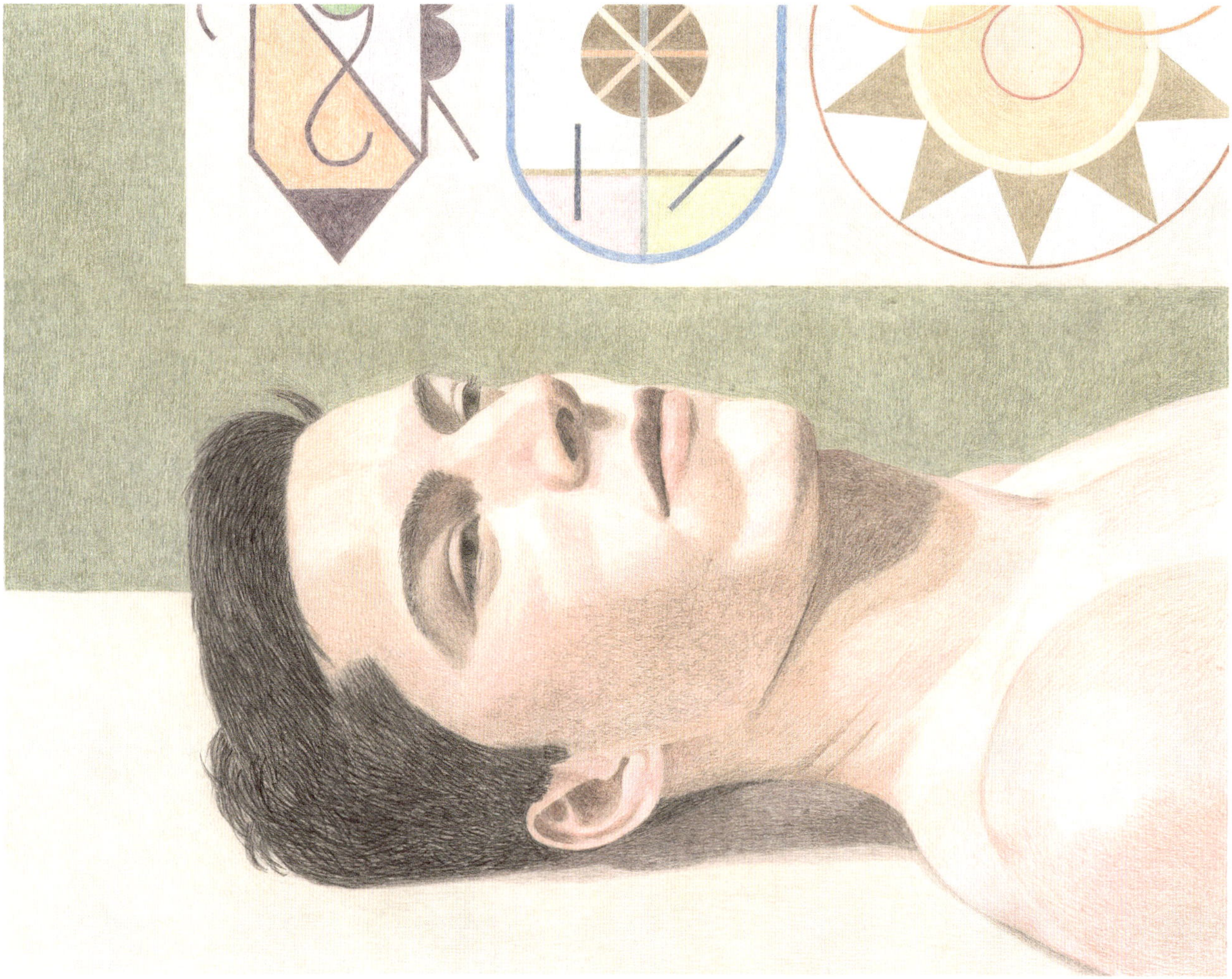

Bachelor (Paul, prone) / 2015 / Colored pencil on paper / 19x24"

REAL FAKE

Robert Heinecken strikes a pose

All images courtesy of the artist and Petzel, New York.

"Subjects" are, of course, those selected and fretted upon by one esteemed artist. But subjects are also those under another's dominion and control. In his series *Lessons for Posing Subjects*, American artist Robert Heinecken (1931–2006) waggishly challenges both definitions. The subjects pictured were never, in fact, modeling for Heinecken. Rather, the images were chosen and lifted by the artist from the annals of commercial portraiture—Heinecken, self-proclaimed "para-photographer" for his frequent lack of actual camera usage, effectively paratrooping these poses from musty oblivion.

From the start, the series's generic title raises the question of whether these "lessons" are intended for the subjects posing or for the photographer posing her subjects, or, in the spirit of upending traditional artist-subject power relations, both. Heinecken's pedantic directives further assume an ironic distance between text and image. As the "one rule" for posing in a teddy, or posing a woman wearing one, is to "tilt the angle of the head to the... right by approximately 15 to 20 degrees," the mutinous left-tilting teddy-donner leaves "an inappropriate projection of tenseness"—as though one wearing said see-through teddy were first and foremost concerned about propriety.

In "Matching Facial Expressions," we are asked to pair the assorted visages of a male and female model—posing solo—with the expressions to which they correspond when the two are paired together. What results is a cheeky seek-and-find, wherein the similarities of these so-called expressions are wryly exposed—the fact that the models can instantly reproduce the same "face" proves surprisingly impressive, if unsettling, insofar as revealing the fact that these "expressions" effectively express nothing at all.

Heinecken's accompanying text, or "lesson," concludes that "[w]hen all ten facial expressions are correctly matched, it is possible to imagine 100 new striking combinations of male/female facial expressions connoting a wide variety of interpersonal relationships." The idea that any natural relationship is connoted, interpersonal or otherwise, becomes hilarious when considering that the expressions each perform when posed together exactly replicate those that appear when they are on their own.

So common, so practiced, is posing in today's near-ubiquitous selfie culture, that virtually anyone can look more convincingly like an underwear model than, well, an underwear model in 1981. There is something charming, even sexy, to how unabashedly fake these models are in their unabashed nape-clutching and hip-gripping; they aren't really attempting the appearance of mid-dress elation, and it's hard not to love them for it.

-Eileen G'Sell

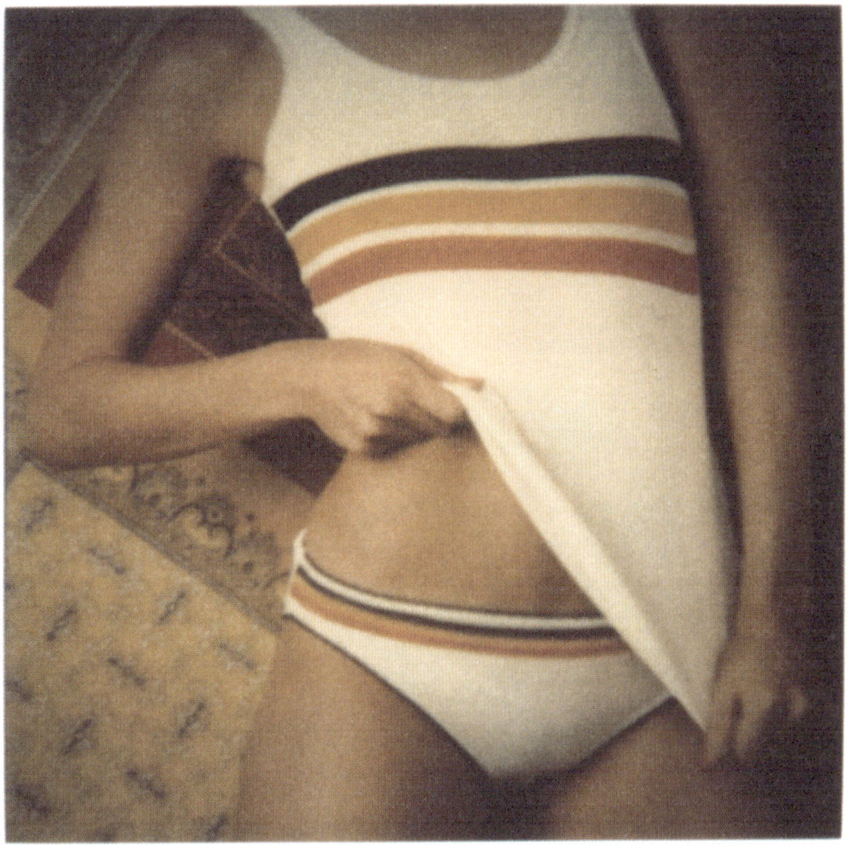

Lessons in Posing Subjects/Lingerie (Tank and Hipster) / 1981 / SX-70 Polaroid

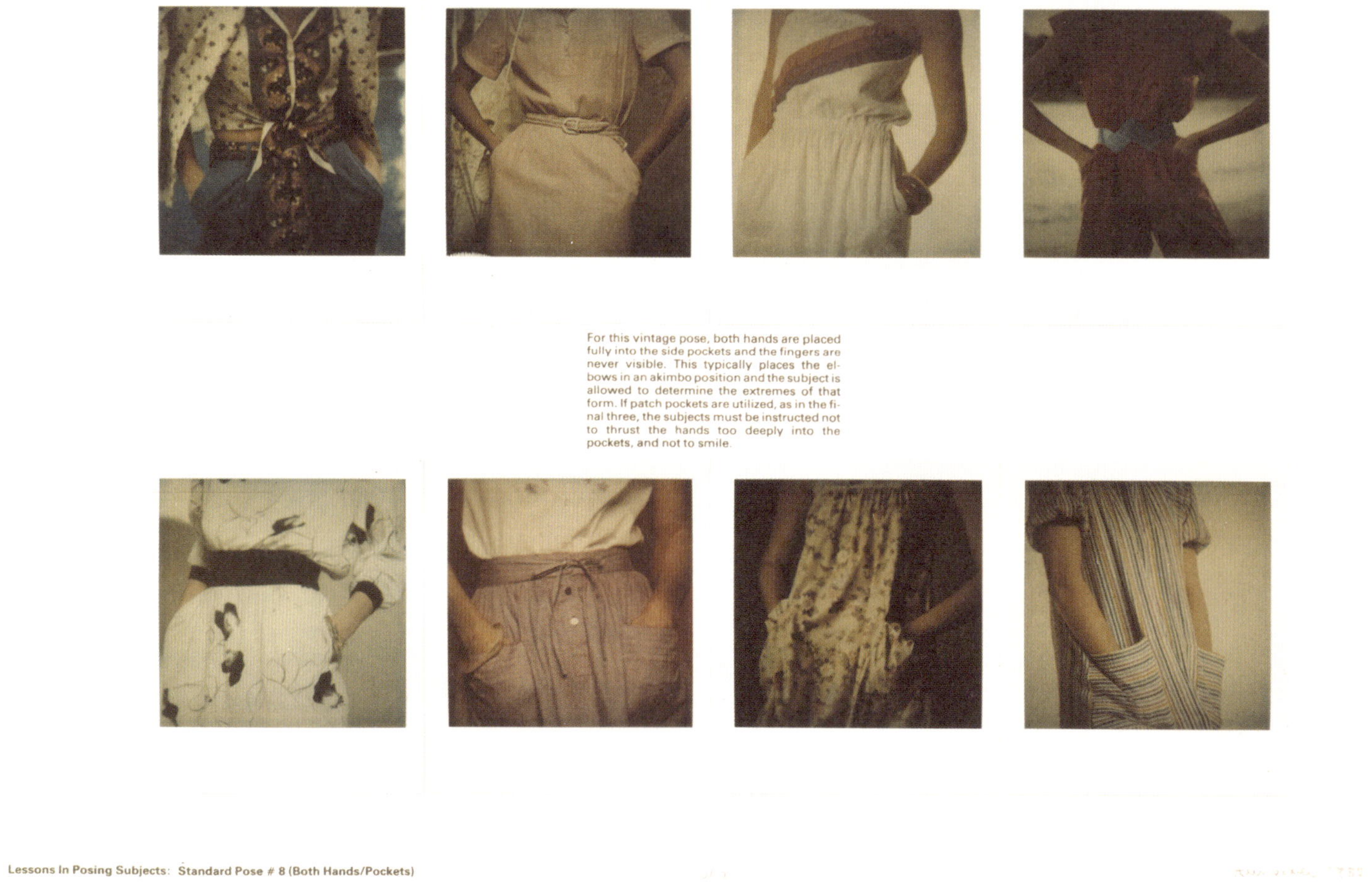

Lessons in Posing Subjects: Standard Pose #8 (Both Hands/Pockets) / 1982 / 8 SX-70 Polaroids, lithographic text / 15x20"

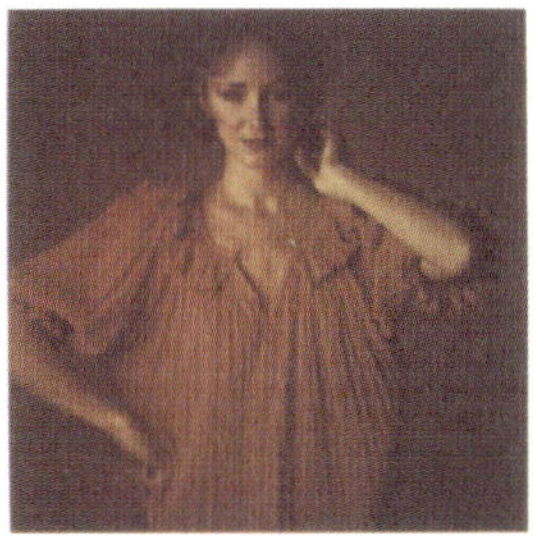
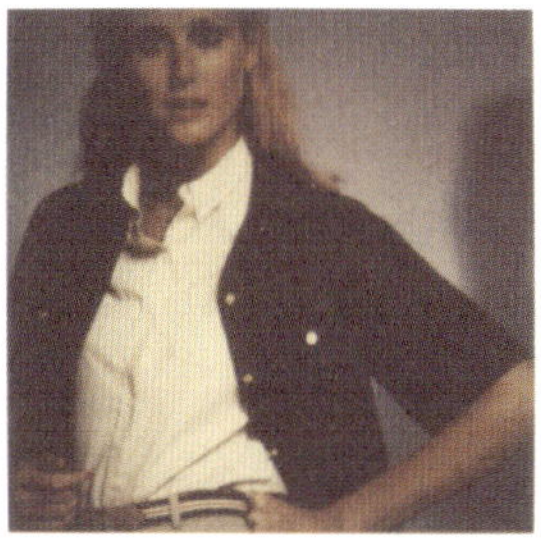
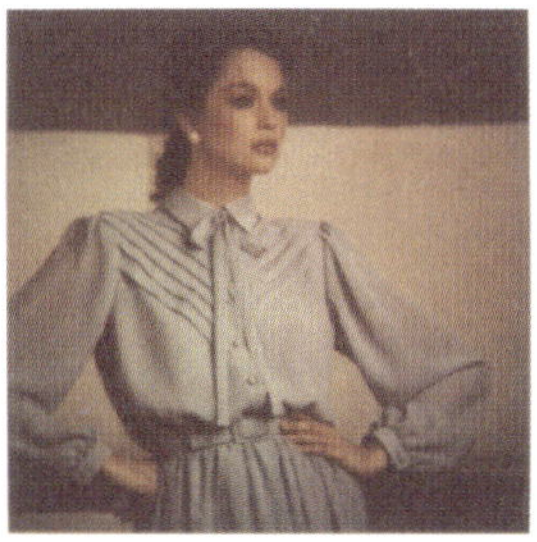
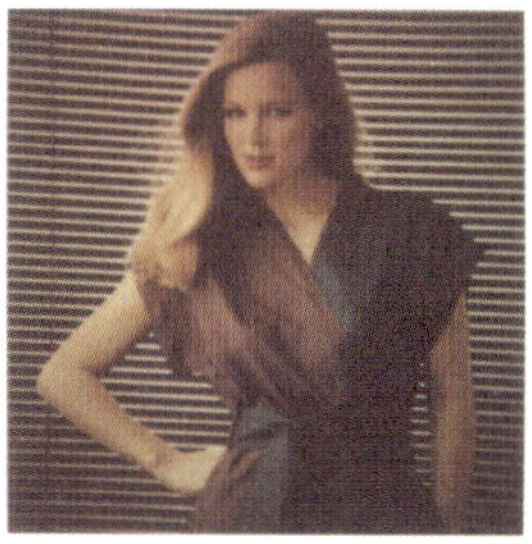

Removing one fist from the hip and placing it in contact with another part of the body completely destroys the full sense of defiance associated with Standard Pose # 11. The subjects here, in each case demonstrate the neutralizing effect of allowing one hand to drift into a position other than the correct one.

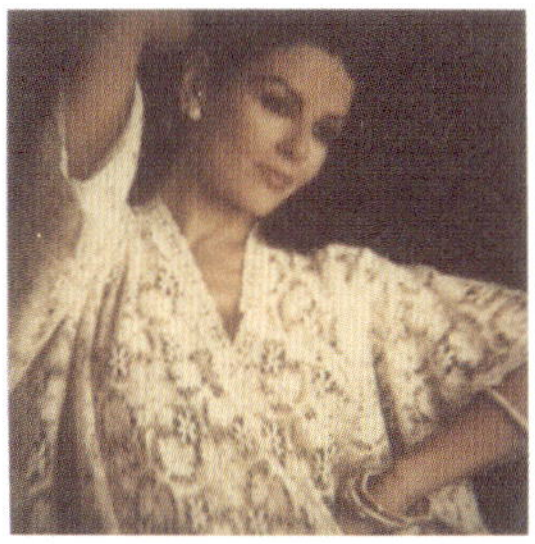
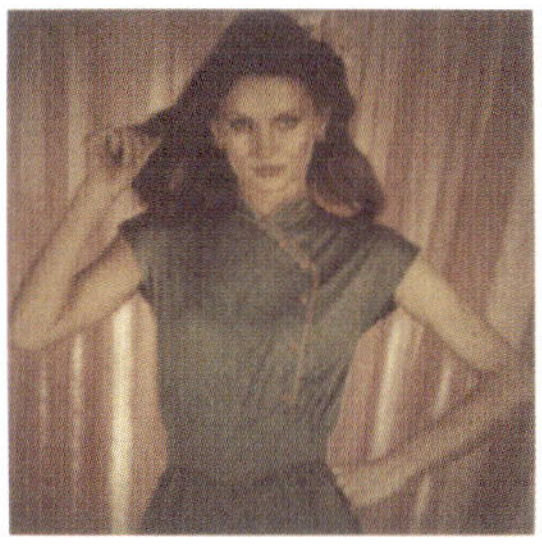
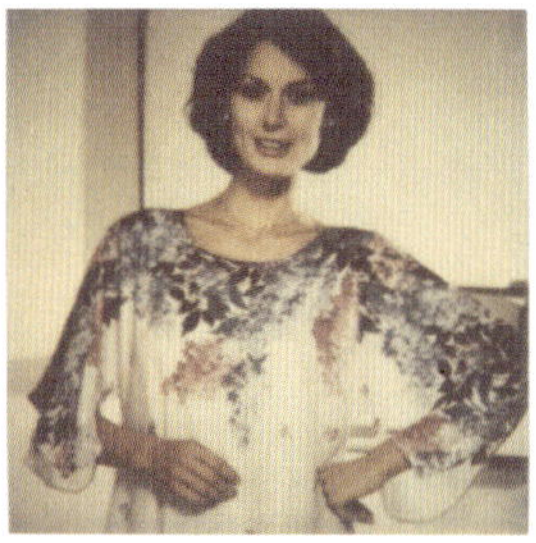
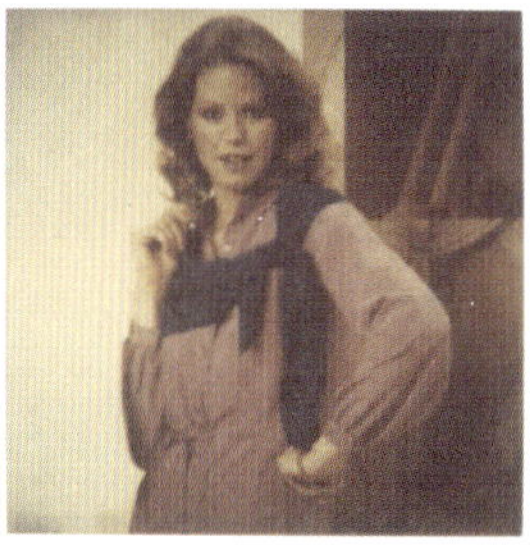

sons in Posing Subjects: (Fist Errors)

Lessons in Posing Subjects: (Fist Errors) / 1982 / 8 SX-70 Polaroids, letterpress text / 15x20"

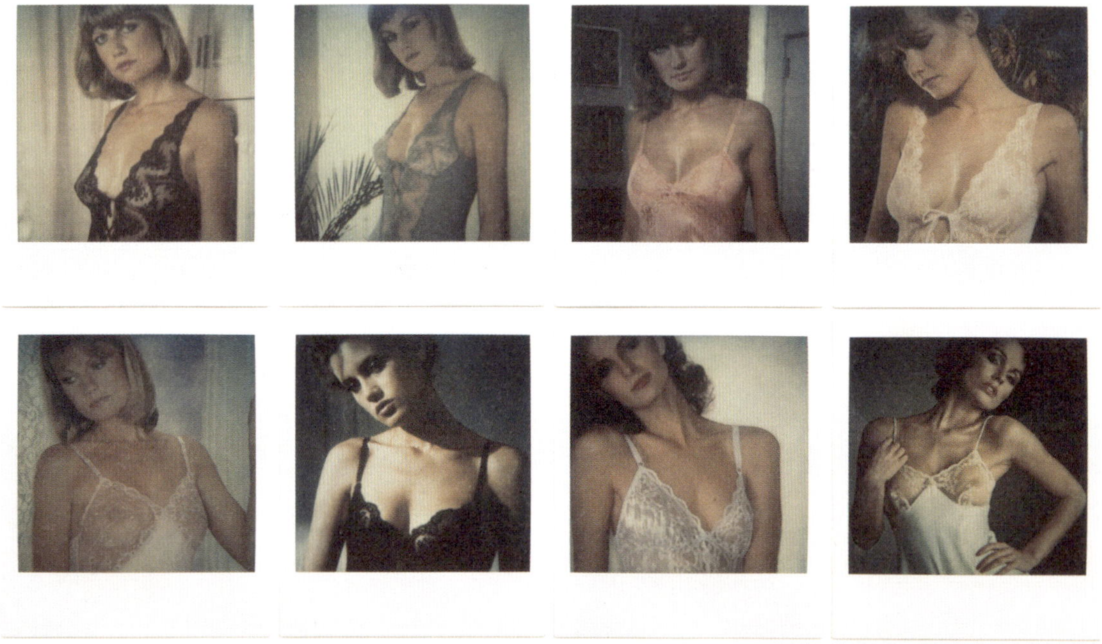

Lessons in Posing Subjects/Lingerie (Teddy)

In posing the Teddy it is necessary to remember only one rule. Tilt the angle of the head to the subject's right approximately 15-30 degrees from the implied axis of the spine. This causes a more or less neutral and serene countenance (lips closed) consistant with the garment itself. Note that in the final sample the failure to cant the subject's head to the <u>right</u> causes the mouth to open, creating an inappropriate projection of tenseness.

Lessons in Posing Subjects: Lingerie (Teddy) / 1981 / 8 SX-70 Polaroids, letterpress text / 15x20"

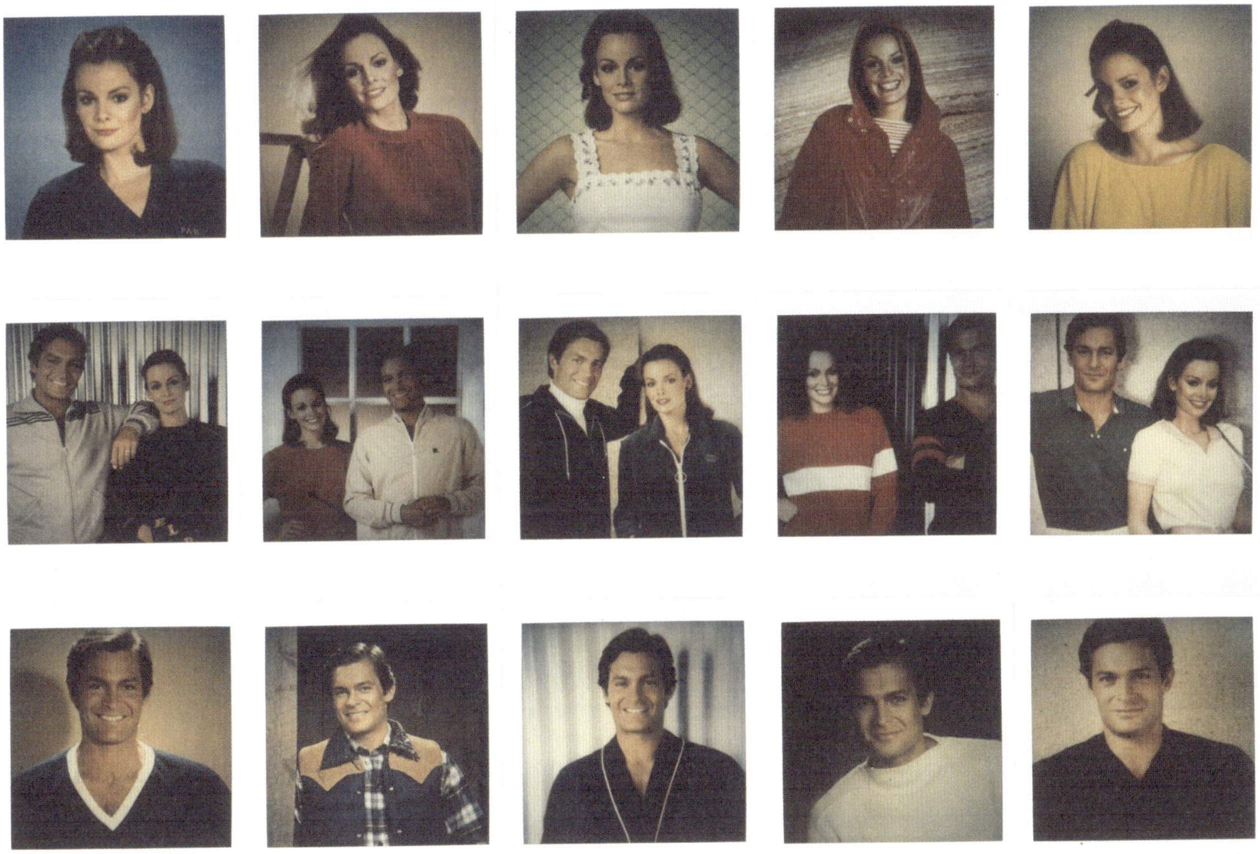

Lessons In Posing Subjects/Matching Facial Expressions

Match each of the five distinct facial expressions projected by the female subject in line #1 (top) with those expressions to which they most closely correspond in line #2 (center) which depicts the interaction of the female and male subjects. Then similarly, also match the five facial expressions projected by the male subject in line #3 (bottom) to his in line #2 (center). When all ten facial expressions have been correctly matched, it is possible to imagine 100 new striking combinations of female/male facial expressions connoting a wide variety of interpersonal relationships.

Lessons in Posing Subjects: Matching / 1981 / 15 SX-70 Polaroids, lithographic text / 15x20"

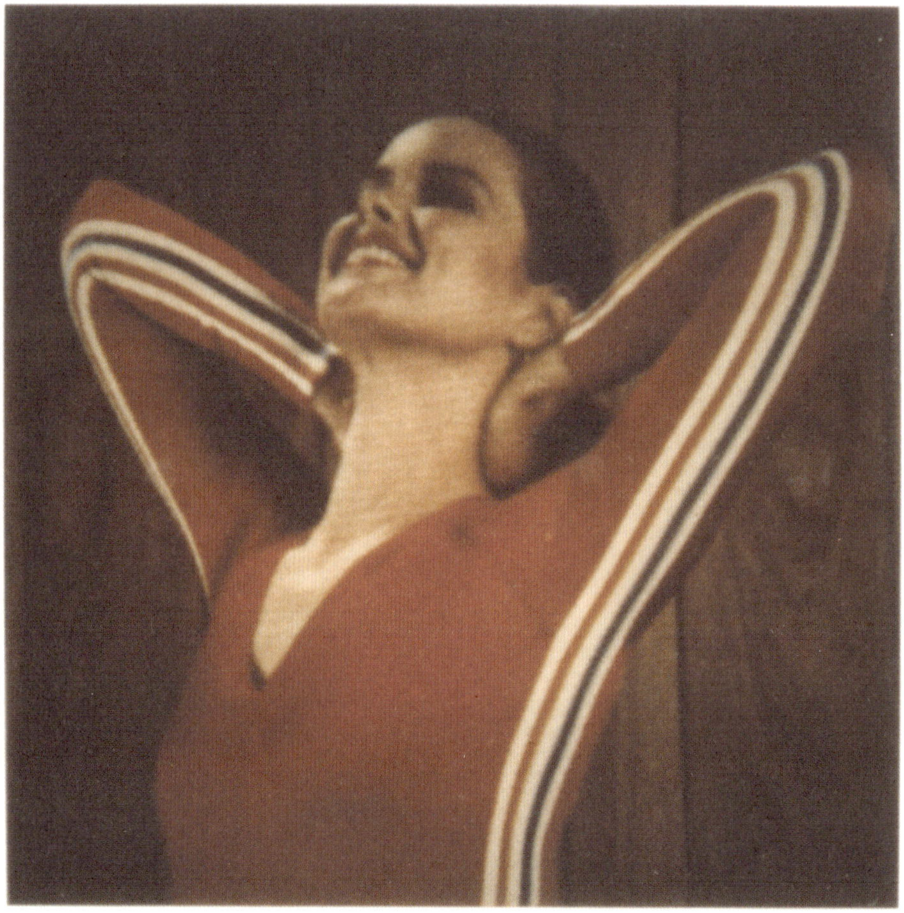

Lessons in Posing Subjects: Standard Pose #1 (Hands/Neck/Head) / 1982 / SX-70 Polaroid

E
XP
LO
RA
T
IO
N

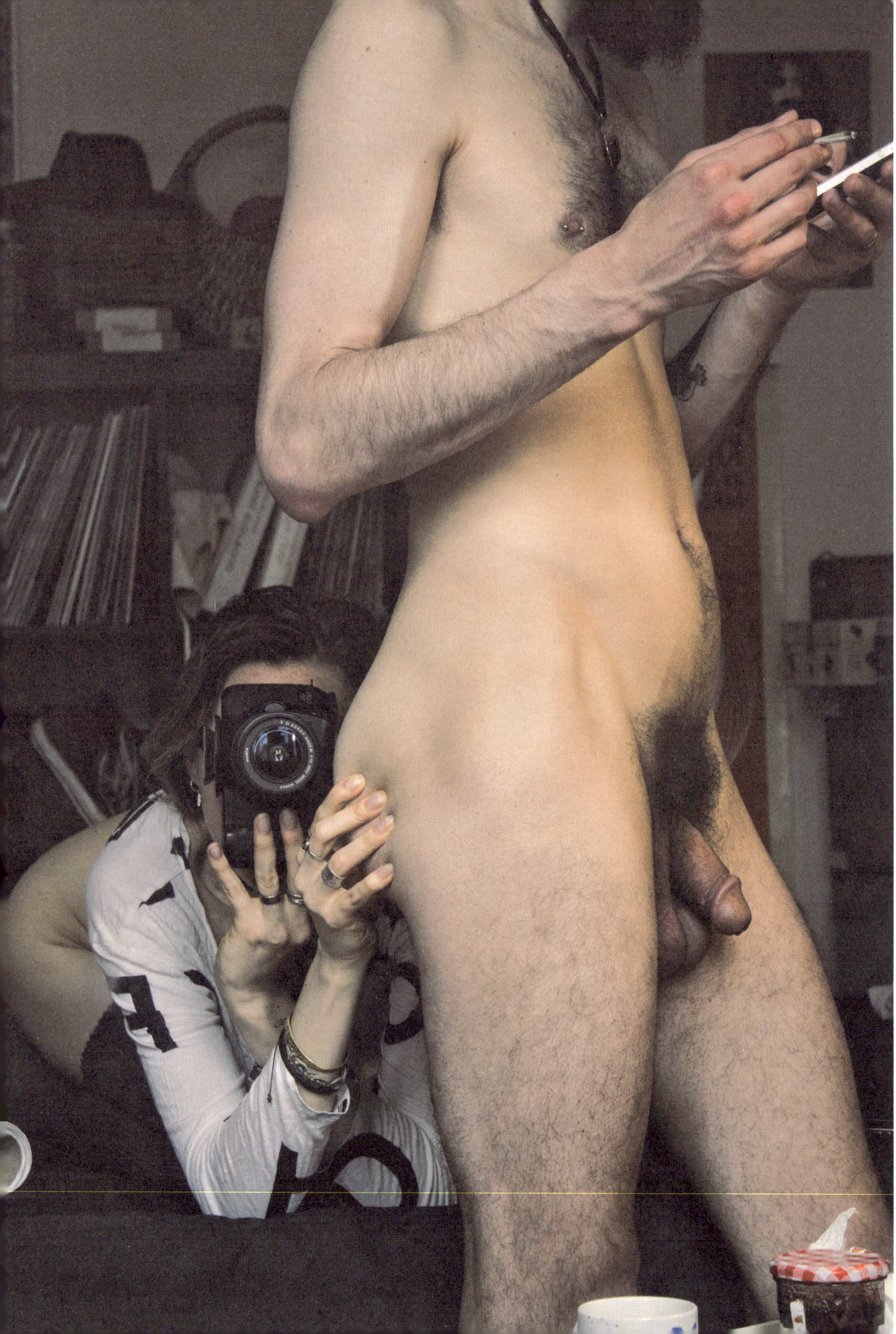

EXPLORATION #1

#SEXLIFE

The ups and downs of online intimacy with Sugar Magnolia and King Snake

I find myself visiting Sugar Magnolia and King Snake on a more-than-regular basis. It's a comforting feeling to drop in on these two. Never mind that I don't know their 'real' names, or have never met them in 'real' life... I've seen them cuddle and bathe and fuck.

Sugar and King have become quite popular in the year since launching Slide-2-Unlock, an anonymous Tumblr site filled with the beautifully intimate photographs they take of each other. These two are a handsome, free-spirited, thirty-something couple, together for fifteen years, living in London, raising kids, working creative jobs and being passionate about things like love, sex and art.

With some persistence I was able to get a message through to Sugar and King, not an easy task as their inbox overflows with all sorts of fan mail, notes from bloggers, letters from people seeking advice about sex, relationships, careers, parenting, fashion, body issues, mental health, nutrition(!), and the unavoidable hate mail from trolls and all-around unhappy people. During my written correspondence I discovered a couple traveling together on a journey of self-discovery. Sugar, an avid photographer, informed me that she doesn't "take pictures for others, I take them for myself. It's therapeutic, it's transformative. It's part of exploring my sexuality in a visual form, and it's also liberating because of its transgressive aspect."

She continues "until very recently I had never seen another woman with a body that resembled mine, and that always made me very uncomfortable. I wish a better world for my children, a world where they won't feel bad about their bodies because they think they're different. So I feel like I'm just doing my bit to change that."

As for King, he is in it for "the liberating feeling of being your true self naked – literally – in body and mind. And producing art in this process of self-investigation. It gives us focus in all aspects of life; from how we raise our kids to how we work and what we create."

I found it interesting that they both love looking at their beautiful images as much as their fans do, and have been known to revisit and relive some of their favorite documented moments. "It is like a journal, from time to time you go back and indulge in some sexy nostalgia." They went on to let me know that "creating the images is a very nice process... the shoots are always an excuse to have more sex," which in turn becomes its own "addictive cycle."

As is to be expected, there are some unwanted aspects of sharing your private parts and intimate moments with the world. Although Sugar and King enjoy most of their interactions with followers and fellow bloggers, they've had some unfortunate negative experiences, forcing them to limit their interactions with their audience, and to disable the ability for commenters to post anonymously.

It's not easy to put yourself out there and I often feel the need to protect these two sensitive artists. But how does one do that in this new digital world we live and play in? Sugar and King deny that they are part of a new digital movement at all. "We are part of a movement, yes, a social movement [...] happening in every media [...] of correct human values and the nurturing of individual human potential."

-James Gallagher

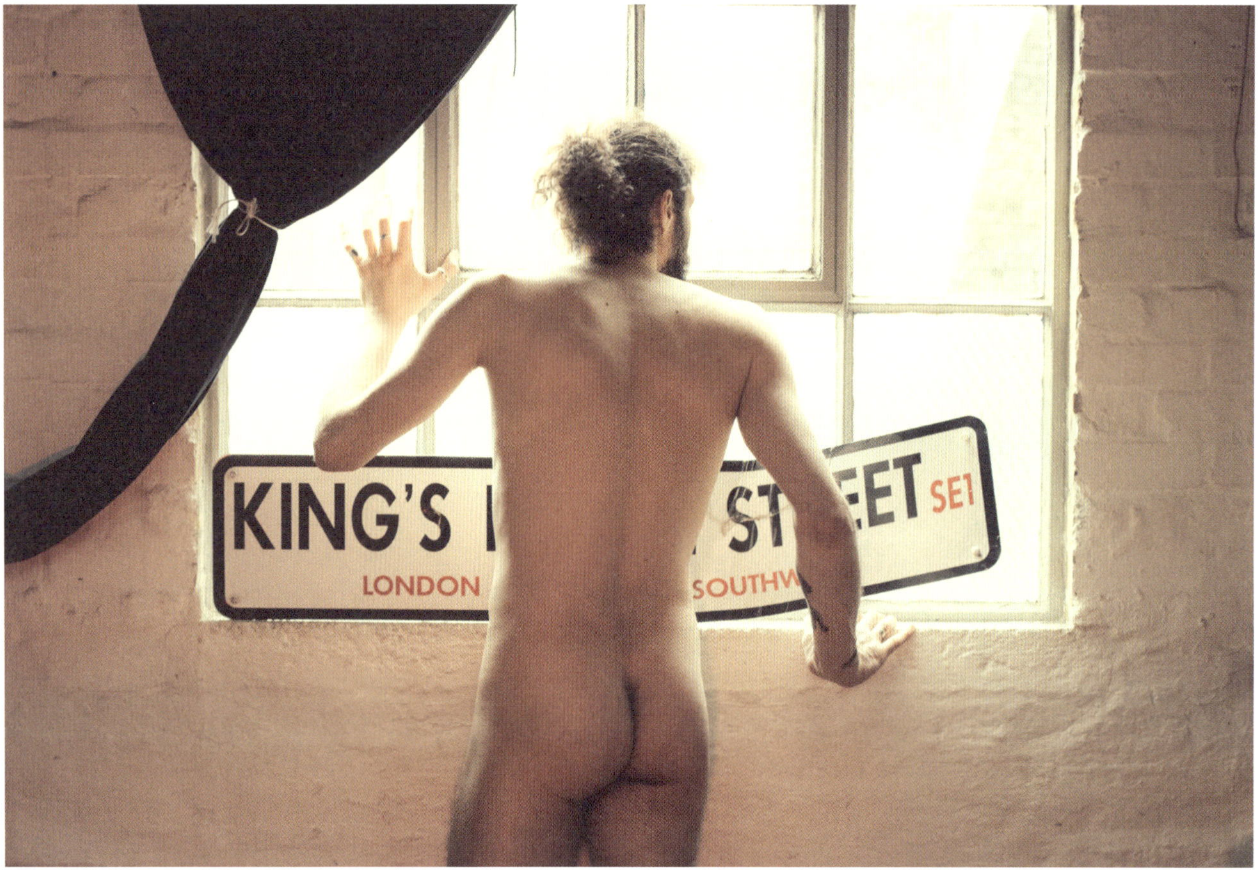
KING'S
SE1
LONDON

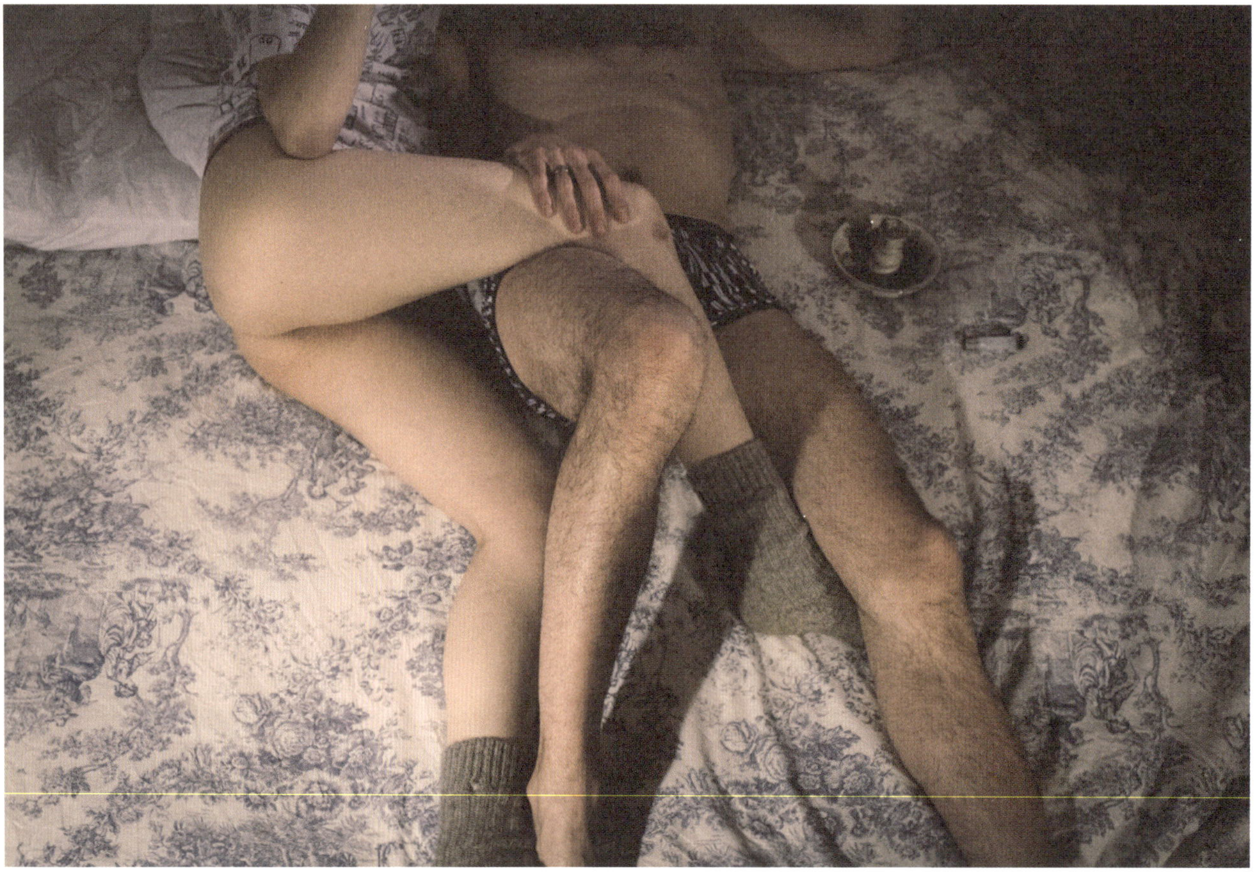

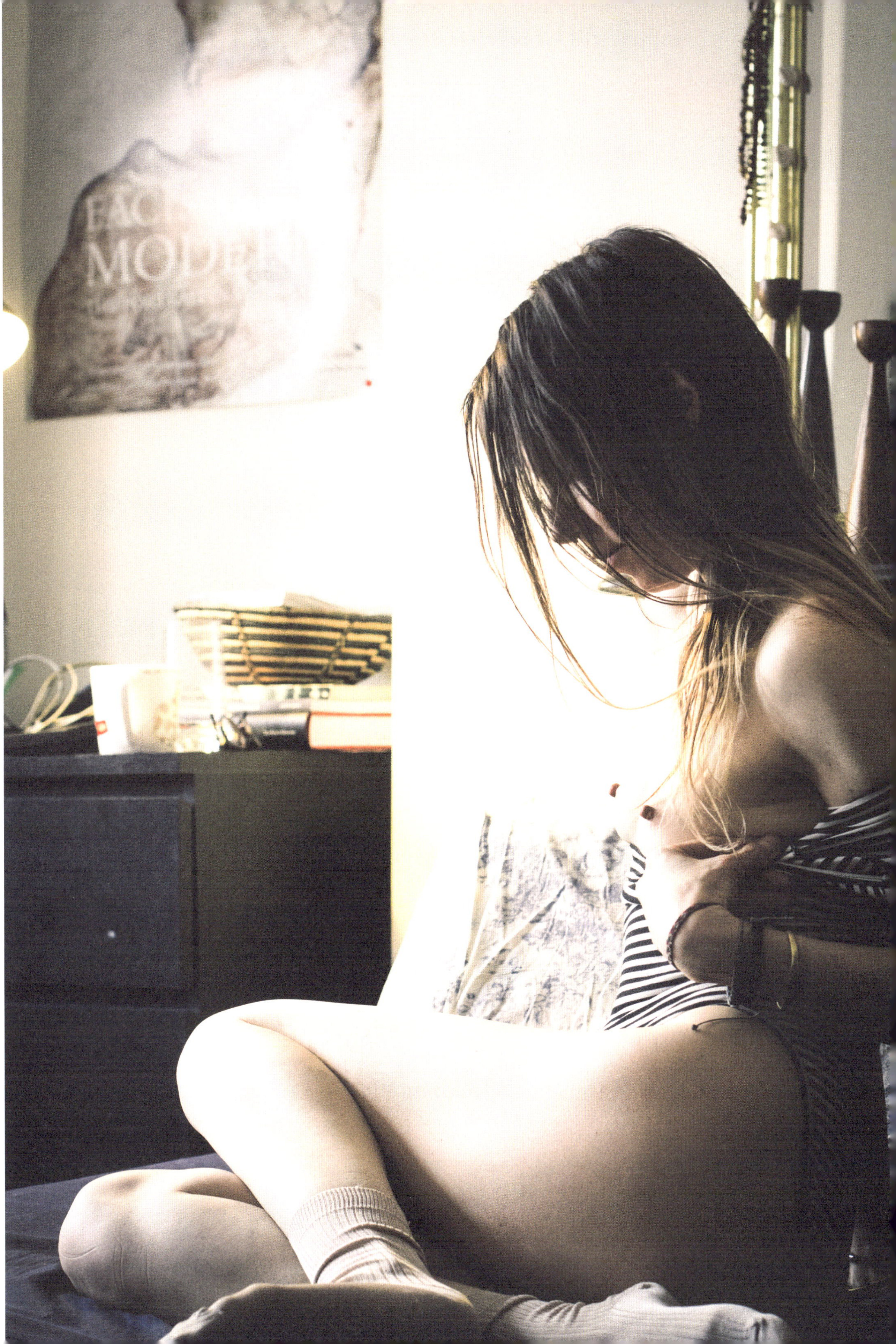

"It's interesting how photographs of sex can evoke virtually all emotions, and likewise portray virtually all. Love is so clear in all of your photographs, and what I love is that we don't need to see your faces to feel it, you hands tell the story. Of course I'm also projecting my own thoughts/stories onto the images, since that's what we do with art."

"I had to cum after watching your shaky ass video I was so turned on. Good god it was hot. Thank you ;)"

"I just wanted to say thank you for the strength and the courage to try new things with my boyfriend and with my bodyhair you gave me. I know it might seem creepy but today i had tons of sex with my boyfriend in honor of your anniversary, happy 15th!"

"You guys must be some fucking awesome parents!"

"Do you have any advice for someone with 32AA breasts? They're so small it ruins my confidence, I don't feel as though anyone could want me in a sexual way because small breasts seem to only be referenced when people are making fun of them… am I just being stupid?"

"I'm really insecure about my labia, wbu? Any thoughts?"

"How do I bring up the fact that my partner is pretty hairy around his cock, and it gets in the way of blow jobs? I feel like he would take it personally and get embarrassed if I asked him to just trim a little."

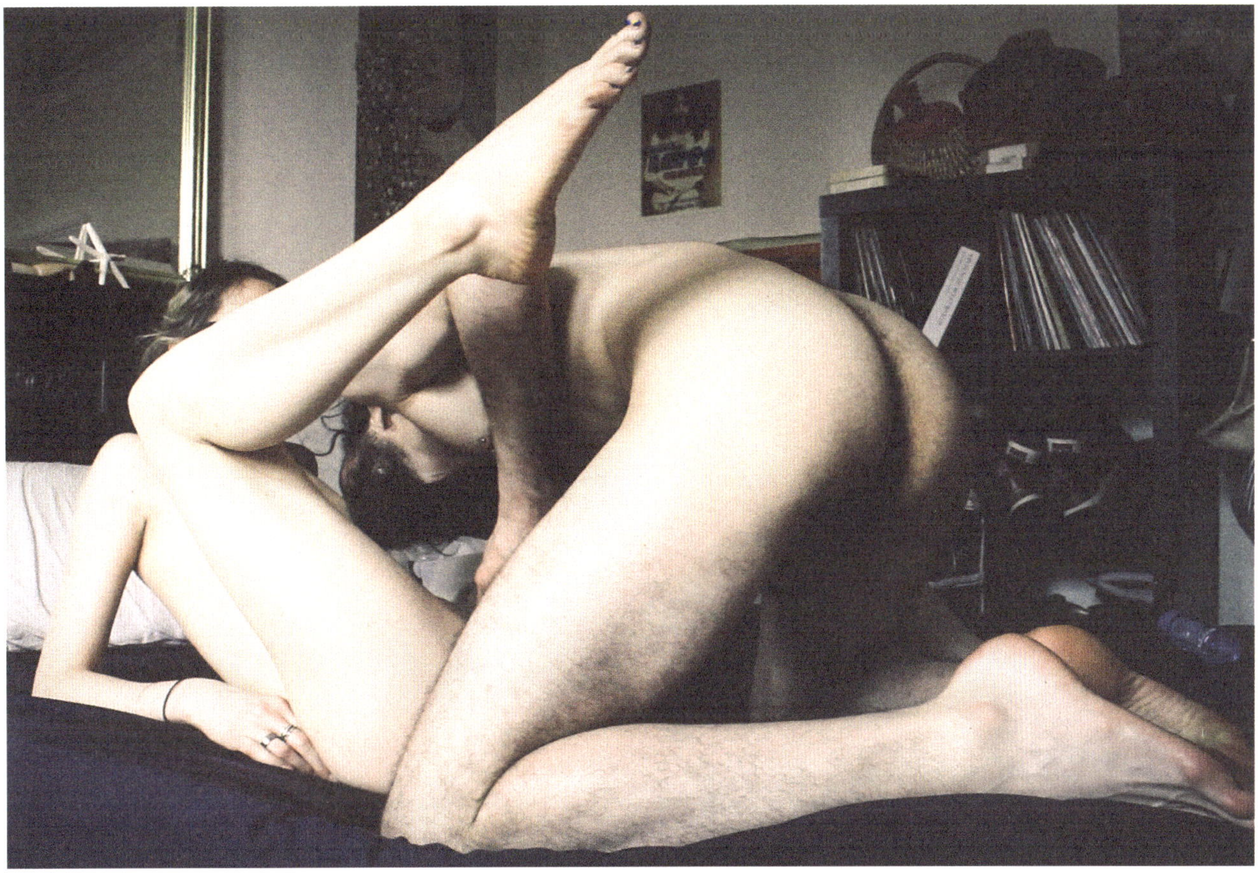

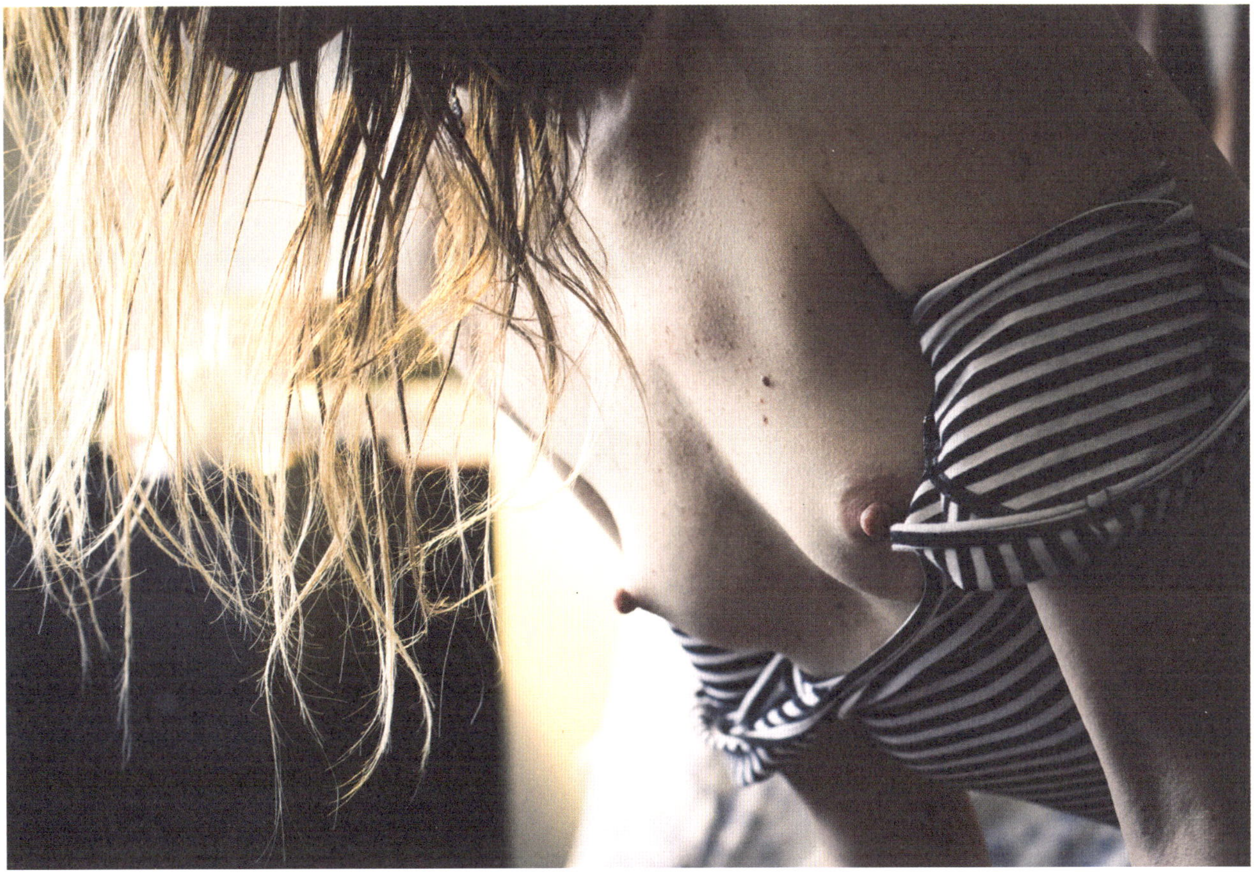

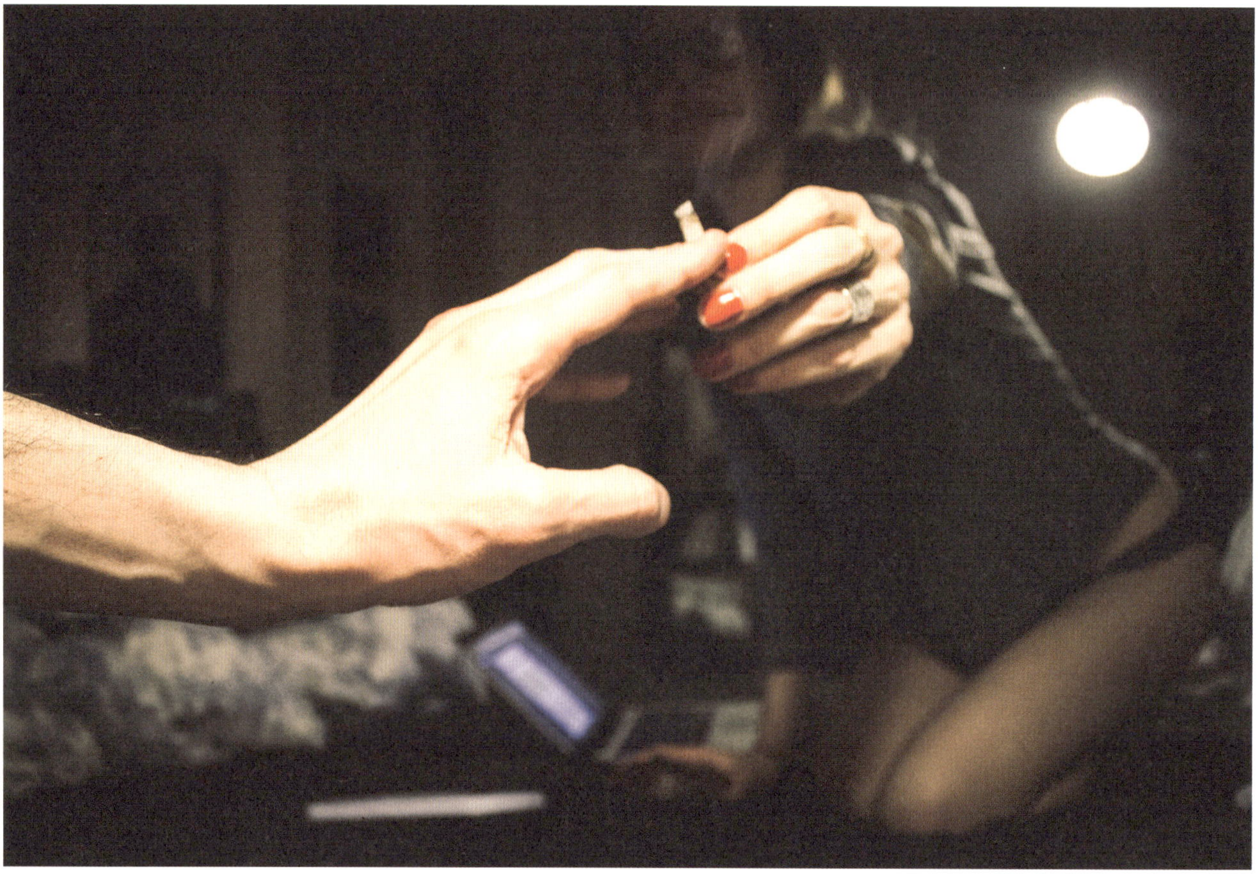

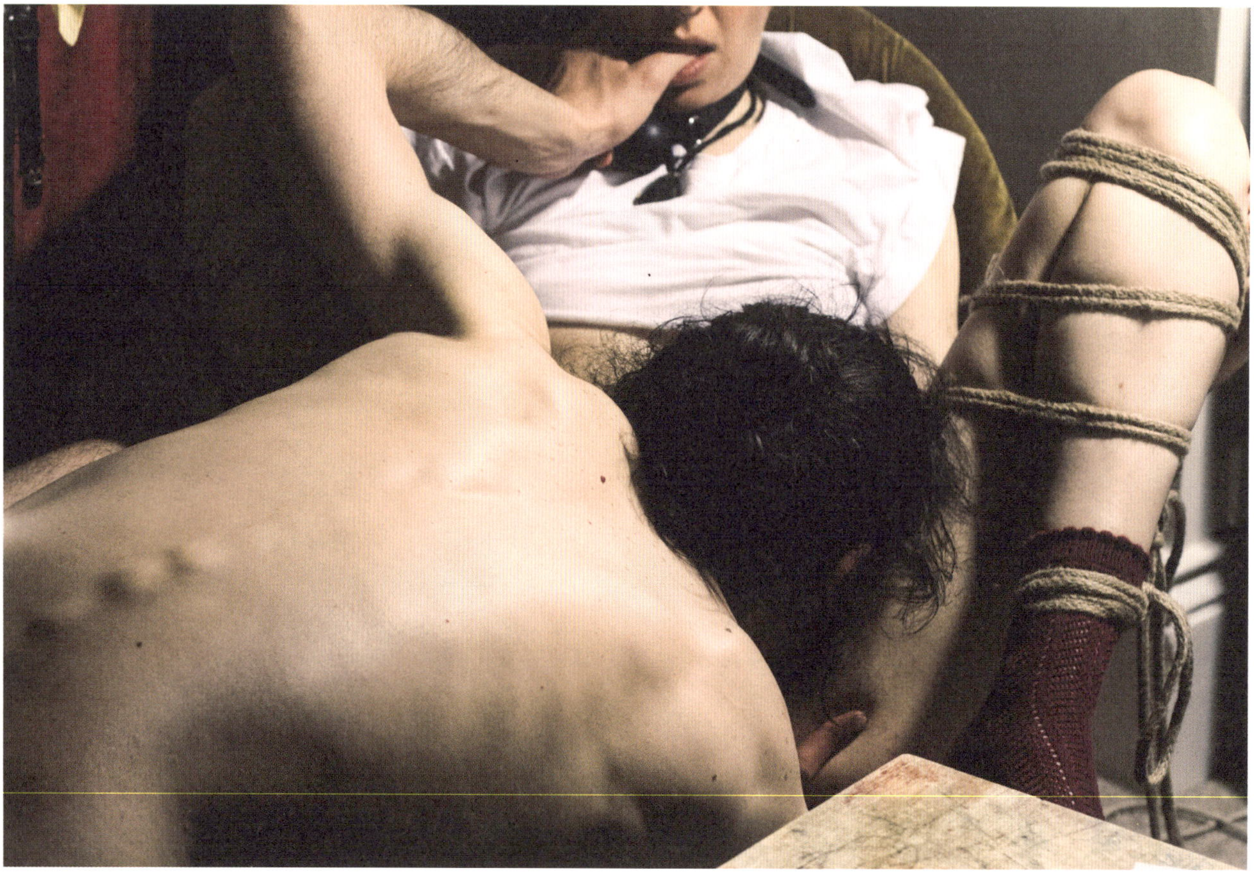

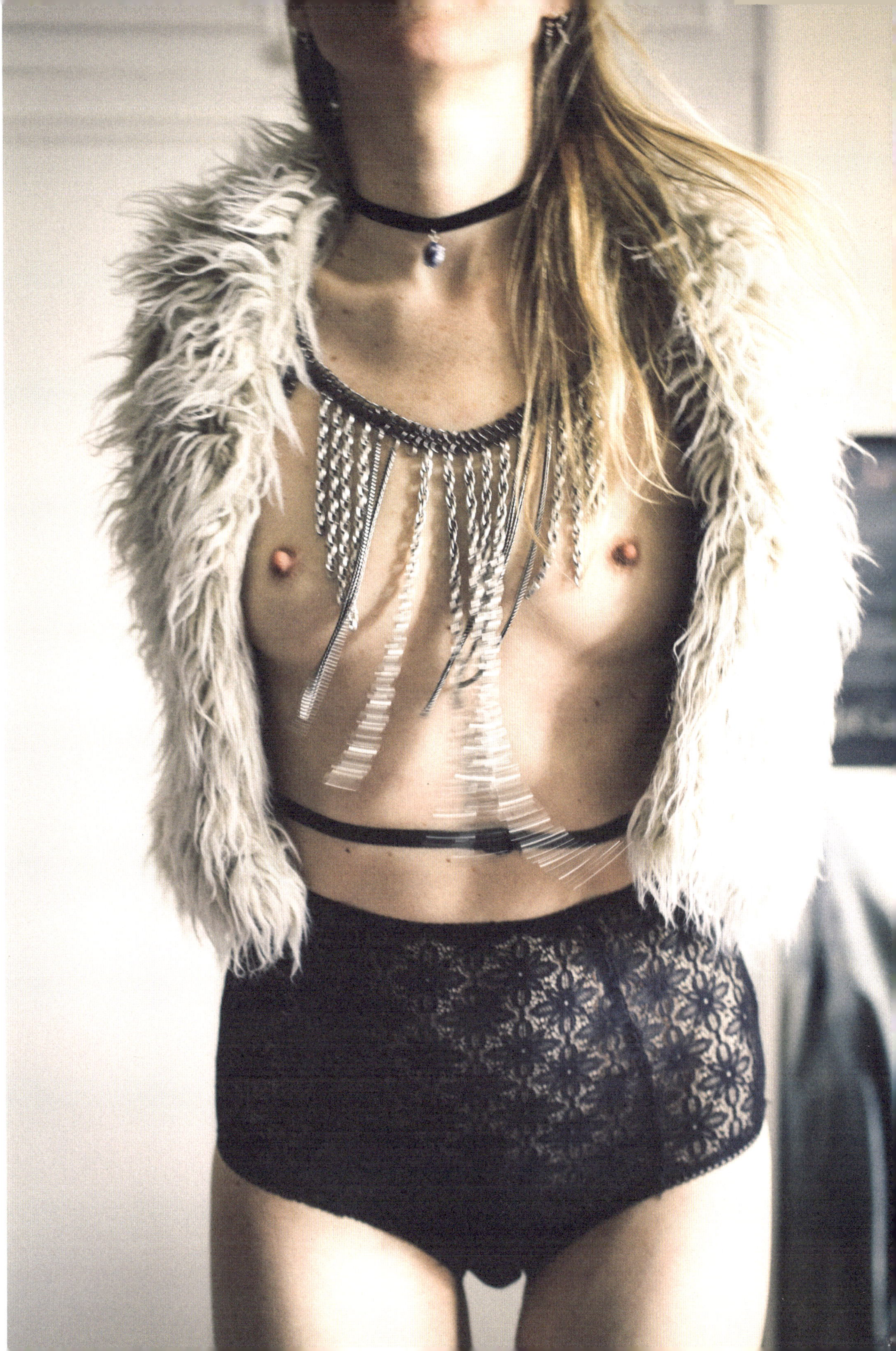

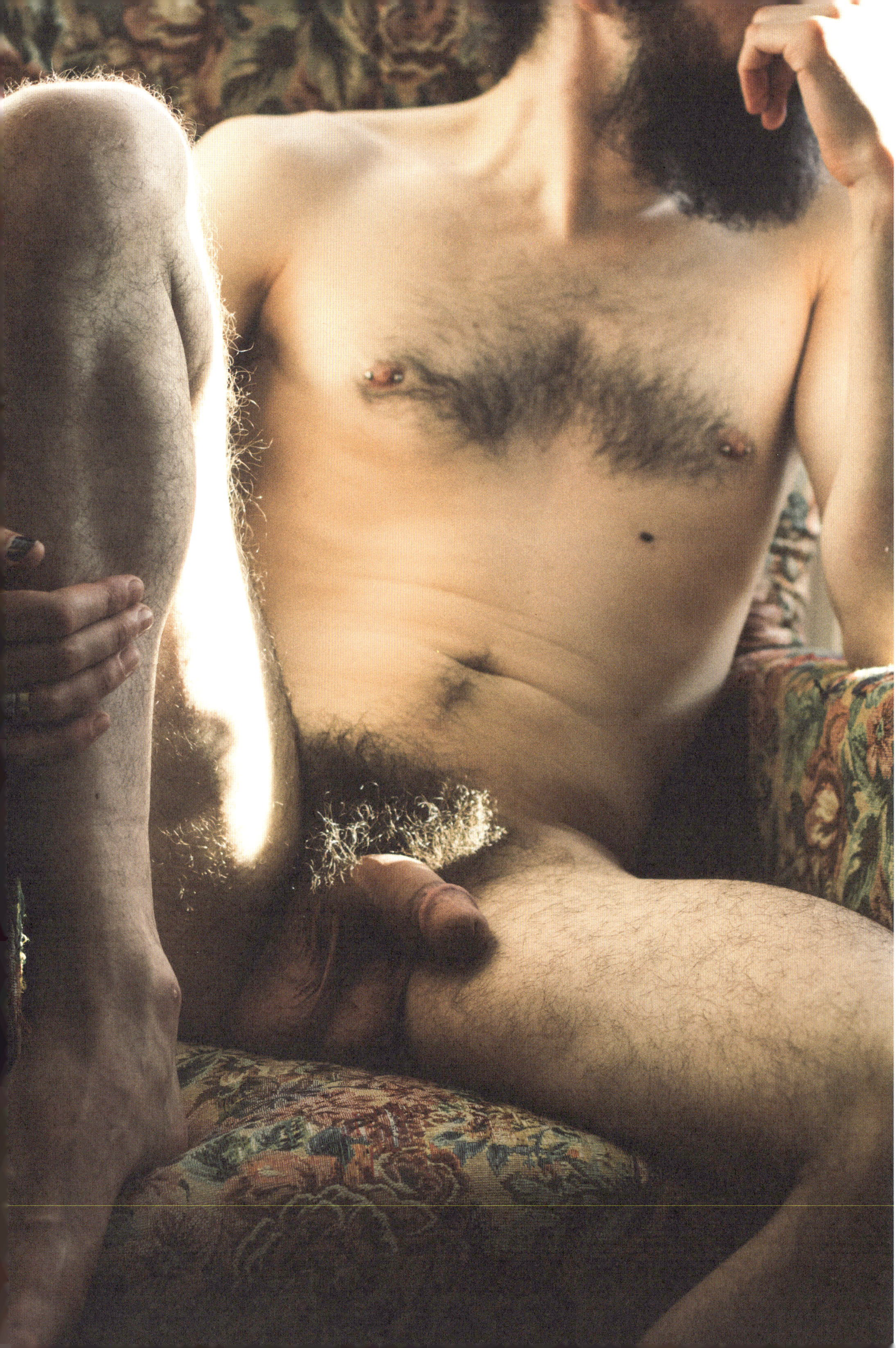

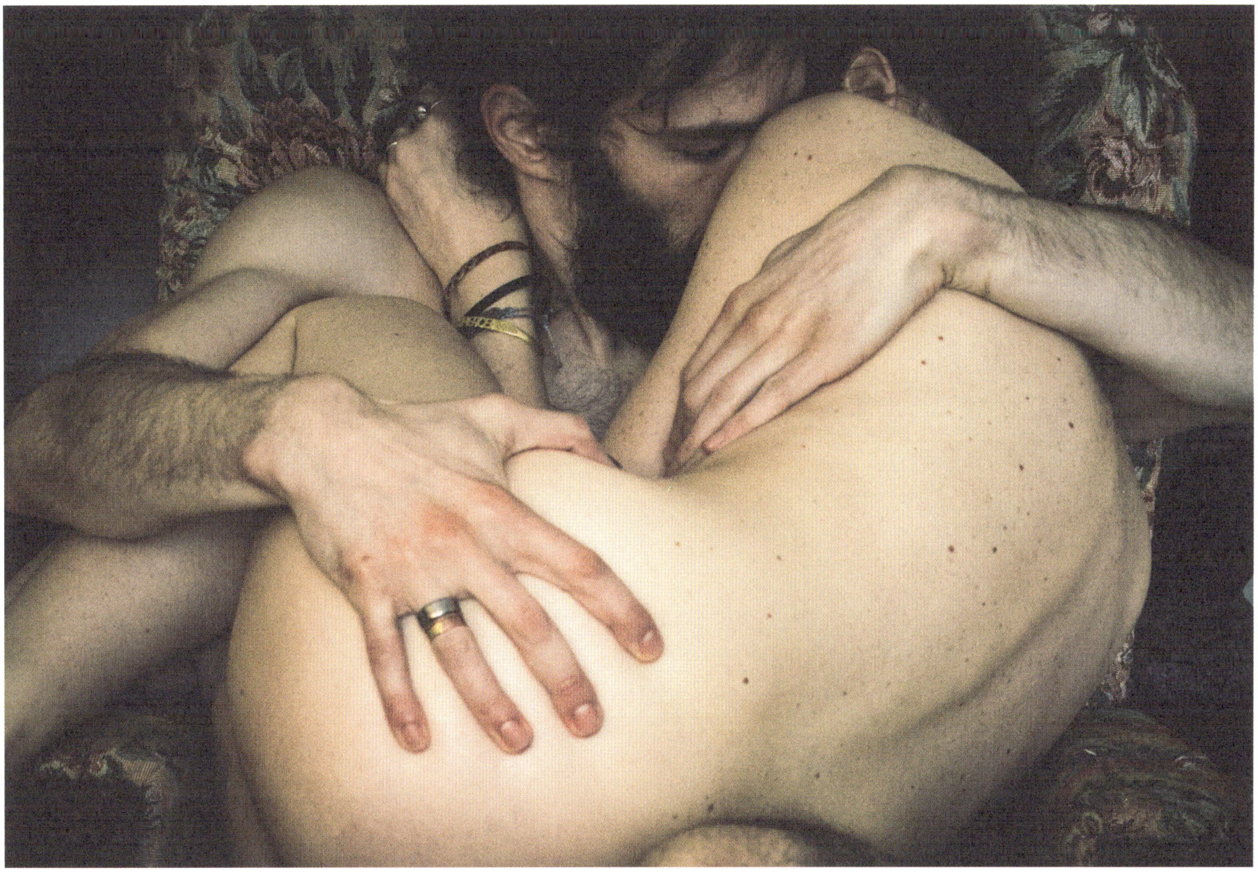

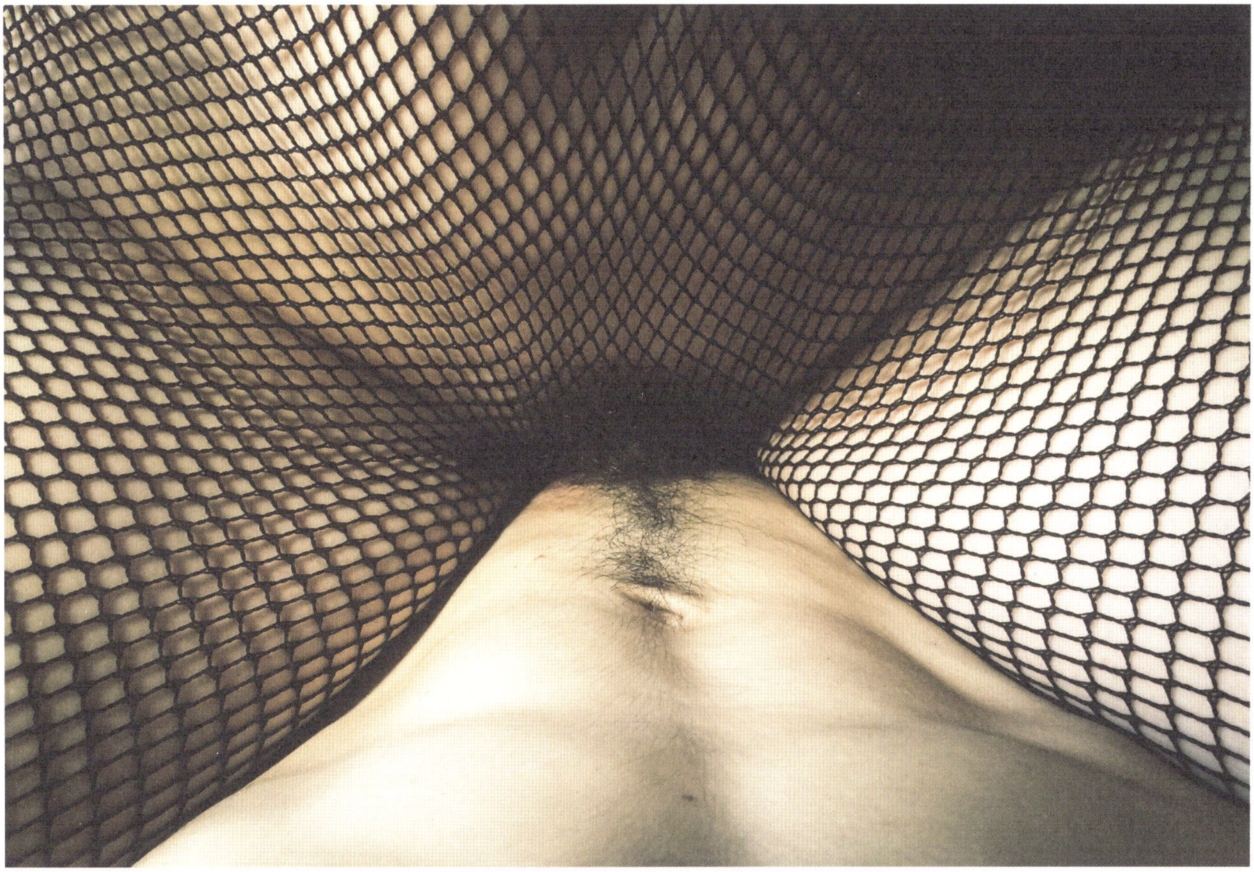

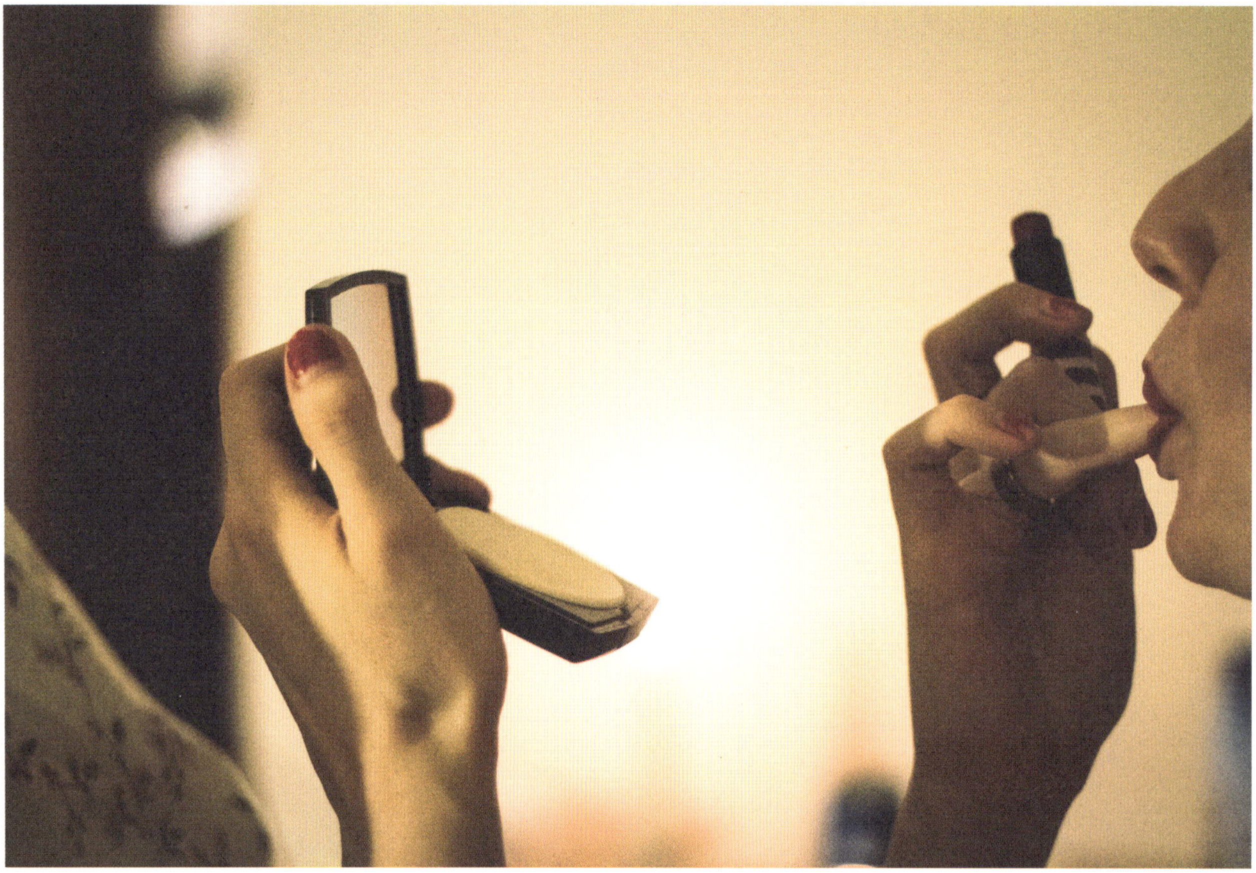

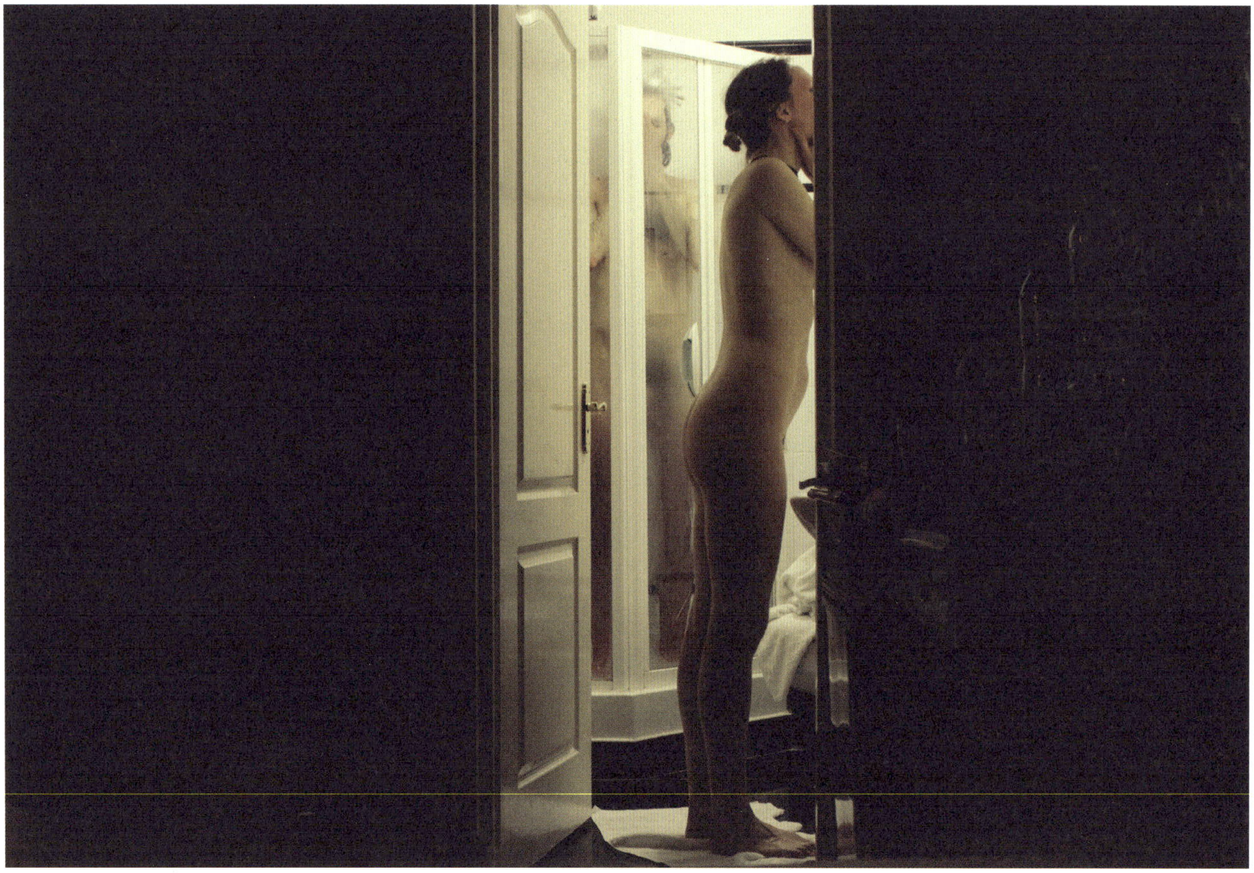

"God knows I should be studying for my exams but I just discovered your blog and I'm stuck browsing it. I love your photography and the warm and intimate feelings it gives off!"

"How do you find time to have so much sex when you have children?"

"Your blog "dared" me to use a significantly larger butt plug than I'm used to during an intense lust and love fuelled session with my husband this weekend. We had the house to ourselves, we'd been teasing/tormenting each other all day. Seeing my husbands eyes light up when he realised what I was planning and doing was fantastic. I will one day find the words to describe the sensation, the whole body experience was immense. Thank you for inspiring us. We've been together 23 years!"

"Do you both have butt hair? I don't see a problem with it, but I'm worried future partners would. What's your thought on a (no so super) hairy butt?"

"I came across your blog a few days ago and it's almost becoming something of an addiction. I'm currently 8 months pregnant and I wanted to say thank you for reminding me that just because my partner and I are about to become parents doesn't mean we'll stop being lovers. You both seem like genuine, tender and caring people and it's lovely to see that coupled with your beautiful photos. All the best x"

"Is it strange that your blog makes me horny?"

EXPLORATION #2

FUCK YES

The loud, fast, sweaty, orgiastic, life-changing arrival of punk as told (and torn) by Paul Burgess with Louise Colbourne

The full force of punk hit me at my most impressionable. In 1976, I was a fifteen-year-old growing up in the suburbs not far from London, and punk spoke to me like nothing else. It had an urgency that sucked me in. The music was fast, immediate, direct, and the attitude—that everything was possible, that you could 'do it yourself'—was life-affirming in exactly the way I needed. Making music, making art, making film and clothing and everything in between—the idea that you could do it all yourself, that you didn't need anyone else's permission or approval—that was a manifesto by which to live your life. And man, it was exciting.

Life seemed to move at an incredible pace in those years. Everything felt urgent, each day mattered more than the last, like time was running out and nothing should be wasted. Every day there'd be conversations in the street, coins pushed into the phone box, hurriedly written notes and letters sent to the press and anyone else who would listen. Maybe it was the speed that got to us? Everyone was creative. We wanted to communicate, to collaborate, to pass on information, person to person. We didn't want to miss anything.

Punk was a beckoning finger. Start a band, pick up a camera, make a zine. No drawing and painting, that was for the hippies. Collage and appropriation were the tools. Snip with scissors, cut 'n' paste. The cinema was empowering: *Taxi Driver*, Warhol, John Waters, *Cabaret*, *The Texas Chain Saw Massacre*, *A Clockwork Orange*, The

Opposite: Johnny, Jordan and Lou / Collage by Paul Burgess / 2015

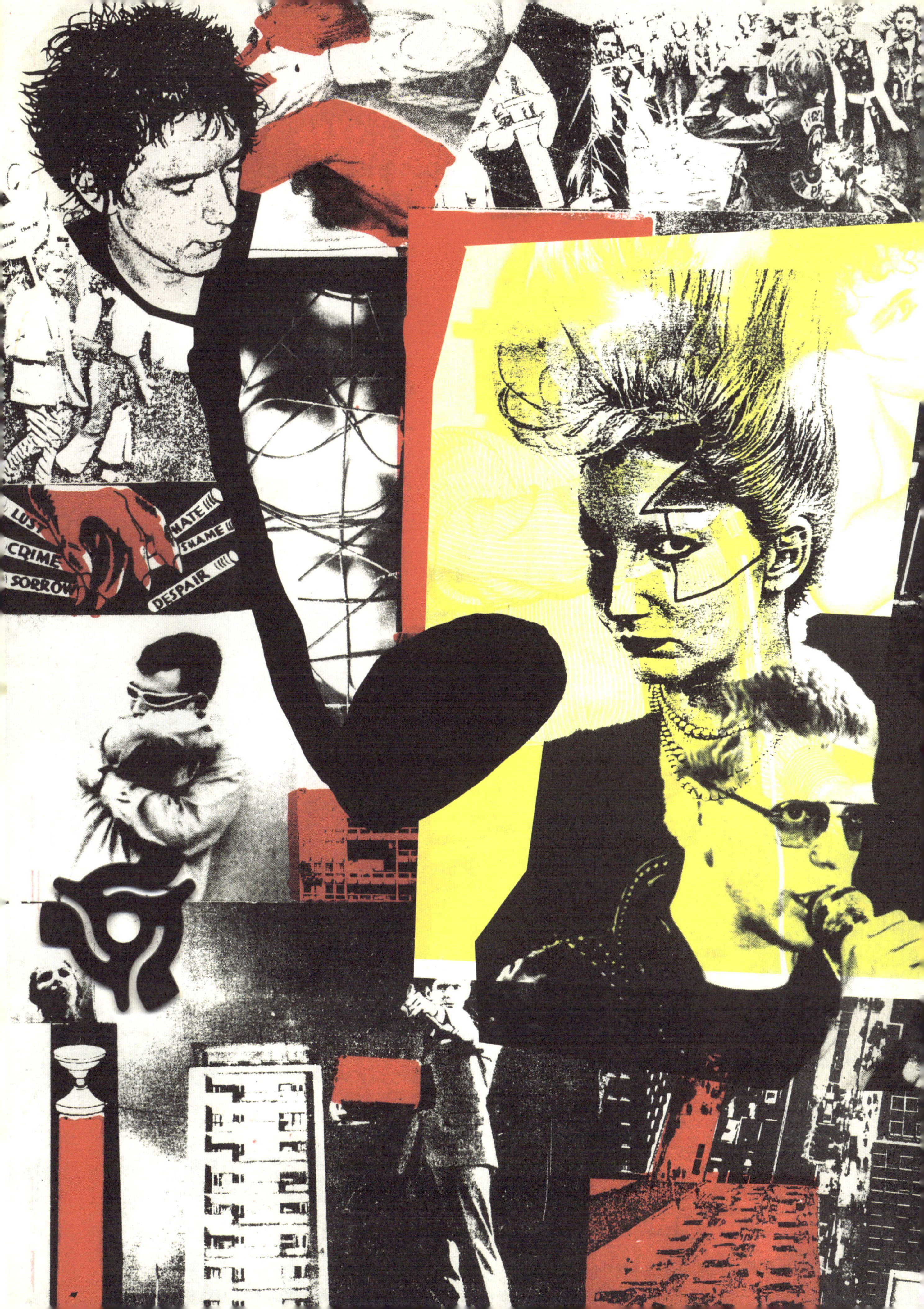
LUST
CRIME
SORROW
HATE
SHAME
DESPAIR

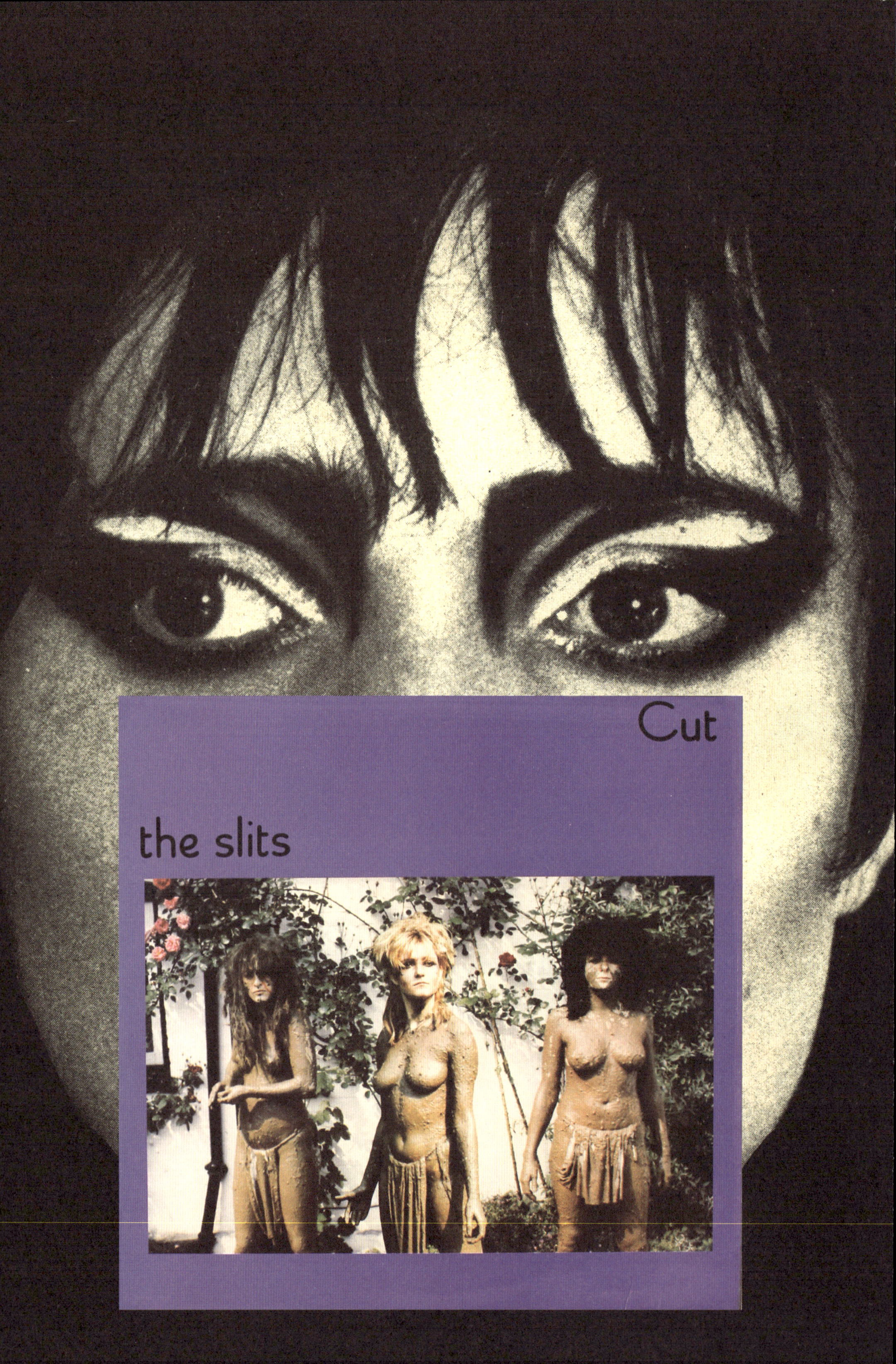
Cut
the slits

Rocky Horror Picture Show, Kenneth Anger, *Eraserhead*, Derek Jarman. Underground film was our library, it set us off in different directions, a myriad of twinkling signposts. We made our own clothes for the first time and it felt good to dress ourselves—to wear our clothes, not theirs.

We felt charged, potent, our fingers on the trigger. We pissed people off in the street with the way we looked. Youth was hot and bothered again, and for a couple of years at least, wild, wild, wild youth stood up and got noticed by the older generation. Part disbelief, part jealousy.

Every weekend we would run rampant on the streets of London. The markets were the place to steal cheap clothes, the records shops the meeting place for like-minded souls. The Kings Road, Acme, Boy, and Seditionaries—that's where we would meet, drink, and fuck up the old-school farts. Gigs were loud, sweaty, and in your face. No bouncers, no boundary between stage and audience. The bands were the same as the people in the crowd. It was a two-way thing. Gobbing was rife. Spit flying everywhere, like a thousand tiny darts whizzing through the air toward their target. It was like a battle, a siege. At the gigs, two or three a week, that sound in your ears was fierce and relentless . . . pure energy. Just like stepping onto a roller coaster ride that you couldn't stop. The gigs are burnt into my brain, even now. Manifestos streaming from the stage, everything up for grabs. Change your clothes, change your hair, change what you think, what you say, what you do—change society by changing your life. It's all in your hands. Learn to destroy in order to create, and then create in order to live.

Beyond the dyed cropped hair and piercings, the bin bags and duct tape, the truly scary thing about us was the sex. After years of repression, sex was out in the open at last. Romance was sneered at, and we craved sexual honesty and directness. Foreplay was functional, intercourse optional. Orgasm addict? We were always at it. S&M? The imagery and language were everywhere. Dog collars, wristbands, belts, studs, and pins. "Venus in Furs." "Oh Bondage Up Yours!" "Whip in My Valise."

History tells us that punk challenged the established order not just by presenting the inner angst and gritty reality of life in the UK and USA, in the 1970s, but also by applying an ethos of protest and even combat to every area of life and art. The pop-and prog rock-loving public were suddenly confronted with music that was vitriolic, performances that were confrontational, clothing that was messed-up anti-fashion, and graphic art that was cut out, cut up, re-purposed and re-appropriated. It all changed overnight.

The punk movement may very well have been the most outrageous act of self-expressive defiance the modern world had ever encountered, but what is the point of exhibitionism that is so self-destructive? Is it merely a form of extreme attention-seeking, an act of egocentrism and self-absorption? Or does it share the sacrificial vision of the shaman, suffering alone to be an influence and inspiration for others? Well, poverty had a lot to do with it. In the UK in 1976 there was a dustman's strike, with piles of trash on every street corner. And what did they do, the punks? They wore the trash. They wore the problem, in order to draw attention to the problem. Bin bags became make-do tunics embellished with pins, duct tape, and badges, as a visual statement of discontent with the way things were.

Exhibitionist performance was key to the punk movement. Performance art from the 1960s and 1970s had an impact, along with a heady mix of Situationist theory,

Learn to destroy in order to create, and then create in order to live.

Opposite: Siouxsie and the Slits / Collage by Paul Burgess / 2015

radical politics, and underground publications and collectives ranging from *OZ* and *International Times* to *King Mob*. In "Cut Piece," an early piece of feminist art first staged in 1964, Yoko Ono knelt on the ground and laid down a pair of scissors. The audience was invited to come forward and cut off any piece of her clothing. It started politely but became more and more threatening as her clothes were reduced to rags and she kneeled in her underwear. Performance artist Chris Burden, who was the inspiration for David Bowie's "Joe the Lion," was famous for having himself nailed to a car in 1974 ("Nail me to my car and I'll tell you who you are") and for having an assistant shoot him in the arm at an art gallery in 1971 ("Guess you'll buy a gun / You'll buy it secondhand")—all pretty radical and daring in Bowie's mind.

Other artists who have pushed the boundaries of exhibitionism, body art, and public self-destruction include Marina Abramovic, Throbbing Gristle, Bas Jan Ader, and Bob Flanagan, a performance artist and poet whose writings and bizarre, sadomasochistic performances centered on his lifelong battle with cystic fibrosis.

Among the many barriers punk broke down was the dominance of male rock bands. A tide of strong-minded women formed bands, and for the first time in the history of rock, female bands existed alongside male bands on an equal footing. Patti Smith released *Horses* in 1975, and The Slits, X-Ray Spex, Siouxsie and the Banshees, The Raincoats, and Kleenex were all formed between 1976 and 1978.

On the cover of their debut album *Cut*, the Slits embody exhibitionism as a feminist statement. Slits guitarist Viv Albertine describes it like this: "The album cover was shot in the rose garden of the recording studio. We wanted a warrior stance, to be a tribe. We were egging each other on, and the next thing you know we were sitting in the mud, smearing it over each other. We knew, since we had no clothes on, that we had to look confrontational and hard. We didn't want to be inviting the male gaze."

That nakedness can be "confrontational and hard" is a vital insight of punk. Nakedness is a disturbance we find hard to deal with, and there are many examples of the unease that an apparently fearless naked person can cause, from Scottish warriors with nothing under their kilts to performance artists, streakers, and nudists. Stephen Gough, the Naked Rambler, walked the length of Great Britain naked in 2003-04 and again in 2005–06, but was arrested in both England and Scotland. He subsequently spent six years in prison, having been repeatedly re-arrested for public nudity within a short period, since each time he was released, he would do it again.

Yet as revolutionary as punk was at the time—and for all the ways its spirit of rebellion is alive in new forms such as the Guy Fawkes masks worn by the hacker collective Anonymous—the movement quickly became a commodity. In particular, the fashion industry has been employing the punk aesthetic in various ways over the past decades, turning punk into a look, a style, a posture, even a cliché. But the truth is that from the beginning punk walked the line between dissent and commodification.

It all goes back to Malcolm McLaren. During his first visit to New York in August 1973, the American sexual revolution was in full swing. The rise of the gay clubs on Christopher Street, along with the clothing and pornography that was readily available in the Village, made a big impression on McLaren. It was during this visit he first met the New York Dolls and started to supply some of their stagewear.

Punk was a beckoning finger. Start a band, pick up a camera, make a zine.

Opposite: Malcolm McLaren / Collage by Paul Burgess / 2015

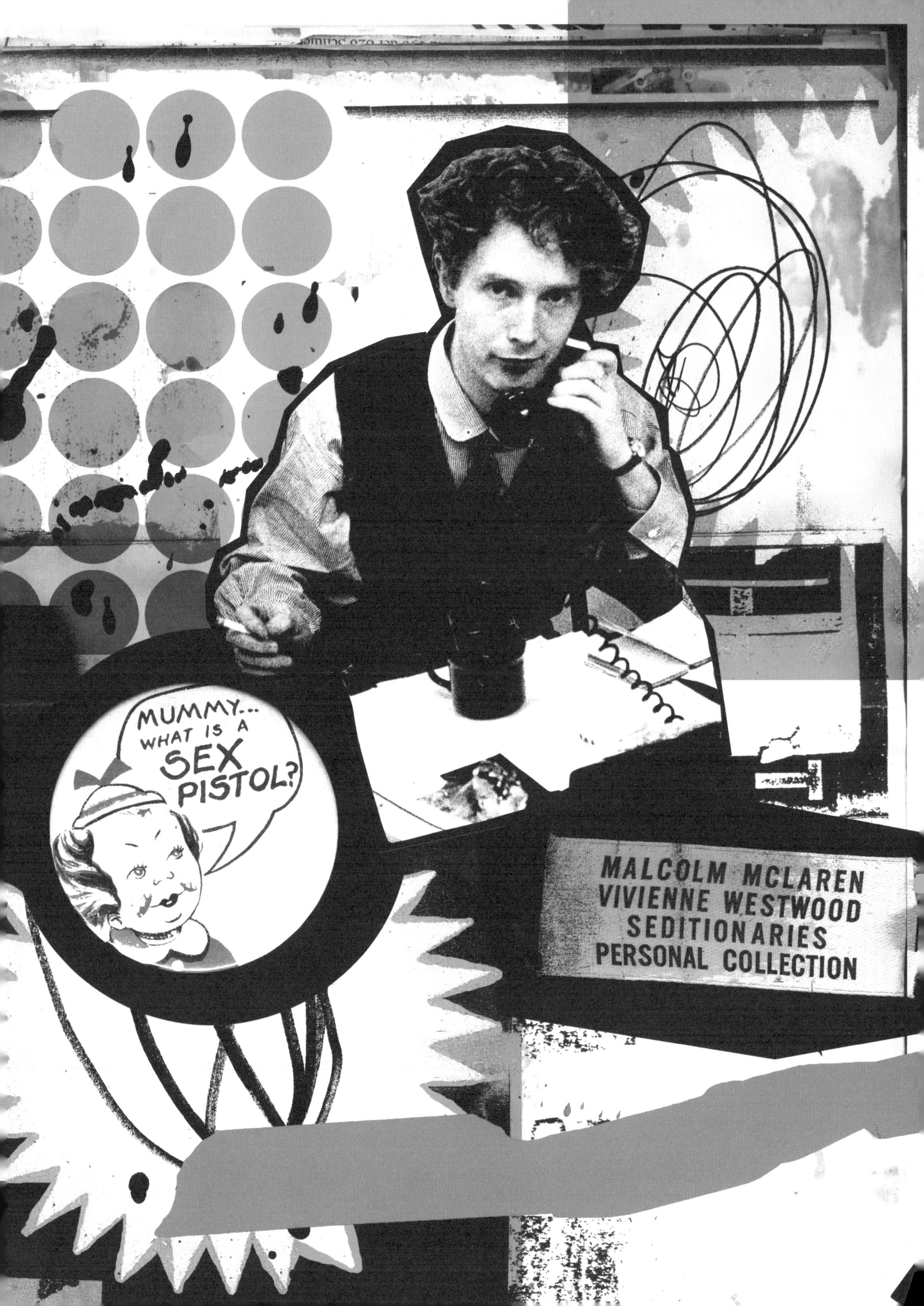
MUMMY... WHAT IS A SEX PISTOL?
MALCOLM MCLAREN
VIVIENNE WESTWOOD
SEDITIONARIES
PERSONAL COLLECTION

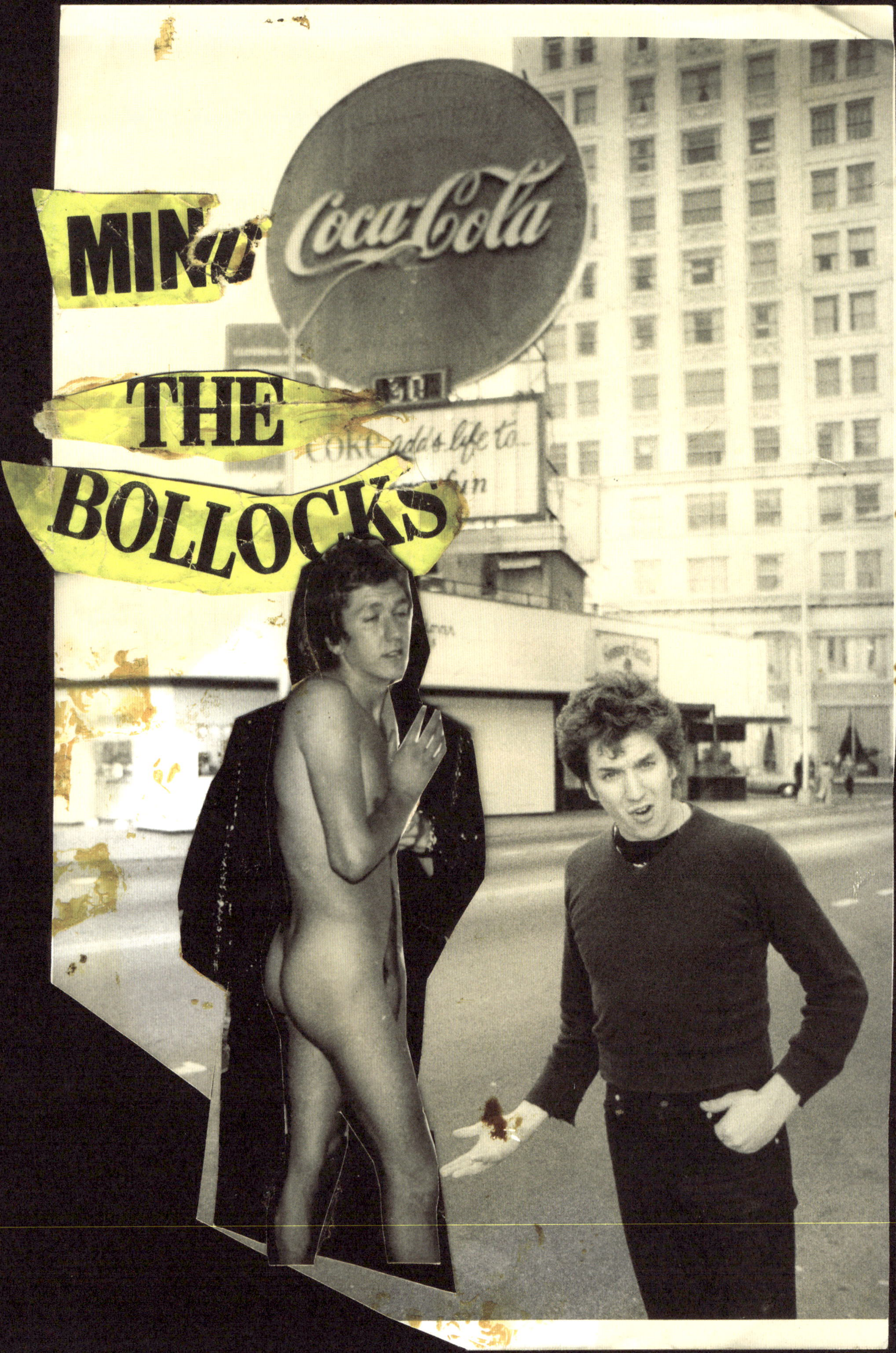
MIN
Coca-Cola
THE
Coke adds life to
fun
BOLLOCKS

Malcolm McLaren and Vivienne Westwood's first shop, called Let It Rock, opened in 1971 at 430 Kings Road, Chelsea. At first it sold clothing left over from the repressive postwar 1950s, including Teddy Boy threads, rock 'n' roll cast-offs, and dusty memorabilia. Swiftly moving on from Teds to rockers, the shop began selling biker leather, studs, and "Dominator" motorcycle chic, with McLaren and Westwood renaming the shop Too Fast To Live Too Young To Die in 1973. Then in October 1974, the store was once again re-branded, this time as SEX, with a new focus on fetishwear and a four-foot-high lurid pink sign spelling out the name in foam rubber. The hand-sprayed text above the SEX sign was a quote by Thomas Fuller: "Craft must have clothes, but truth loves to go naked."

It was really New York that changed McLaren's mind about the direction he should take. SEX came about because of New York. Radical politics in the UK had failed and were now just a distant memory of musty patchouli oil, just as the smoke had long since cleared from the 1968 uprisings in Paris, Chicago, Mexico City, Prague, and elsewhere. In New York, McLaren was put in touch with the beginnings of the punk scene. He had met Richard Hell, the New York Dolls, and the Stooges, and had become enamored of the Velvet Underground. Lou Reed would later wear stage clothing from SEX, to affirm the connection. In the UK, the landscape was already changing. A postcard sent to McLaren by his old friend Fred Vermorel in October 1973 stated "Malcolm! Stop wasting your time. Time is running out, there are better things to do". McLaren took notice right away.

What McLaren wanted was to blow the lid off British repression, sexual and otherwise. This was to be done through the exhibitionism of punk. Capitalising on the growing market for chic sadomasochism and the accelerating sexual chaos of the 1970s, McLaren used SEX to fulfill a mission—to bring what was supposed to be hidden out into the open, to bring the private out into the public, to bring sexuality out into the streets. Let people have a look at your repression with the aid of sexual commodities. Turn your alienated privacy into a public display—and let the press spread the word. By channeling the idea of "creating a situation," of forcing people to react, McLaren's Sex Pistols became the musical extension of SEX the shop. Create a situation they did—and the country reacted.

The notorious *Today* interview with TV host Bill Grundy, in December 1976, was an exercise in punk exhibitionism in four short minutes. Siouxsie Sioux, Johnny Rotten, Steve Jones, and Glen Matlock all show off gloriously, to the watching public, and for days the sensation caused chaos across the British tabloids. Like every other school kid watching that night, I knew that the touch paper had been lit. Whether inspired or repelled, we all knew there was no turning back. It was up to us now what to make of the new world we suddenly found ourselves in.

Nearly 40 years have passed since that night, and the movement has become something of a cultural industry unto itself. Hell, you can even get a 'Never Mind the Bollocks' Virgin credit card these days. What is remarkable, though, is the way that punk had an irreversible effect on many of the people it touched. Through McLaren and SEX, commodification was built into the punk movement from the beginning, but for those of us who were there, for those of us who said yes to the punk attitude, it was like saying yes to life. It gave us our freedom, our identity, our sexuality. It gave us ourselves.

What McLaren wanted was to blow the lid off British repression, sexual and otherwise.

Opposite: Mind The Bollocks / Collage by Helen Wellington-Lloyd / 1978

RAISING THE SKIRT

The empowering project by artist Nicola Canavan, in collaboration with photographer Dawn Felicia Knox

In Greek Mythology we have the story of Baubo and Demeter: after the traumatic abduction of her daughter Persephone, Baubo reveals her vulva and belly to cheer up Demeter so that she could replenish her superhuman power. Baubo's return to strength enables her to rescue her daughter and bring her back to the land of mortals and away from the wicked grasp of Hades, the god of the underworld.

In 16th Century France, scholar François Rabelais described a story about a woman who put the devil to flight by showing him her vulva. This story would eventually become an illustration – one of my all-time favourites – by Charles Eisen, created for the 1762 publication of Jean de La Fontaine's fable The Devil of Pope-Fig Island.

'Raising the Skirt' began as a fight to repair the damage done to the body image of women over many centuries; particularly, damage done by the continued pushing of the external anatomy of the female genitals into the dark, tucking away the reality of the labia to depict women with hairless, fleshy mounds whilst the cock is out there, pissing in water fountains. There comes a time when someone needs to revolutionize and throw caution to the wind, instead of going around and around in a hair-free, vulva-less circle.

The drive of this project came from a very personal place, being told that my body was not normal and, later, that my labia are too large, made me feel nothing but discomfort in and about my body, which continued for more than a decade into my adult life. This shame has had a negative effect on the intimacy that I have shared with others and the commitment to my own sexual explorations and needs. It's time the world stopped naming women's genitals incorrectly. It saddens me that women feel so ashamed of their cunts that, for example, cosmetic surgeries like labiaplasty (the trimming of the labia) have rapidly increased over the last 5 years. After a very long battle with my body and with sex I decided I'd had enough of all of these stigmas and that it was time to shed it. It was important that this should be a shared experience and an inspiration to others.

My research began as a way to inform my solo artistic practice, where I began this journey by delving deeper into the historical links between the vulva and power, where I dug up the inspiring act of raising the skirt which is buried deep into many of our cultures.

The depiction of female genitals, and of raising the skirt, goes right back to the early Neolithic period, in pottery, in stonework, and even on graves when bodies were returned to the womb of the Great Mother for rebirth. The representations of women in these early works are marks of respect and ways of honoring the divine goddess; the artifacts served as a reminder that women bore equal power to their male companions. The cunt was a place to marvel.

On stone slabs, on potsherds and limestone statues, the enlarged vulva were earnestly carved and painted into 'fish' figures from Serbia, the 'Sheela-na-gigs' of Ireland and Europe, Greek and Chinese pottery, and the dancing goddesses of Tibet. The gesture of lifting the skirt to reveal the vulva was the inspiration for these relics, and has been translated through various mediums across the world. It is known as Anasyrma or Ana-Suromai (Ancient Greek), Anlu (Kom Communities), and many other names. A flash of the cunt has been known to calm forces of nature; in Madras (India), women were known to subdue storms by exposing themselves. In other folklore, women

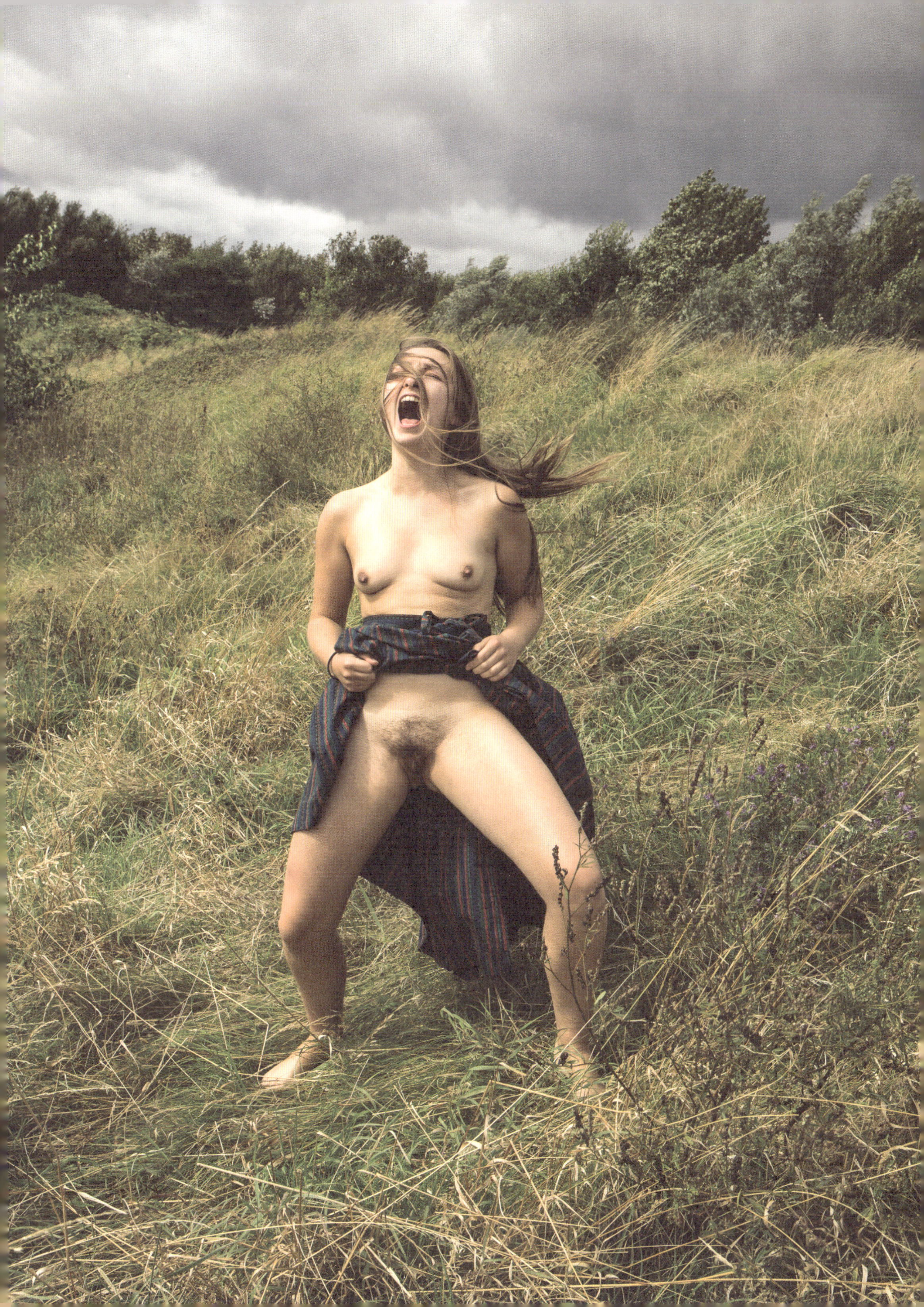

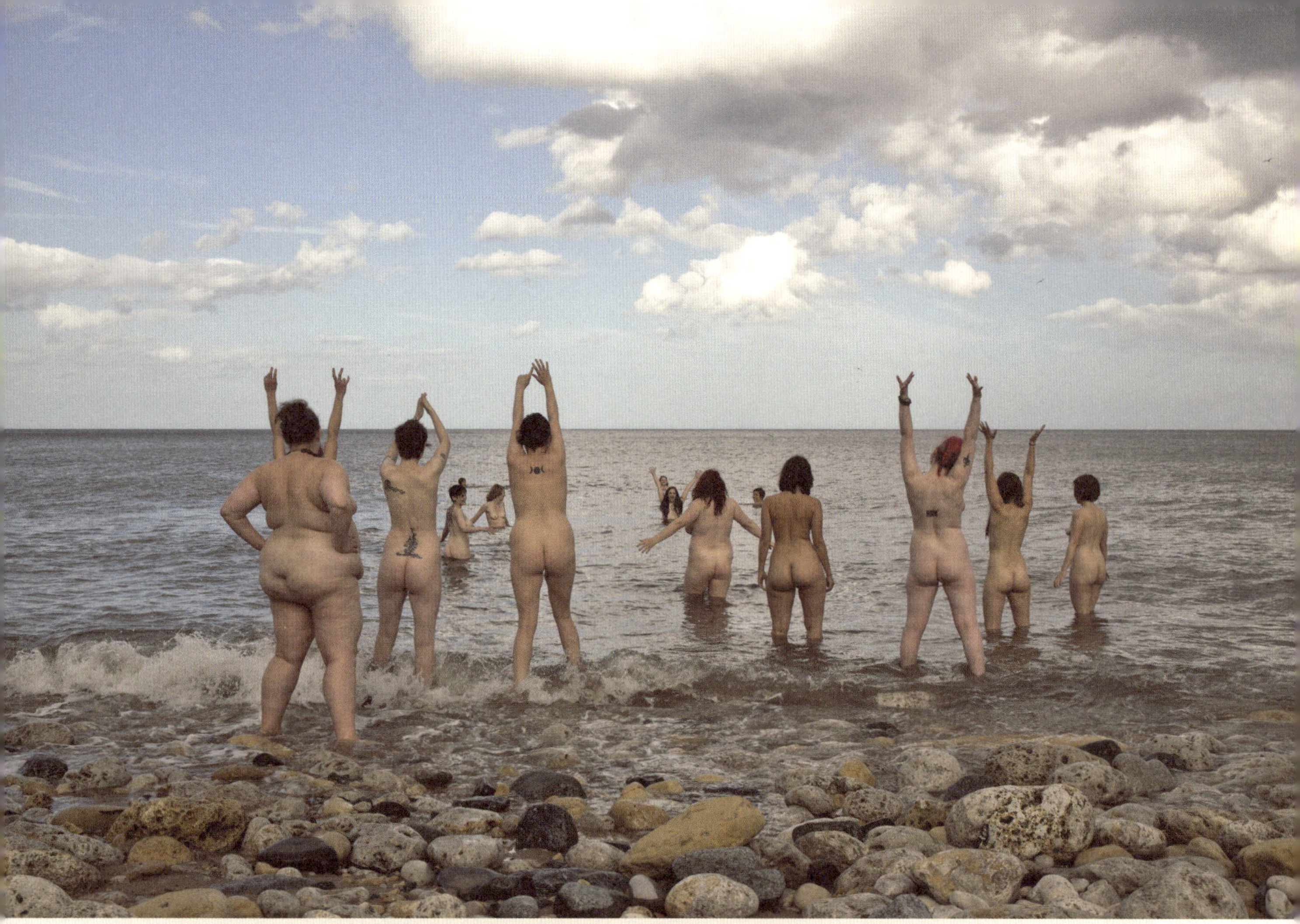

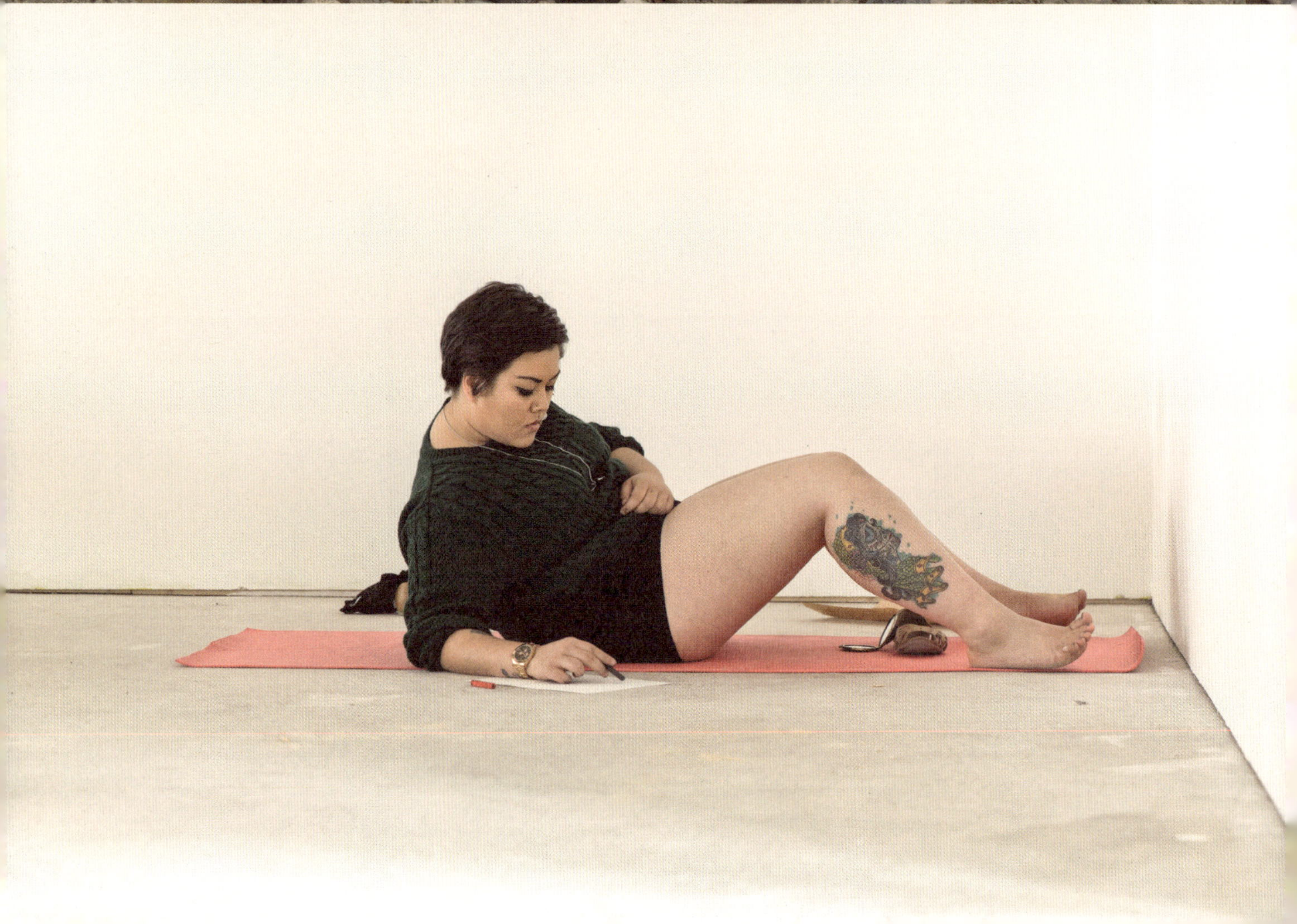

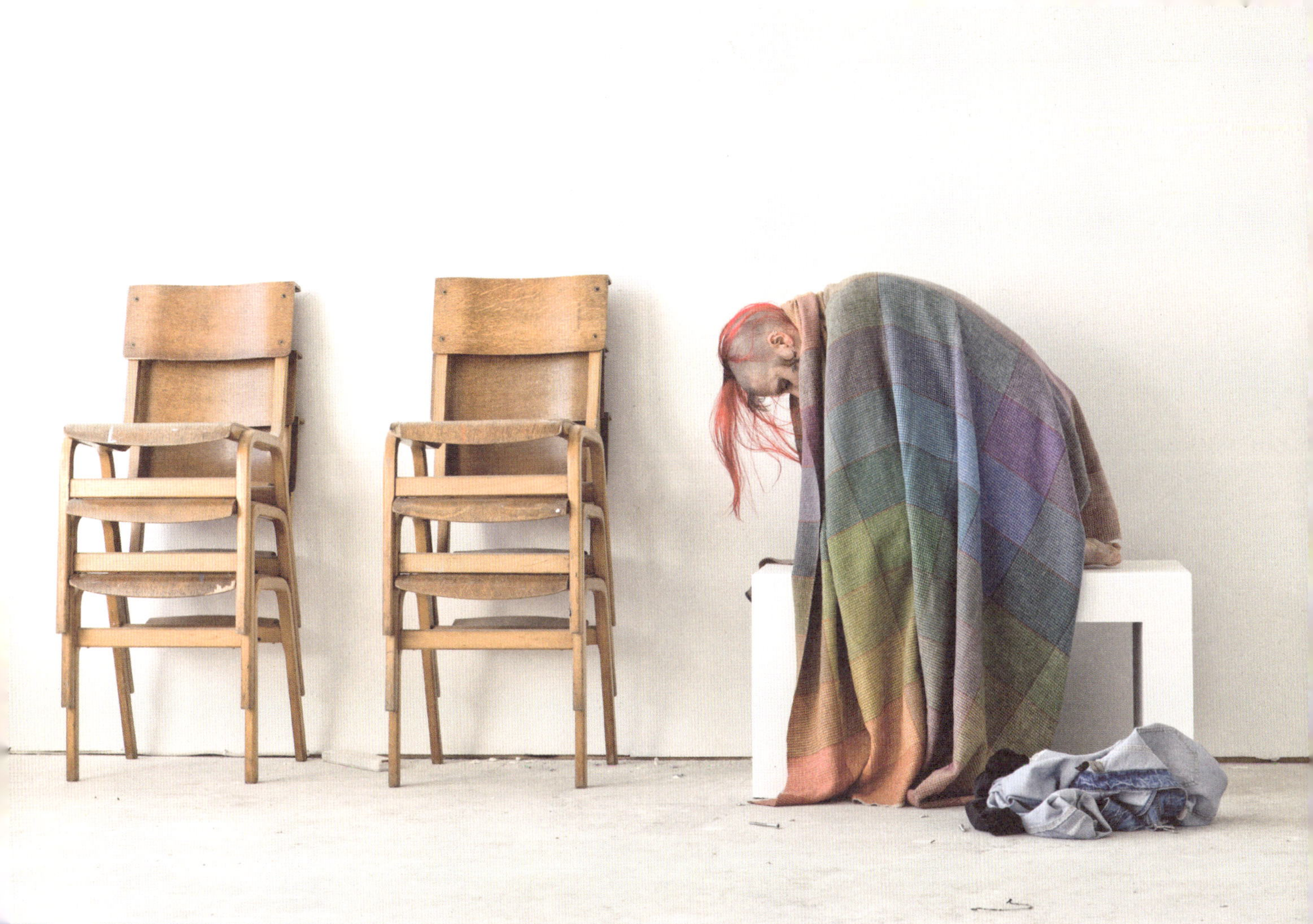

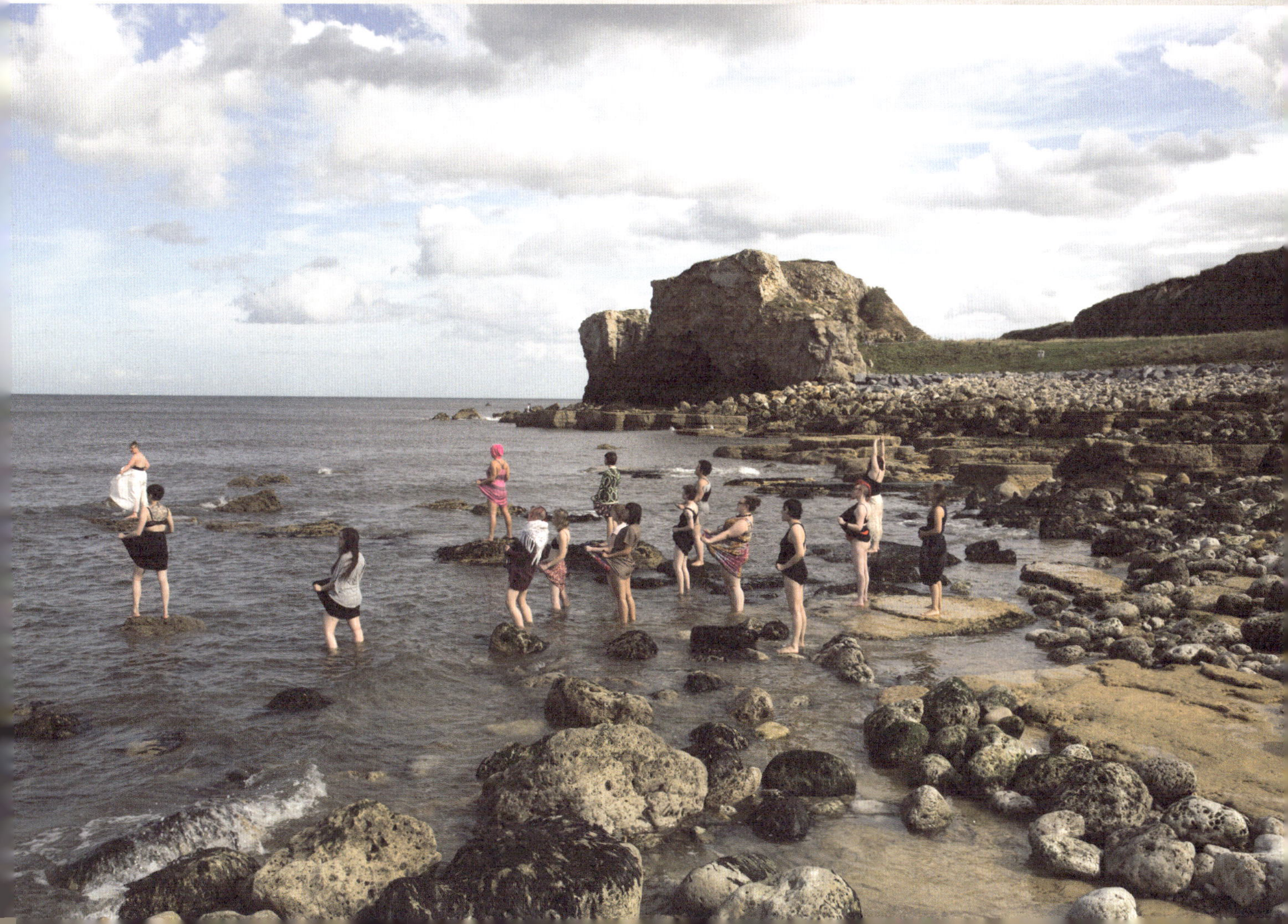

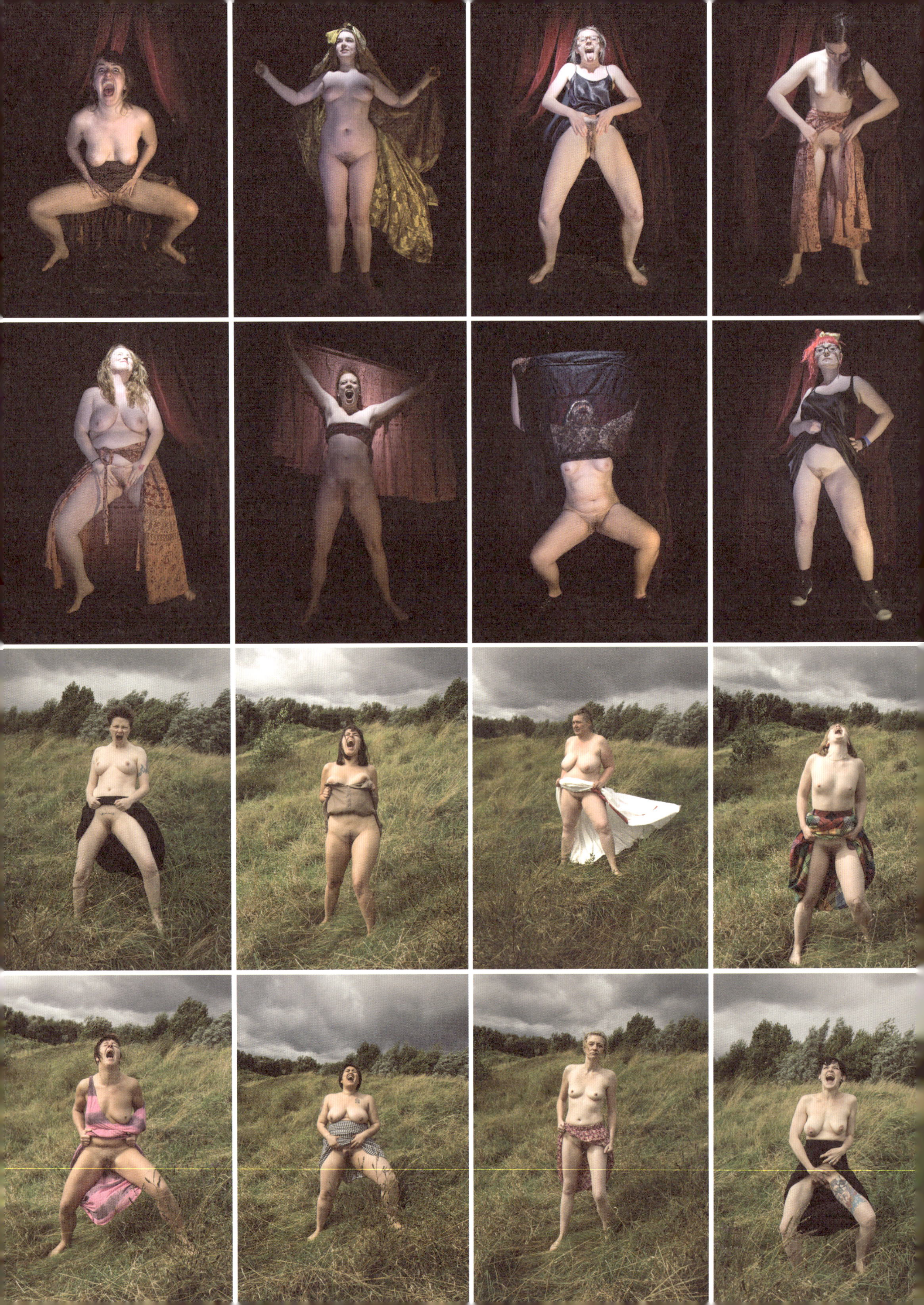

could drive away devils and evil spirits, all through the power of their fierce femininity.

More recently, Leymah Gbowee – a Liberian activist – used anasyrma as an act to bring peace during the Second Liberian Civil War. Her efforts to end the war, with her associate Ellen Johnson Sirleaf, helped initiate a period of peace and, in 2005, enabled a free election that Sirleaf won. They later went on to be jointly awarded the Nobel Peace Prize.

I devised a workshop, co-facilitated by friend and collaborator Dawn Felicia Knox. Pulling together my research into the act of raising the skirt keyed our experiences as artists and performers. Seventeen women came together in August 2014; each participant brought their own strength, memories and creative flare to the circle. Through challenging activities and a peaceful unity, we formed our own Anasyrma Army. The transformation and rejuvenation was astounding, and felt by all of us.

The past year has seen so many successes for 'Raising the Skirt.' The project continues to change and grow. We are very grateful to all participants, who have committed and contributed on many levels. You all continue to amaze us.

'Raising the Skirt' leaves more than just images, it is a project raising questions, it is a resource tool and a community, which aims to represent women from all communities and origins, those strong and passionate women all fighting for the same cause.

I want my Anasyrma Army to grow and for us all to have peace within our bodies but fire in our hearts.

-Nicola Canavan

GLASGOW: I went to my knees there, on that stage. After the talking, the listening, the preparing. I went to my knees and looked up through my lens. See, that is where I want you, viewer. Looking up at each woman as she enacts the ritual, as she inhabits the divine feminine. Look, she becomes the Sheelanagig. She becomes the Greek goddess. The archetypal, the divine and the deeply individual all held in the folds and curves of her and her cunt. The women often spoke about who would look, who would see. 'I want my daughter to see these images' one woman told me. 'I never want her to be ashamed.' One woman wanted to see herself, to remember and truly see how strong she could be. Another woman talked about the unintentional viewer – the ones she didn't do this for. She let her hair fall over her face and held her skirt in front of her like Judith holding the head of Holofernes and quietly waited for me to take the photograph.

The images are there, the powerful, the fearless, the joyous. I didn't say become Judith, become Baubo, become Kali. There is no need. The archetypal image of the fully inhabited woman is in our history. It is there, beneath the skirt. Bear witness to the ritual, the transformation. Bear witness to the fearless, courageous display. Look. Do not turn away. See.

Each woman stared intently into herself like she was staring into the sea. I recorded to the looking. I bore witness to the seeing. Then when we make the images and perform to camera we engage more directly in the dialogue. Every image becomes a collaboration. How do the narratives of the projects resonate with you, I would ask? Where does it vibrate? How does it sound? What does it look like? How can we make an image that captures that? I hold the space as I hold the camera. There is so much joy there, laughing, howling, dancing, humming, arriving and revealing. I feel profoundly honoured to bear witness to the whole of it. All of it. Unashamed.

JARROW: In the field, I began with sound. Find your home tone, I said, the one that comes naturally, the one that resonates through your mouth, that fills your head like a light. Now, on to your heart. Find the sound that expands the hollows, vibrating the space between your breath and pulse. Now, let's find the resonant frequency of your cunt. Your cunt's home tone. A gentle humming, an open toning, a deep earth droning. The mouth and the cunt a mirror. Then a channel. How do you move that deep rumbling tone up through the body and out the mouth as a fearless roar? Your whole body holds the roar then releases it.

It was raining the day we made those images, in that field. Fierce swirling skies. Fierce, defiant women. Back behind the metro station in Jarrow, we stood. It is rough as you like round there they say. Not the place to make art out in the open like that. But there is a history of defiance there; the Jarrow men marched on London through day and night when they closed the shipyards, when they took their work away. Yes, rough and defiant. That is where we chose to create our action, enact our ritual. That is where they raised their skirts and where I bore witness. In that field, in that place. They calmed the sky. They unleashed the warrior's cry. I recorded it.

-Dawn Felicia Knox

Opposite Top: Glasgow portraits. Opposite Bottom: Jarrow portraits. All photographs by Dawn Felicia Knox.

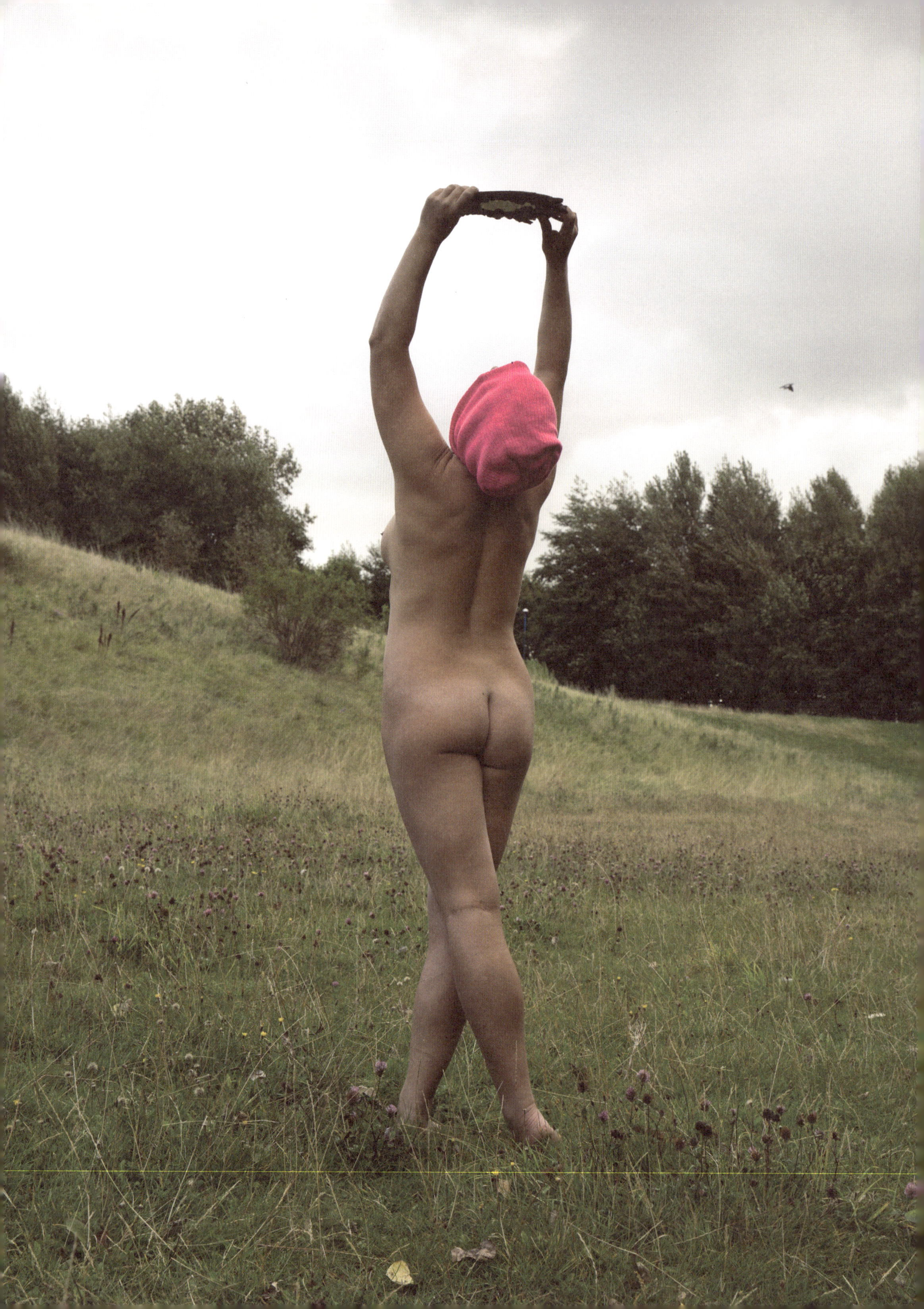

‘La mar es posa bona si veu el cony d’una dona’ is a Catalan saying, meaning ‘the sea calms down if it sees a woman’s cunt’.

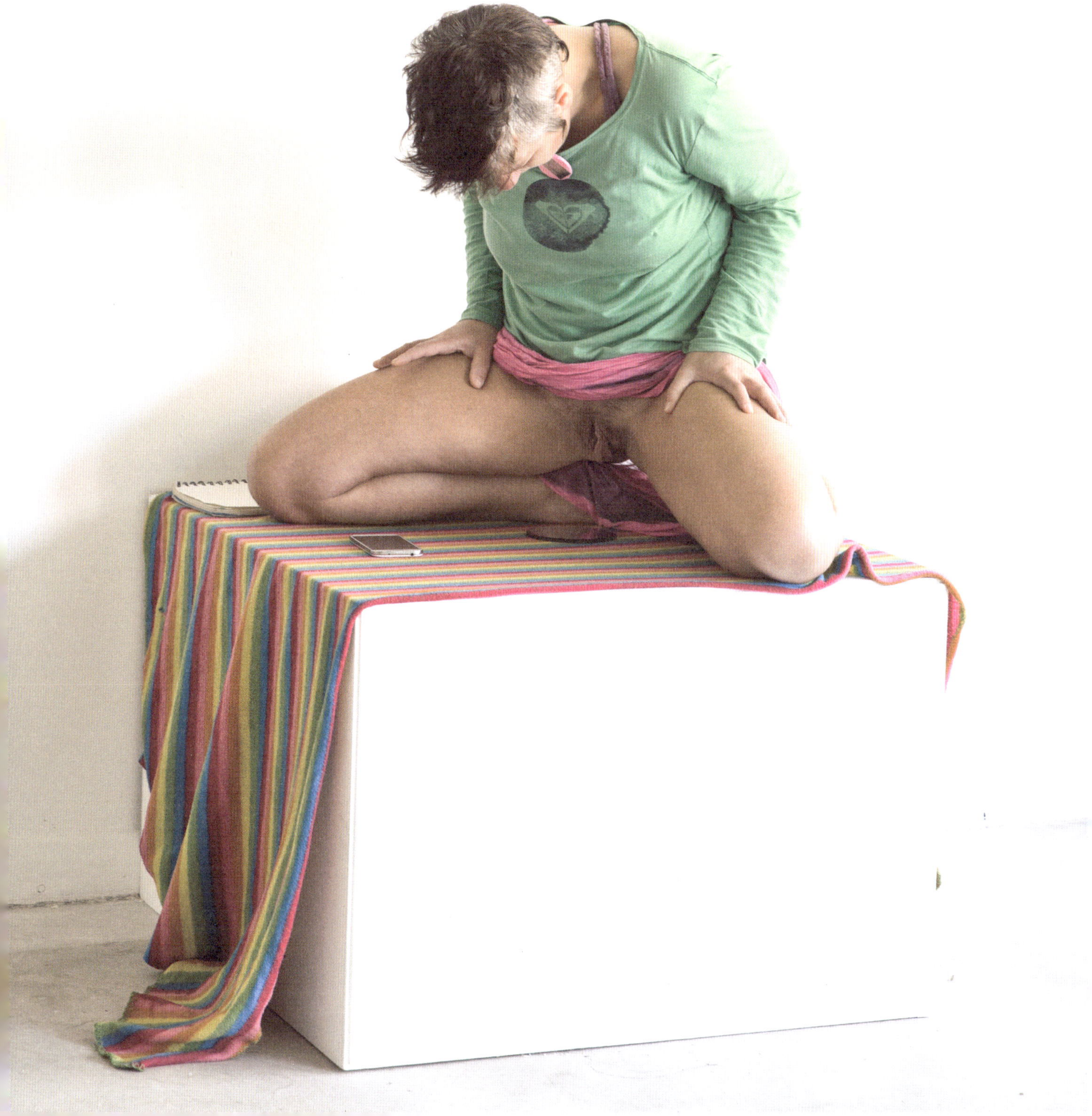

"Dear Nicola, I love this project and I think this type of work is so important for women and for men. I believe in the sacredness of a woman's yoni and all too often it is not treated the way it should be-it should be celebrated and loved and adored!"

"Hi Nicola. As somebody who has suffered from an eating disorder and with my body image since my teen years, I would like to participate in a liberating experience with other women. I want to feel proud of my body and my skin. This project resonates with me and my curatorial practice."

"Stumbled upon your work only yesterday and felt an obvious and immediate connection..very timely for the world picture right now..leading/enabling an empowering, courageous and honest opportunity for raising our awareness of the power of our own bodies and our potential for change in our selves, our lives and in the world."

"I feel significantly more connected with the experience of owning and embodying my vagina, but most of all, I feel attracted and lured to its appearance and nature more and more by the day. I can appreciate its honesty, authenticity and history, and feel excited about our future together, as opposed to feeling like it was just an arousing orifice for my own and others pleasure. Its more than that now, and I would like to have the opportunity to delve deeper into its 'being' whilst sharing the experience with others."

"I think your workshops are essential to help women to be reconciled with the centre of their femininity (= with their deep self). I've been making pictures of this wonderful part of the female body, as a tribute, and I'm very happy to have discovered that most women who saw them acknowledged this tribute and the beauty of this intimate part of their body."

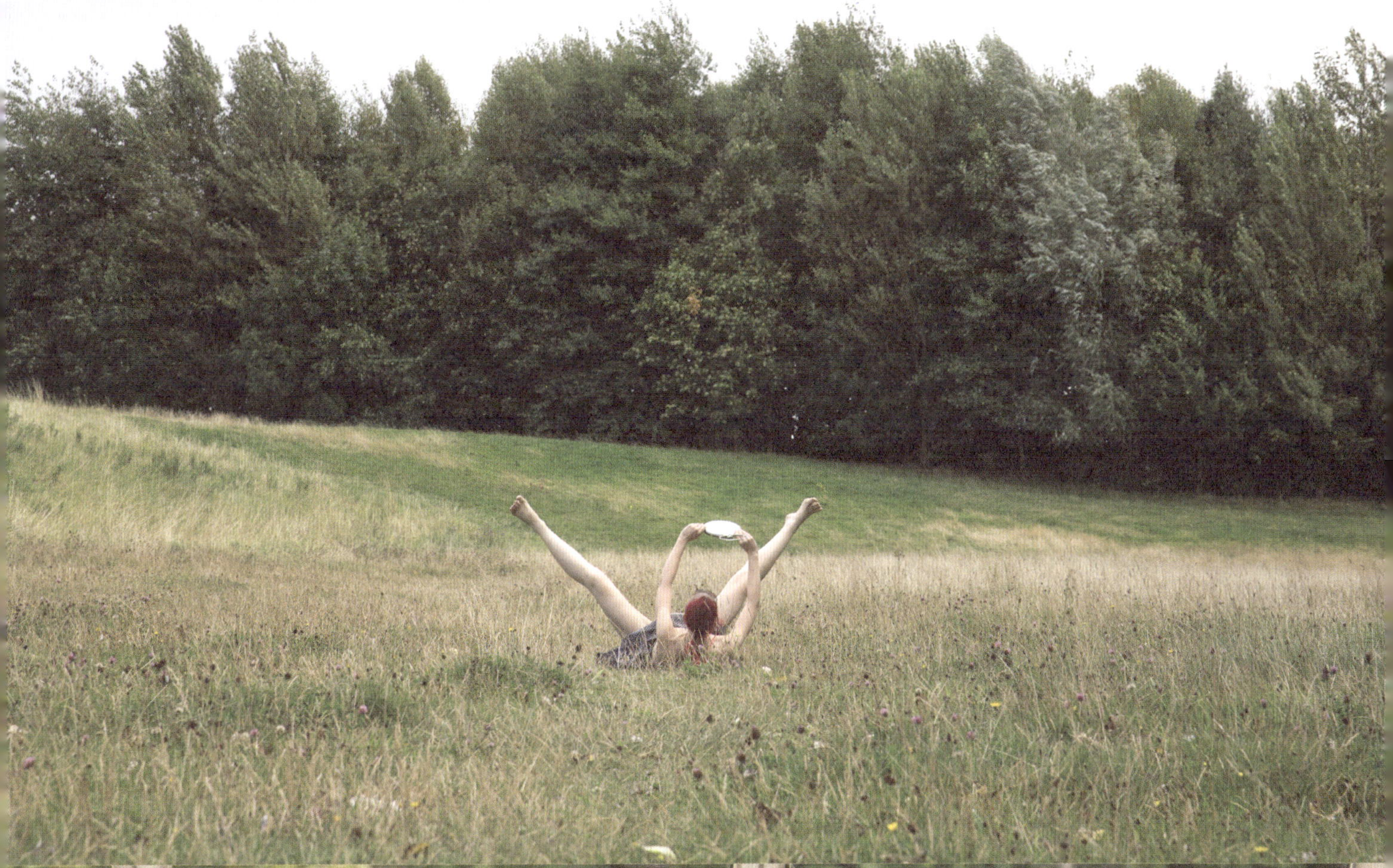

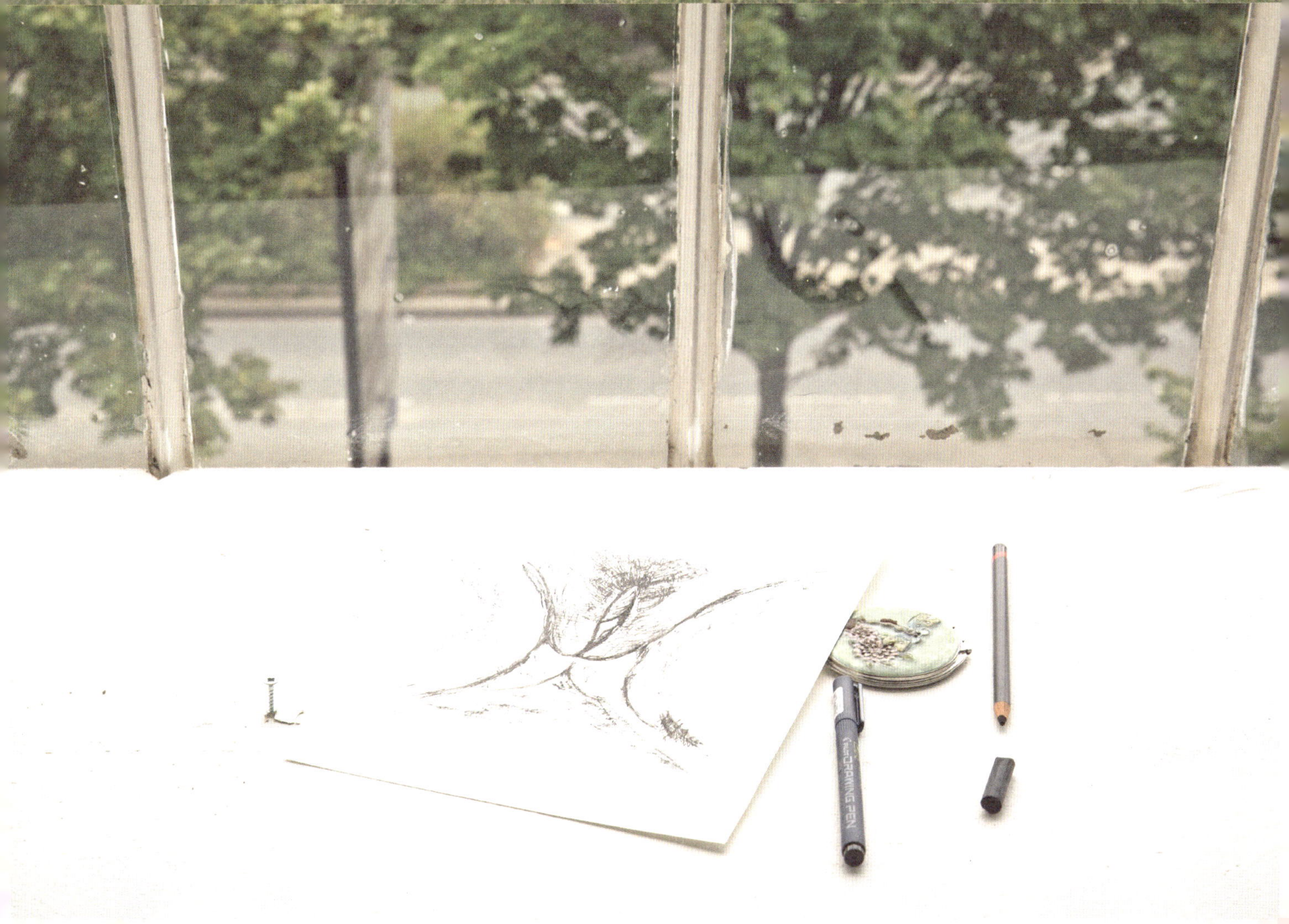
DRAWING PEN

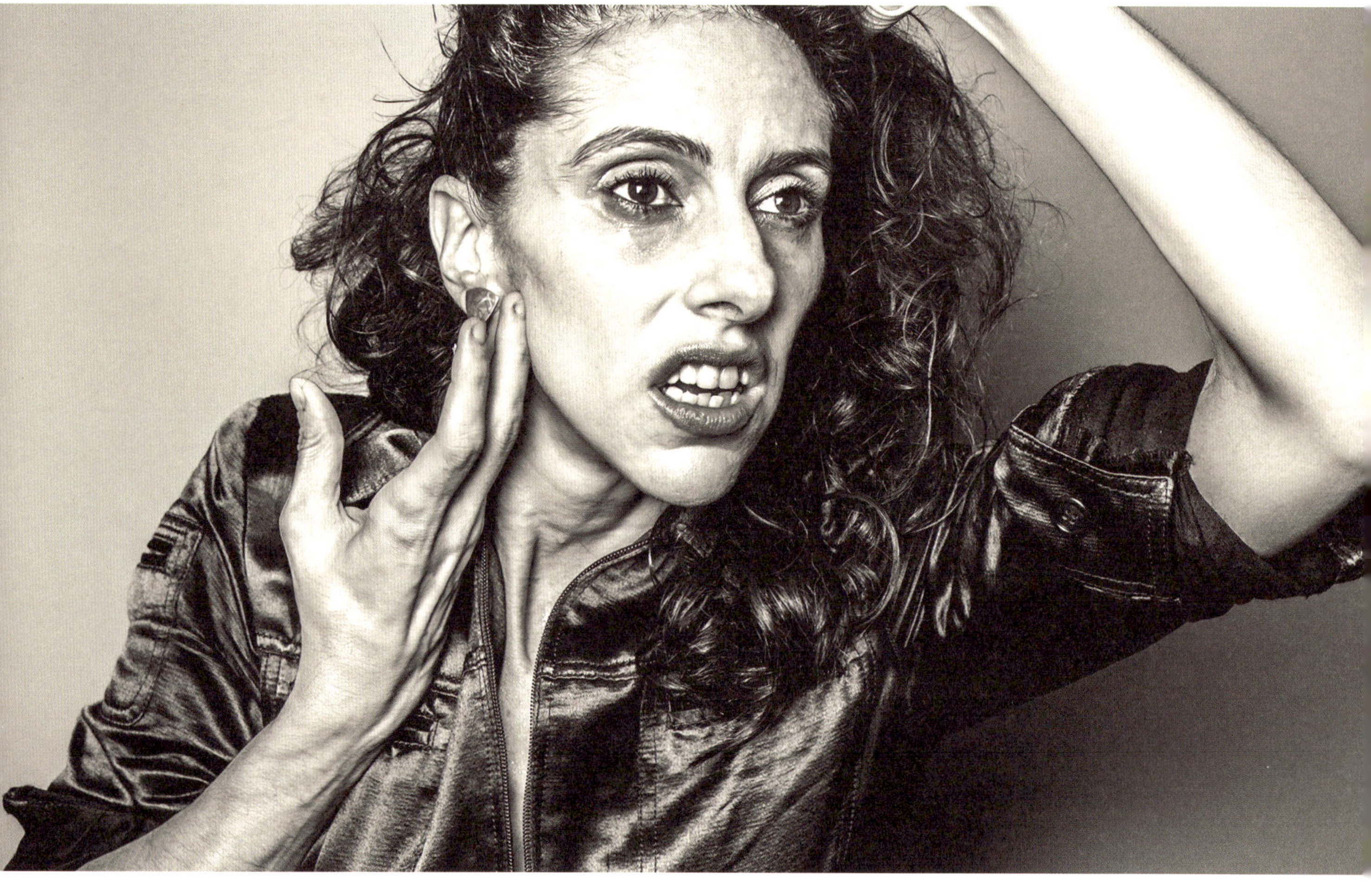

Dina Seiden / Photographed by Erin Albrecht / 2015

POSTINGS

by Dina Seiden

Sort of bummed out, I cleaned my house for my sister-in-law and her family before they came to visit us and now I see that we forgot to remove the big bottle of "Macho Friction Oil" from the 70's that is in an absolutely unmissable spot in our bathroom, right in the eyeline of any urinating guy. now my brother-in-law and adorable twelve year old nephew, who is like a son to me, I love him so much, is now thinking that his Auntie Dina is walking around with a pathologically massive vagina. it was just a gag ornament for our bathroom to make guests laugh. now I'm thinking my brother-in-law and nephew were sort of treating me different after they relieved themselves. they had that you-obviously-have-a-massive-vagina look in their eyes. oh god.

So my mother just called me to ask me why I talk all the time about my vagina on facebook. she said she went out for a lovely meal with an old friend who herself friended me a while ago on facebook and that person told her that I endlessly gas on about my vagina on facebook so despite a lovely meal, my mother came to worry that I was Mileying all over facebook. this wouldn't be so concerning if three other friends on facebook hadn't mentioned to me or others how often I talk about my vagina. I just skimmed my posts, went back a long while before I got bored (shit, do I ramble on) and I can't find a single reference to my vagina. of course this is a reference, but really, what do you know about my vagina after this post? that I call it a vagina? that I am possessed of a vagina? big fuckin whoop. and anyway, I never talk about my vagina but rather talk about people talking about how I talk about my vagina. granted there was a request made now years ago for referrals to gynecologists because I couldn't go back to the clinician who had ordered all sorts of crazy-expensive tests on MY VAGINA when I went in for a routine pap smear after she told me how healthy MY VAGINA seemed during the examination and after I'd told her how I'd had no weird symptoms to speak of. when I confronted her, she told me she routinely tests for gothic vaginal diseases but I told her she'd been aware that I hadn't insurance and that she should have told me she was testing for vaginal rickets and all this other shit for which Quest was billing me. tangentially, I miss you, Linda Echols (former Swarthmore Health Center Director) you treated my vagina as if it were her own. she never tested me for vaginal scurvy and other crap without my consent, and she was very Rogerian: she listened, she wasn't judgy, she offered lubricant. Linda Echols, you gave great, warm-clamped, consensual pap smears. I miss your pap smears, Linda Echols. you showed me a great time during those pap smears. and you were in an out of there. you didn't overstay your welcome. the pamphlets you published were always informative. I liked all the plants. I've had only one other good gynecologist, Kathi Sanders, who ran Columbia's health center. Kathi was fuckin awesome. she even came to one of my shows. she once had a urologist pry open my recalcitrant urethra, that was Kathi. ah, Kathi, peach among paptologists. where was i? oh yeah, stop telling me I talk too much about my vagina!!!

Joseph Akel is a freelance writer and editor. His writing has appeared in *Frieze*, *The New York Times*, *Interview*, *The Paris Review,* and *Artforum,* among others.

Shane Book, a poet and filmmaker, is the author of *Congotronic* and *Ceiling of Sticks*.

Ana Božičević came from Croatia and lives in New York. Her books are *Stars of the Night Commute* and *Rise in the Fall*.

Paul Burgess is a freelance illustrator, designer, photographer, artist, and writer. He lives and works in St Leonards-on-Sea.

Nicola Canavan, born in North East England, has been performing and showing her action-based work internationally since 2007.

Julia Cohen is the author of *Triggermoon Triggermoon* and *Collateral Light*. She lives in Chicago.

Louise Colbourne, based in St Leonards-on-Sea, is an artist and curator with a particular interest in interdisciplinary film practices and expanded cinema.

Todd Colby has written six books of poetry. His latest is *Splash State*. He lives in Brooklyn.

Andy Fitch is the author of multple books based on walking, talking, and making audio recordings.

Benjamin Fredrickson is a photographer whose work centers on portraiture and subcultural taboos. He is represented by Daniel Cooney Fine Art New York.

Eileen G'Sell's poetry and cultural criticism has appeared in *Salon*, *Boston Review*, and *The Rumpus*, among others.

Rachel Kash is a writer of fiction and non-fiction. She tweets under the name MomsBitching.

Dawn Felicia Knox is an artist and curator. American by birth, she is now at home in North East England.

Anna Moschovakis, a poet and translator, is an editor at Ugly Duckling Presse.

Keith Newton is the author of *A Week of Kindness*, based on the work of Max Ernst.

Mike Newton is an artist and writer living in Brooklyn.

Danielle Pafunda's most recent book is *The Dead Girls Speak in Unison*.

Niina Pollari is the author of *Dead Horse*.

Harling Ross is a footloose and fancy freelance writer.

Marcelle Sauvageot (1900-1934) was a French writer and teacher.

Christine Schwartz Hartley is a writer and translator based in Brooklyn.

Dina Seiden is a New York-based performer combining comedic schtick, performance art, a therapy session, and hyperbolic and mannered drawing room readings.

Jeremy Sigler is the author of numerous books of poetry, including *Crackpot Poet* and *ABCDEFGHIJKLMNOPQRSTUVWXYZ*.

"Commentary" by Marcelle Sauvageot is an excerpt from her book *Commentary*, published by Ugly Duckling Presse in 2013 in a translation by Christine Schwartz Hartley and Anna Mochovakis.

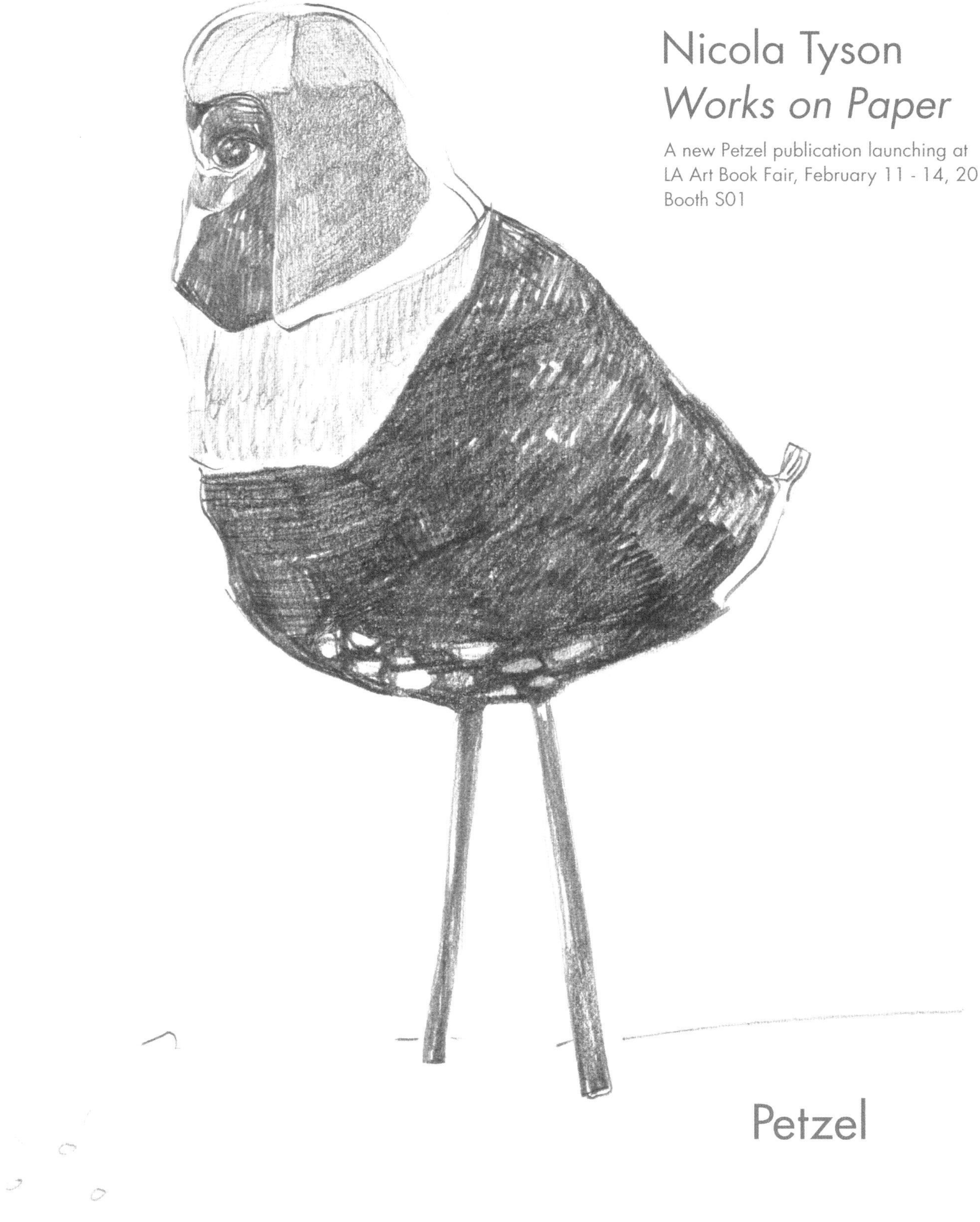

Nicola Tyson
Works on Paper

A new Petzel publication launching at
LA Art Book Fair, February 11 - 14, 2016
Booth S01

Petzel

Publisher, Editor-In-Chief, Creative Director:
James Gallagher

Editorial Director: Keith Newton

Editor: Mike Newton

Contributing Writers: Joseph Akel, Paul Burgess, Nicola Canavan, Louise Colbourne, Dawn Felicia Knox, Benjamin Fredrickson, Eileen G'Sell, Rachel Kash, Keith Newton, Mike Newton, Harling Ross.

Secret Behavior Issue 03: Exhibitionism / 2016

Published by Secret Behavior, LLC.

ISSN 2330-0590

Printed at Heidel.

Distributed by ARTBOOK | D.A.P.
155 6th Avenue, 2nd Floor New York, NY 10013
www.artbook.com

For more information visit www.secretbehavior.com
or write us at info@secretbehavior.com

Secret Behavior invites submissions but cannot promise replies.

Special Thanks: Annie Baltz, Andrew Black, C. Sean Horton, Holly Jenkins, Chris Manzanedo, Rose Shoshana, Morgan Taylor.